The Embroidered Tent: Five Gentlewomen in Early Canada (1982)
Redney: A Life of Sara Jeannette Duncan (1983)
Below the Peacock Fan: First Ladies of the Raj (1987)

MARIAN FOWLER

BLENHEIM

BIOGRAPHY
OF A
PALACE

VIKING

VIKING

PUBLISHED BY THE PENGUIN GROUP
27 WRIGHTS LANE, LONDON W8 5TZ, ENGLAND
VIKING PENGUIN INC., 40 WEST 23RD STREET, NEW YORK, NEW YORK 10010, USA
PENGUIN BOOKS AUSTRALIA LTD, RINGWOOD, VICTORIA, AUSTRALIA
PENGUIN BOOKS CANADA LTD, 2801 JOHN STREET, MARKHAM, ONTARIO, CANADA L3R 1B4
PENGUIN BOOKS (NZ) LTD, 182–190 WAIRAU ROAD, AUCKLAND 10, NEW ZEALAND

PENGUIN BOOKS LTD, REGISTERED OFFICES: HARMONDSWORTH, MIDDLESEX, ENGLAND

FIRST PUBLISHED 1989
1 3 5 7 9 10 8 6 4 2

COPYRIGHT © MARIAN FOWLER, 1989

FILMSET IN MONOPHOTO SABON
PRINTED IN GREAT BRITAIN BY
BUTLER & TANNER LTD, FROME AND LONDON

A CIP CATALOGUE RECORD FOR THIS BOOK IS AVAILABLE FROM THE BRITISH LIBRARY

LIBRARY OF CONGRESS CATALOG CARD NUMBER: 89–51104

ISBN 0–670–82027X

THIS BOOK IS DEDICATED
WITH LOVE AND GRATITUDE
TO GERARD GAUCI
WHO LIMNS MY PROSE

CONTENTS

ACKNOWLEDGEMENTS

My main source of research for this book was the vast collection of handwritten letters, journals, receipts, invoices, account books and other miscellanea known as the Blenheim Papers. Formerly housed in the Muniments Room of Blenheim Palace, where they were initially sorted by Archdeacon William Coxe in the 4th Duke of Marlborough's time, then re-sorted by Stuart Reid in the 9th duke's day, these papers were offered to the British Library in 1973 by the 11th Duke of Marlborough. In 1978, the Blenheim Papers were allocated to the 'Additional Manuscripts' collection of the British Library, and in the years since then they have been beautifully bound in 610 red-leather volumes, and expertly catalogued in three printed ones. I spent many happy hours dipping into this exciting treasure trove, and am most grateful for the help I received from Mr J. Conway, Executive Officer of the Department of Manuscripts, and other British Library staff members. I also worked extensively in the London Library, whose staff, as always, were unfailingly courteous and efficient. Like all Blenheim scholars, I leaned heavily and gratefully on the work of the late David Green, who devoted years of perceptive and patient study to the Marlboroughs and their grand house, and who produced many of the best books on the subject.

I am grateful to His Grace, the 11th Duke of Marlborough, for access to the Blenheim archives, for graciously permitting me to see rooms not open to the public and for permission to reproduce photographs in his collection. Paul Duffie, Palace Administrator, Patrick Garner, butler, and other staff members at Blenheim were also most helpful and obliging.

Friends and relatives who in various ways helped me with this book include my mother, my son Tim, Norma Harrs, Shirley Mowbray, Christopher Kelly, Robert Cramer, Gerard Gauci and Joan Pierson. Michael Pierson deserves a special thankyou for supplying me with photocopies of documents from British libraries when I found myself far away on the Canadian side of the Atlantic.

The sound editorial expertise of Anthony Lacey, Editorial Director of Viking, UK, and Catherine Yolles, Senior Editor of Penguin Books, Canada, vastly improved the text. My agents, Lucinda Vardey and Carolyn

Brunton, gave equally sound guidance and support. I am also grateful to Esther Sidwell and Janice Brent for their contributions.

The individuals, institutions and publishers who granted permission to reproduce illustrative material are listed below.

Finally, I should add that because many eighteenth-century writers who contributed to Blenheim's story were erratic in spelling and punctuation, I have modernized and standardized both when quoting directly from their work.

M.F.

'KILMARA', LISLE, ONTARIO

PHOTO CREDITS

We shape our dwellings,
and afterwards our dwellings shape us

SIR WINSTON CHURCHILL
Speech in House of Commons, 28 October 1943

John Churchill, 1st Duke = Sarah, d. of Richard Jennings
1650–1722
(cr. Duke of Marlborough 1702)

Henrietta Churchill, 2nd Duchess = Francis, 2nd Earl of Godolphin
1681–1733 (suc. 1722)

Charles Spencer, 3rd Duke = Elizabeth, d. of Earl Trevor
1706–58 (suc. 1733)

George Spencer, 4th Duke = Caroline,
1739–1817 (suc. 1758)   d. of Duke of Bedford

George Spencer-Churchill, 5th Duke ———
1766–1840 (suc. 1817)

George Charles Spencer-Churchill, 8th Duke = (1) Albertha, d. of Duke of Abercorn
1844–92 (suc. 1883)   (2) Lilian, d. of Cicero Price

Charles Richard John Spencer-Churchill, 9th Duke = (1) Consuelo, d. of William Vanderbilt
1871–1934 (suc. 1892)   (2) Gladys, d. of Edward Parker Deacon

John Albert Edward William Spencer-Churchill, 10th Duke ———
1897–1972 (suc. 1934)

John George Vanderbilt Henry Spencer-Churchill, 11th Duke ———
b. 1926 (suc. 1972)

THE MARLBOROUGH (SPENCER-CHURCHILL) LINE OF DESCENT

——————— = Susan, d. of 7th Earl of Galloway

George Spencer-Churchill, 6th Duke = (1) Jane, d. of 8th Earl of Galloway
1793–1857 (suc. 1840)   (2) Charlotte, d. of Viscount Ashbrook
   (3) Jane, d. of Hon. Edward Stewart

John Winston Spencer-Churchill, 7th Duke = Frances,
1822–83 (suc. 1857)   d. of Marquis of Londonderry

Randolph Henry Spencer-Churchill = Jennie, d. of Leonard Jerome
1849–95

Winston Leonard Spencer-Churchill = Clementine,
1874–1965   d. of Sir Henry Montagu Hozier

—— = (1) Alexandra Mary Cadogan, d. of Viscount Chelsea
   (2) Laura, d. of Hon. Guy Charteris

—— = (1) Susan Mary, d. of Michael Hornby
   (2) Athina Mary, d. of Stavros Livanos
   (3) Dagmar Rosita, d. of Count Carl Ludwig Douglas

INTRODUCTION

'HOUSES ARE ALIVE,' DECLARES THE HEROINE OF E. M. FORSTER'S *Howards End*, 'alive and listening'; according to Ford Madox Ford, they are 'watching the ways of men with sardonic eyes'. Certainly Blenheim Palace, first conceived in 1705 in the fertile mind of playwright Sir John Vanbrugh, has always been dramatically, decisively alive: a sentient, remembering and, above all, active protagonist. The grandest and most famous house in England, country seat for more than two and a half centuries of the Dukes of Marlborough, Blenheim Palace has always stood at the centre of British history and myth, foursquare in fact and fancy, compelling and compendious. The house itself, not its inhabitants, will be the main focus of this biography, for Blenheim's character is rich and complex and fascinating.

I have divided the biography into five chapters, each one centred on one particular event in the house's continuing drama. Chapters 1 and 2 begin with amateur theatrical productions given at Blenheim in 1719 and 1787 respectively; Chapters 3 and 4 open with banquets given for the Prince of Wales in 1859 and 1896; in the first instance, the future Edward VII was a slim youth attending Oxford, and in the second, a portly, bored playboy. Chapter 5 begins with Sir Winston Churchill's burial just beyond Blenheim's gates in 1965. In addition to Blenheim's physical appearance – external details of décor and furnishings – each chapter will touch on its internal workings, that bustle of servant activity and related technology in kitchen and cellar, dairy and stable, which gives the house its regular heartbeat. Living as most of us do now in servantless, streamlined boxes, we crave that keyhole view of how the rich and titled were kept comfortable in a de luxe atmosphere of frills and formality. More important in this book, however, than either Blenheim's appearance or vital systems will be its soul. 'The soul of a house,' declares Vita Sackville-West, 'the atmosphere of a house, are as much part of the house as the architecture or the furnishings within it.' Houses which have seen as much living as Blenheim tend to have large, distinctive souls, and it becomes evident, as we progress through two hundred and sixty years, that Blenheim has undergone five main changes of mood, or general tone.

Each generation of Marlboroughs had a different view of the house's main function. They left their imprint on its spirit, an imprint conditioned partly by private dictates of temperament and partly by public ones of taste. Dukes and Duchesses redecorated and rearranged; rooms changed function; new hobbies and pastimes were accommodated. How its residents left their mark on Blenheim, however, is not nearly as interesting to chart as the reverse: how Blenheim moulded its inmates. The supporting plinth for this book is my firm belief in the profound influence of environment on character. 'Roofs,' says a character of Ivy Compton-Burnett's, 'seem to give rise to situations.' Roofs do indeed oversee, in more than one sense. Blenheim's roofscape, filled as it is with martial symbols carved in stone – cannon-balls, crossed swords, captured standards – clearly trumpets Blenheim's conquering character. The palace has always been a despot: an imposing, imperious, very demanding presence. 'The house,' Elizabeth Bowen writes, referring to her Irish home, Bowen's Court, 'stamps its own character on all ways of living. I am ruled by a continuity I cannot see.' So it is with Blenheim. 'Blenheim engulfs you,' declares the present Duchess of Marlborough, who came to live there in 1972 when she married the 11th Duke. 'I found it difficult to understand how one could make one's own life here when these walls seemed to dictate a certain kind of life of their own. I was scared rigid for about three years until I came to terms with it.' In each chapter I hope to demonstrate Blenheim's extraordinarily persuasive powers as a living entity, powers which prevail far beyond its park boundaries. Beautiful and beguiling in certain moods, with silk-damask walls and hovering cupids, Blenheim may appear to cajole; it does, in fact, always control.

It also inspires, and uplifts. 'It is a reverent thing,' according to Francis Bacon, 'to see a Castle or other ancient building that is not in decay.' 'The Castle of Blenheim', so called by its early viewers, has always functioned as both house and icon, artefact and archetype. Seen in certain lights, its honey-coloured stone gleams like El Dorado gold, encouraging all viewers to dream the impossible dream. The country house in general, as Elizabeth Bowen recognized, 'embodies that perfect ideal of living that, in actual living, cannot realize itself'. 'Of all the great things that the English have invented,' agrees Henry James, 'the only one they have mastered completely in all its details so that it becomes a compendious illustration of their social genius and their manners, is the well-appointed, well-administered, well-filled country house.' The country house as symbol of civilized living, of ceremony, community and continuity, stands in the heartland of British culture. English novelists such as Fielding, Richardson, Jane Austen, Thackeray, Wells and Galsworthy have kept their eyes fastened firmly, fondly, on the country house. They consistently eulogize its rhetoric and its romance, until the house itself becomes an epic hero. In those novels written during or after the Second World War, such as Evelyn Waugh's *Brideshead Revisited* (1945), a new note of elegy and loss creeps in. It is sad for Waugh and the rest of us to reflect that never again will one man have the means or the panache necessary to build himself an immense dwelling guaranteed to give him, right there on the spot, within his own gates, immense power and prestige and pleasure. Just to know that this neat trick was once upon a time accomplished with such verve and grace and cunning warms our hearts.

Today we are all little better than nomads, shifting our meagre belongings from flat to house, city to city, very few of us living as adults where we lived as children, fewer still living where our great-grandfathers lived. No wonder we are drawn, in ever-increasing numbers, to Britain's stately homes. More than 350,000 people each year make a pilgrimage to Blenheim; 53 per cent of them are British and 14 per cent are on their second visit.

In addition to those who buy their tickets at the gate, Blenheim has always had its parade of distinguished visitors: Alexander Pope, Daniel Defoe, Voltaire, Samuel Johnson, Thomas Jefferson, Lord Nelson, the Duke of Wellington, Nathaniel Hawthorne, Lytton Strachey, Noël Coward. They all paid their respects and formed their impressions. None of them could simply ignore such a forceful presence as Blenheim; they all either loved or hated. Hawthorne is perhaps the most lyrical; he likens Blenheim to the Garden of Eden.

If Blenheim's walls sometimes sing a noble epic of paradise regained, they more habitually paraphrase the wicked world beyond its gates. After the Fall: the rise and decline of the house's fortunes very neatly parallels that of Britain herself. The palace was built to commemorate the stunning victory at the Battle of Blenheim (1704) of British troops led by John Churchill, 1st Duke of Marlborough, the most famous Churchill of them all. By so decisively curtailing France's rise to imperialist power, he 'opened the gateways of the modern world', according to his descendant Sir Winston, the second most famous Churchill. Britain's might rose with Blenheim's. By the time Blenheim's four towers were capped, in the early eighteenth century, the Protestant Succession had been secured and Britain was a world power to reckon with. As the Empire grew during the nineteenth century, so did Blenheim's land holdings. One can argue that the English country house and English imperialist policy were closely linked. All those dukes and earls and lesser landed gentry ruled their hierarchical domains of servants, tenant-farmers and villagers with an iron hand and a superior mien, and their offspring ruled the Empire in exactly the same way. They saw it as one vast estate which, in exchange for firm, paternalistic control, would yield rich material rewards. Having grown and matured and reaped a golden harvest together, Blenheim Palace and the Empire, in musty decline, grew sentimental and nostalgic, both looking back over their shoulders at former paths of glory. The parallel ends there, for the Empire is gone, while Blenheim remains, to be visited and cherished and written about.

The doughty dowager appears now, at first glance, to be in a brash and vulgar mood. I went down to Woodstock from London, one spring afternoon in 1987, to meet my subject face to face. I joined the queue of tourists entering by the East Gate, paid my admission, bought the glossy guidebook. (Those who don't buy it here will have several further chances.) Once through the impressive gateway, I stood in the vast forecourt paved with stone, and craned my neck upwards at the palace. The house does indeed, as Sir John Vanbrugh once wrote, 'stare us in the face with a pretty impudent countenance'. I stared back at Blenheim's north front, and understood at once why no owner has ever dared tamper with its exterior design; nothing has ever been added or removed. I felt awed, ant-like, apprehensive, as I gazed at Blenheim's huge baroque mass, its fearful symmetry, its threatening roofscape of ferocious lions and plunging swords, its trumpeting central portico and tremendous, trailing wings. House and courtyards cover seven acres. This is a dragon of a house which once breathed fire and was turned to stone by some terrible curse. Blenheim sprawls like a petrified dinosaur or beached whale, completely out of scale with the little blue folds of hills that lap it round. Surely the huge stones of its walls were quarried by giants; how they reached the site in the days before cranes and lorries is a mystery as awesome as how the Egyptians built their pyramids.

Feeling rather like Jonah, I entered the cavernous Great Hall and joined the other tourists huddled there awaiting the tour guide. Even the children were hushed. We followed the red carpet from stateroom to stateroom; red ropes on either side kept us from straying. The crowds were thickest in the Churchill Exhibition Rooms, filled with Sir Winston's books and paintings and photos. On one wall was a huge photograph – as oversize as everything else at Blenheim – of young Winston at Harrow, wearing top hat, boutonnière and an expression of arrogant aplomb. His rich, fruity voice on tape pursued us from room to room: 'We shall fight in the fields and in the streets, we shall fight in the hills; we shall never surrender.'

For an extra fee, one can also tour the present Duke of Marlborough's private apartments. (From March to October, when the palace is open to the public seven days a week, he flees across the park to a modest Georgian house at Charlbury.) We were more relaxed, less reverential now, as we inspected the rooms where 'the Dook', as the Americans called him, shaves and eats his breakfast and makes love to his wife.

Right beside the Chapel is a bookshop where one can buy notepaper, match-books, bookmarks and three kinds of lapel buttons, all stamped with Blenheim's outlines. There is a souvenir kiosk on the water terraces as well, and a green wooden stand bearing the legend in gold: 'Ice Cream, Hot Dogs, Cold Drinks'. The exit from the palace takes all tourists through the main gift shop, where the hoary old house is embossed on copper wall plaques and imprisoned in paperweights made on the premises by the London Paperweights Company, owned jointly by the present Duke and an American.

Blenheim, I was beginning to realize, as I turned my back on the palace and went to explore the grounds, is now Big Business; nostalgia wears a price tag. Over two hundred and eighty years old and increasingly infirm, Blenheim is being kept alive by a complex life-support system, a team of almost two hundred administrators, secretaries, guides, cleaners, gate-keepers, gardeners, all rushing about in garden cafeteria, adventure play-ground, putting green, plant centre and butterfly house, as well as the palace itself. Repairing Blenheim's roof and stonework has eaten up £1,500,000 since 1950. The scaffolding on the roof, perpetually there, covered with green plastic, looks like a giant oxygen tent. Somehow, in spite of its disfiguring ganglia of metal tubing and printed signs and cash registers, Blenheim keeps her dignity. The proud palace prevails; Big Business trails behind.

I lingered as the other tourists bought their last postcard, took their last snapshot, and sped away. The light began to fade. The clumps of ancient cedars on the lawn grew almost black, placed two centuries ago there, and there, exactly where smiling Capability Brown pointed a correct finger. The cedars turned into covens of crouching witches, with matted hair and elbows all askew. As the sun set, sparks flew from the great golden balls on Blenheim's towers, and its obdurate stone melted suddenly into rivers of honey. Herons flapped silently homewards; the glowing sky cooled to grey ash; Blenheim's stones grew pallid again, splotched like aged skin. A damp chill and a tinge of malevolence crept out from the base of every pillar. Shadows hung like bats in all the crevices. The palace was alone now with its soul, its obsidian, stoic, brooding, great soul. The house in repose, like an elderly person, turns in on itself and shuffles its memories. The present blurs and is forgotten almost as it happens; only the distant past still glows in its true colours. As silence and night settled round it, Blenheim Palace remembered...

1
GROWING PAINS

Some violent bitter man, some powerful man
Called architect and artist in, that they,
Bitter and violent men, might rear in stone
The sweetness that all longed for night and day,
The gentleness none there had ever known.

W.B. Yeats, 'Ancestral Houses'

INSIDE THE HOUSE THERE WAS A BUSTLE OF ACTIVITY, A FLUSHED air of anticipation. In the Bow-window Room in the eastern wing, a footman was arranging carved chairs covered in white embroidered fabric into neat rows while a second footman filled the wall-sconces with wax candles. In the kitchen, the cook was taking pans of rosquillions and marchpane cakes from the brick wall-oven. In the Duke of Marlborough's dressing-room, one of his two valets was helping him into his best waist-coat, the one with diamond buttons.

Outside, the sun gilded the western towers as it disappeared behind them and the first coach bringing guests rumbled towards the house over the storeyed arch of Vanbrugh's vast bridge. On that early evening in August, 1719, Blenheim Palace felt itself, at long last, quickening into real life and some semblance of lightheartedness. The house was getting ready for its first party. Fourteen years old, it was still growing, still ungainly at its western extremities; they presented a calm enough exterior, but they were filled with scaffolding and turmoil within. Fourteen years ago, when it was very small, being then a foundation stone only eight feet square, Blenheim had experienced one brief moment of tearing high spirits, of dancing and laughing and general merriment; after that it had been all *Sturm und Drang*, one long identity crisis, as three people fought to raise it according to three different concepts of what Blenheim should become.

All conflict and confusion; a muddy battleground filled with broken stones and the rumble of rebellious workmen. Until today. Now the first coach was clattering into the huge north courtyard with a silvery jingle of harness. It looked very tiny, like a toy carriage, in that huge acreage of paving stones. A lady and gentleman, splendidly powdered and brocaded, climbed down slowly as a blue-coated footman held the door. As they looked up at the house, they were, as all future guests of Blenheim would be, momentarily transfixed, rooted to the spot by that basilisk eye.

The house couldn't help itself; it bristled and glowered. The Battle of Blenheim had begotten it and left its imprint mainly on the roof; fourteen years of a different kind of battle had raged around it. No wonder Blenheim Palace's habitual expression was fiercely belligerent as it stood braced for

East colonnade, quadrants and central portico

the next attack. The palace's north front was 480 feet long and its weight and density suggested a medieval fortress. 'Lie heavy on him, Earth, for he/Laid many a heavy load on thee,' was Alexander Pope's playful epitaph for Sir John Vanbrugh, whose militaristic baroque style at Blenheim struck all beholders, at first glance, with the megalomania of its sheer mass. Its symmetry was severe, both externally in its façade and internally in its arrangement of rooms. To left and right of the central portico, Blenheim's long lines of windows stood at attention like so many foot-soldiers under the command of four mounted officers, the four tall towers at its corners. Nothing broke rank. The corners of the four towers were capped with thirty-foot pinnacles (carved by Grinling Gibbons for £20 apiece). Each pinnacle consisted of the Duke of Marlborough's heavy coronet crushing the French fleur-de-lis, proclaiming to soft skies above and uplifted eyes below that in 1704 the British had thoroughly trounced the French. Over the central portico stood Minerva, goddess of defensive warfare, with a chained captive on either side. Atop the two ends of the east and west colonnades bristled twin trophy-piles of pikes, armour, cannon-balls and drums, so magnificently carved in stone by Grinling Gibbons that the drum cloth stirs and wrinkles there for ever in an unseen wind. Two ferocious stone lions on the east-court towers faced two more on the west; all four were sinking their rapacious British teeth into the ruffled feathers of French cocks. All the roof ornaments, lions and warriors, cocks and captives, were gilded or painted in bright colours, a garish and grotesque troop parading through the air high above gentle green verdure and veiled elms.

Other carriages were arriving in the forecourt now; other gentry who lived in haphazard ivy-covered manor-houses tucked into the Oxfordshire hills were standing stock-still to stare upwards, before proceeding slowly up the wide steps and in through the huge double doors beneath Minerva and the Marlborough coat of arms.

There to greet them, just inside the door, stood the groom of the chambers and the butler. Like all the Marlborough menservants in the house, they wore blue coats, waistcoats and plush breeches – plain liveries, not expensive 'laced' ones trimmed with gold braid. They wore laced liveries only at Marlborough House in London; that way, they lasted two years. The plain liveries had to be replaced annually. The Duchess paid for their making, buying the cloth from Mr Nash for 8s. a yard, 'better cloth than I have ever had of the drapers for ten'.

The groom of the chambers and the butler slept in plain basement rooms under the kitchen court, 'boarded and wainscoted in deal'. They deserved their £15 a year salary, for the Duchess was not an easy mistress. She never gave her servants 'board wages' when the family wasn't there to be tended. After all, the staff had the dairy produce to feed them and there was plenty of venison on the hoof in the park. She also made the menservants buy hats, shoes and stockings for their liveries, giving them an extra pound a year to do so. And if a servant left, his blue coat and breeches were altered for his replacement, with the Duchess haranguing the tailor if he charged a penny too much.

The blue-coated butler bowed to the guests as they entered the Great Hall, motioning them with a gloved hand to proceed down the corridor to the left. All of them instinctively lowered their voices as they entered the Hall.

Like all the rooms at Blenheim, it bore witness to the three egos battling for dominance during its construction. Its flamboyant architect, Sir John Vanbrugh, had made it large – 70 by 45 feet – and dramatic, with a cathedral's solemnity achieved by having daylight come only from a clerestory of windows at the top of its sixty-seven-foot walls. Vanbrugh had also seen to it that here, as elsewhere in Blenheim, masonry and the geometry of space dominated, overpowering all furniture and ornaments, no matter how grand. Blenheim's owner, John, 1st Duke of Marlborough, on the other hand, insisted that the Great Hall bear his image. He made it into a giant billboard advertising himself, the self-made man, the remarkable Duke who had raised himself, from humble beginnings as poor, untitled John Churchill, by various kinds of warfare, to the very pinnacle of power and patronage and wealth. Everywhere in the palace, in stone and marble, tapestry and paint, loomed the Great Hero, Victor at the Battle of Blenheim, raised to mythic heights. The guests craned their necks upwards in the Hall. Look! the Duke, in shining cuirass and blue mantle, was kneeling to Britannia seated on a globe, offering him a wreath. At Britannia's feet sat Plenty, pouring out her cornucopia of fruits. To the right of the Duke, a winged genius displayed a large plan for the battle of Blenheim, while Mars and Hercules looked up from below in attitudes of wonder. Above them all hovered a winged female called Fame, with trumpet and laurel-wreath at the ready. Off to one side Clio, the Muse of History, grasped a huge pen and inscribed the words: 'Anno Memorabili, 1704' into a huge volume. It seemed significant that History's feet were turned in a different direction from all the rest.

Sarah, Duchess of Marlborough, Blenheim's other parent, for her part, saw to it that Sir James Thornhill painted this grand allegory on the ceiling for 25s. per square yard. When he sent in his total bill for £978, she paid it reluctantly, calling it 'a higher price than any thing of that bigness was ever given for Rubens or Titian'. She did not invite Thornhill back to Blenheim to paint the ceiling and walls of the Saloon.

As the guests passed solemnly through the Hall, the heels of the ladies' satin slippers echoing on the hard Portland stone, some of the standards captured over the years by the conquering Duke waved above them, and more than a dozen lascivious gods and goddesses leered from the walls. Hung there were nine large paintings on leather, attributed to Titian, which had been given to the Duke by Victor Amadeus, Duke of Savoy. A flushed Pluto was embracing Proserpine, an avid Apollo grabbing Daphne, an inebriated Bacchus tickling Cupid; all of them very large and pink and sensual. Like Blenheim's martial roofscape, the Titians reflected the raw passion of the age which sired the palace: a crude age of sex and violence,

---

OPPOSITE: South end of Hall and eastern corridor

The Bow-window Room, showing capitals and frieze carved by Grinling Gibbons

in which animal spirits were openly expressed. Blenheim was raised in a stench of smoking cannons and blood-streaked sports, an aggressive age when Englishmen abroad revelled in war, in killing and looting and bringing home the spoils, and at home in cock-fighting and in sword-clashing duels. More than a hint of all that whoring and warring was right there in Blenheim's Great Hall.

When the guests reached the Bow-window Room, the softer charms of the palace began to take effect. If Blenheim ever came close to a youthful skip and smile, it was here. Placed in the exact centre of the eastern wing, where the Duke and Duchess had their private apartments, the Bow-window Room served as Sarah's sitting-room and was the only room in the palace which she liked. All the others were too cold and formal, too right-angled and ostentatious. The very first command she had uttered to Sir John Vanbrugh in 1705 when he was designing Blenheim was to give her a comfortable room with a bow-window. Accordingly, he had made the room 41 by 18 feet, small enough to be cosy, and had placed Blenheim's foundation-stone directly beneath the bow. The room invited conviviality and intimate conversation; it was the true heart of the house.

Inside a pillared alcove at its eastern end, the pretty bow of three arched windows curved outward with a playful spontaneity as if to embrace the delightful garden outside, which Queen Anne's head gardener, Henry Wise, had planted in 1708 with damask roses, marigolds, 'black-eyed hotspurs' and 'coxcombs'. Sarah had hung the windows with blue silk damask from Venice, doing some of the stitching herself to make sure it was properly done. She and the Duke had only moved into Blenheim a few weeks before; there was still a great deal to see to, but she had furnished this room first. There were two white marble tables with gilded frames and large gilded mirrors above them; an easy chair covered with blue silk embroidered with gold wheat sheaves; fourteen chairs – on which the guests were seated – covered with white Dutch fabric embroidered in coloured flowers.

The most beguiling feature of the room was not its curvaceous bow or fine furniture but the four fluted pillars which stood in pairs on either side of the alcove. Grinling Gibbons, delighted to find a piece of wood under his hands at last rather than stone or marble, had carved the delicate leaves of their Corinthian capitals, and the charming frieze above – for £36. No other man, as Horace Walpole recognized, could give to wood 'the loose and airy lightness of flowers'. Gibbons had already been practising his craft for forty years when he came to work at Blenheim. His wood-carvings of primrose-wreaths, sea shells and luscious fruit curled round the kingdom, but the only naturalness the hard-nosed Marlboroughs had allowed him at Blenheim was in the Bow-window Room's pillars. His other work at Blenheim, all in grim stone and marble, shouts the palace's pugnacity from its rooftops, or sweeps severely round a fireplace.

On that soft August evening, Gibbons's fluted pillars and lilting leaves were about to turn themselves into a proscenium arch, for the Marlboroughs' guests were to be entertained with an amateur production of Dryden's *All for Love*. First produced in 1678, the year in which John Churchill and Sarah Jennings were married, the play was an apt choice, for like Blenheim itself, it is cast in heroic mould, its noble blank verse richly rhetorical.

Since the palace was still in a makeshift state, still in the process of becoming, it was fitting that the production was an unsophisticated affair, all very impromptu, with screens placed before the bow-window to suggest scenery, and with three Marlborough granddaughters taking part. Since the Marlboroughs' third daughter, Elizabeth, Countess of Bridgwater, had died in 1714, her daughter Lady Anne Egerton had come to live with them. When, two years later, the Marlboroughs' second daughter, Anne, Countess of Sunderland, had died of pleurisy at thirty-two, Sarah had eagerly taken her two daughters Lady Anne and Lady Diana Spencer into the household. Sarah enjoyed her power over them; she strictly supervised their manners, dress, and when the time came, choice of husbands. She would marry them, as she had her own daughters, into the highest, richest families in England. Her iron will had lately cut a swathe through rehearsals, for she had excised all the amorous passages from *All for Love*.

The company hushed as Lady Anne Spencer stepped forward to recite the specially written prologue. The Duchess had asked her house guest Sir Richard Steele, sitting behind her, his plump face glistening, to write it. He had, after all, written three comedies and was Master of the King's Players at London's Drury Lane. Sir Richard, however, declined, preferring to act as stage-manager for the Blenheim production; his muse flowed best in close, dingy coffee-houses, not in Blenheim's antiseptic acres. Another house guest, Bishop Hoadly, had rushed forward eagerly, pleased to be able to do the great Duke a service. The Bishop was, like most men of the time, fiercely ambitious for wealth and status, a whig and low-church leader working his way up from small bishopric to larger. It was also typical of the age that since he'd become Bishop of Bangor in 1716, he'd never been anywhere near his diocese. 'Little Ben', as Steele called him, had come down to breakfast at Blenheim that very morning with the prologue in his hand. Now, as Lady Anne declaimed it, he grinned proudly, a rather rodent-like grin that showed his 'nasty rotten teeth', as his monarch George II would later describe them. The prologue began with a compliment to Her Grace; from his seat beside Steele, Little Ben watched the back of the Duchess's head closely to see if she would deign to nod and smile in his direction.

> O Marlbro', think not wrong that I thee name,
> And first do homage to thy brighter fame,
> Beauty and virtue with each other strove
> To move and recompense thy early love.
> Beauty which Egypt's queen could never boast ...

Her imperious Grace nodded ever so slightly to the air above the Bishop's head, but didn't smile. She was conscious of her high office: chatelaine of the grandest house in Britain, and constrained by so much unaccustomed magnificence stretching out, through room after echoing room, behind her. At fifty-nine, Sarah still had that glow of vitality, that sparking nimbus of energy that had made young John Churchill, himself cast in more phlegmatic mould, fall passionately, permanently in love with her. It was in 1677 that he'd first seen her dancing a saraband at the Duchess of York's ball at St James's Palace. Born on 29 May 1660, Sarah Jennings, with 'a fury temper and a fairy face' was, at seventeen, still something of a tomboy. Handsome Jack, then twenty-seven, the youngest – and most ambitious – colonel in the English army, wanted to marry her at once, but Sarah was scornful and teasing, blew hot and cold, kept him on tenterhooks for a year and a half. Then she married him, became fiercely loyal and loving, bore him seven children, and never looked at another man again.

For the first four years of their marriage, the Churchills had had no proper home, shifting from quarters in John's parents' house to rented ones in London's Jermyn Street. As soon as he could afford it, in 1683, John built Holywell House for Sarah at St Albans, the town in which she had been born. It was always her favourite dwelling, no matter how many others they acquired, with its sprawling informality and fruit trees spilling over the garden walls. 'However ordinary it may be,' Sarah decided in 1714, 'I would not part with it for any house I have seen.'

Poor Sarah. She was born with a high brick wall between herself and her fellow man, keeping her from all empathy and insight. She could never put herself in the other person's place, and this natural obtuseness made her tactless and suspicious and more than a little paranoid. 'I find it a perpetual war in this world to defend oneself against knaves and fools,' she declared, from inside her beleaguered garrison. From time to time, she fired fusillades of rage and invective over the walls, letting them fall where they might. (A goodly number landed on Blenheim.) Once, after she and John had had a terrible row, she had snatched up a pair of scissors and hacked off her long golden hair, which she knew he adored. It was still golden; she kept it that way with frequent applications of honey water. Alexander Pope was probably referring to the Duchess when he wrote of Atossa, 'Who, with herself, or others, from her birth/Finds all her life one warfare upon earth.' Jonathan Swift proclaimed that 'three furies reigned in her breast, sordid Avarice, disdainful Pride and ungovernable Rage'. Sarah was sharp and sarcastic to her children and her servants, and would never, ever admit that she was at fault. She prided herself on her common sense, her pragmatism and her sense of order. Even the pockets of her gowns were subdivided into four compartments so that her scissors, thimble, vinaigrette and snuff-box, with its two enamelled portraits of the Duke, were always in their right place. All these qualities of thrift, pride, hot-headedness, stubbornness and practicality had, for the past fourteen years, converged on Blenheim as it grew larger and more imposing. Sarah would have liked to have been born a man; she would have made a first-rate architect, lawyer or financier. When it came to Blenheim, she was determined to be its master.

The Duchess was dressed for her party in gold-worked brocade, fine lace and an excessive complement of diamonds. On one finger she wore the diamond ring which Queen Anne had given her to commemorate John's stunning victory at the battle of Blenheim. Under a huge flat diamond was a miniature of the Duke, with smaller diamonds clustered round it. In the 1716 inventory of her jewels, Sarah had drawn 'the exact bigness' of the diamond and noted its value: £800. She sat very erect in her embroidered chair as Lady Anne recited the prologue, with an eye on her grandfather:

> This heap of stones which Blenheim's palace frame,
> Rose in this form a monument to thy name.
> This heap of stones shall crumble into sand,
> But thy great name shall through the ages stand.

The Duke of Marlborough slumped in his gilded chair, his mouth slack and dribbling, his face the colour of old ivory. Two strokes had impaired his speech and left him partially paralysed. 'Thy great name ...' The Duke tried to square his shoulders but his flaccid right side wouldn't obey. There was a snail-trail, Sarah noted with dismay, of spittle down his flower-embroidered waistcoat. Still, his were the only diamond buttons in the room. The other guests were in their best silks and velvets, for one dressed

---

OPPOSITE: Sarah, 1st Duchess of Marlborough. Portrait after Kneller

John, 1st Duke of Marlborough. Portrait attributed to Closterman

in the country exactly as one dressed in town, but their buttons were gold or silver. Sir Richard Steele's were mere brass. He was quite as greedy for material gain as the rest of the nation but he hadn't yet achieved it. His latest get-rich-quick scheme, conceived a year before, was for a ship which would bring fish alive from the sea by means of a salt-water 'fish pool' flowing through the hull. To date he had found no investors. He had penned some fulsome praise of Marlborough in No. 139 of the *Spectator* papers, thus securing entrée to the Marlborough circle of sycophants, not as large now as it had once been.

For his part, the Duke hoped that the splendours of Blenheim, now that he could, at last, show them off, would add fresh lustre to his somewhat tarnished image. His Grace had been shrewder than Sir Richard at the game of winning wealth and status. From the start, John Churchill had been an opportunist, switching his allegiance from Jacobite to Hanoverian according to which party had the fattest purse and the biggest plums to offer a devoted follower. 'Faithful but unfortunate' was the Churchill family motto; John gave it an ironic twist. In a society traditionally based on ascribed rather than achieved status, young John Churchill, with no one to help him, had to climb the slippery stairs leading to titles and riches, and, having reached them, to climb one step higher on to the secure landing of a country estate, whose property could be passed on to his heirs in perpetuity. John's father was Sir Winston Churchill, who could trace his ancestry back only three generations and whose family name came from a village in Somerset, not, as later Churchills liked to claim, from the Norman 'Courcelle'. Sir Winston had married cannily; by choosing Elizabeth Drake from a famous old Devonshire family, he had secured not only money but also Ashe House, an Elizabethan E-shaped manor on the main road from Axminster to the sea. Born in 1650, Jack grew up, with twelve brothers and sisters, in that unpretentious seat of plain country squires, part of which lacked a roof. In appearance, he himself lacked nothing, for he was tall and well-built, with fair hair, blue eyes, a finely chiselled nose and a firm mouth. 'Handsome John Churchill' began his career serving the Duke of York as an ensign in the foot-guards, and began his money-hoard with £5,000 given him by Barbara Palmer, Duchess of Cleveland. It was John's reward for having jumped out of her bed and through the nearest window with great dispatch when Charles II, whose mistress she was, arrived one day unexpectedly. John prudently invested the whole £5,000 in an annuity, giving him £500 a year, and after that he never looked back. When the Duke of York came to the English throne as James II, he created faithful John Baron Churchill of Sandridge, and sent him off as Ambassador Extraordinary to the court of Louis XIV. Louis was building

Versailles, and John's vague dreams suddenly became concrete: some day he would have a house as grand as Louis's and would live there like a king. In 1689, William III gave Baron Churchill a boost up by making him Earl of Marlborough. But it was hard for a man, in those shifting sands, to know which king to stand by. In 1692 John found himself clapped into the dank confines of the Tower of London for five weeks on a charge of conspiring to murder William and restore James to the throne. Nine years later, however, when King William III was embarking on the War of the Spanish Succession, he trusted Marlborough sufficiently to appoint him commander-in-chief of the armies in Flanders, and just before the king died, in 1702, he told his successor, Queen Anne, that Marlborough was the only army leader capable of keeping the greedy French from swallowing Europe. When Queen Anne made her first appearance as sovereign in the House of Lords, looking uncertain and ungainly in her heavy purple robes, the handsome Earl of Marlborough, carrying the Sword of State, walked ahead of her and the handsome Countess of Marlborough walked behind. Both of them were silently resolving to squeeze from Her Majesty as many places and pensions as possible.

Sarah and John were well-matched, for they both craved money, power and fame, in that order. In that cock-fight age everyone, not just the Marlboroughs, kept a beady eye on possible state sinecures, and scrabbled for them shamelessly. (The graceful pursuit of culture would come later in the eighteenth century, and a sense of public duty later still, in the nineteenth.) In that same year, 1702, Queen Anne granted John his dukedom. The Duke was not a clever man – Lord Chesterfield pronounced him 'eminently illiterate' – but he had a positive genius for waging war. The men in his army were a scruffy bunch of former gaol-birds, but the Duke made them loyal and invincible. He never lost a battle. His dreams of the affluent life drove him forward to victory after victory. If he faltered or felt lethargic – for John could be, according to Sarah, 'intolerably lazy' – she was always there, with her Lady Macbeth iron will, to give him a push. Many of the pamphleteers of the day – for the higher up the ladder a man scrambled the more enemies appeared to knock him down – reported that the Duke of Marlborough ordered his officers to certain death so that he could sell their commissions and that government funds, earmarked for secret-service operations and consequently not having to be accounted for, went straight into the Duke's pocket. How he got his vast wealth is, however, not as well documented as how he hung on to it. Once he chided his orderly for lighting four candles in his tent when his ally Prince Eugene of Savoy came to confer with him; another time when the Prince couldn't read the Duke's handwriting and passed the letter to a colleague, the latter remarked that the Duke didn't dot his i's. 'Oh,' said the Prince, 'it saves his Grace's ink.' Since his recent strokes, the Duke had gone frequently to Bath to take the waters. More than one diarist records that the infirm Duke always walked home from the pump-room, even 'in a cold, dark night', to save sixpence in coach hire.

Like most rich men, the Duke loved what he possessed, so as he sat in the Bow-window Room, with his granddaughters and his house both in pretty, playful mood, both bent on pleasing him, he felt happy for the first time in weeks. The house seemed to give him its blessing.

Lady Anne Spencer had finished the prologue now, and the players began to roll forth Dryden's rich rhetoric. Lady Anne played Octavia; Antony's children were played by her sister Diana, only nine years old, and by Lady Anne Egerton. A family friend, Lady Charlotte Macarthy, made a rather too virginal Cleopatra. All four looked splendid in the silks destined for Blenheim's windows and bed-hangings. On 17 May 1708, the warring Duke had written to Sarah from Brussels in one of his despondent moods: 'Though I have many melancholy thoughts, I can't but hope we shall have some time at Blenheim; so that if you have not already writ to Lord Manchester, I should be glad if you would, that he might choose some velvets and damasks, and send them home by some of the men-of-war this winter.' Sarah had written at once to Charles Montague, 4th Earl and later first Duke of Manchester, then serving as Ambassador Extraordinary to the Court of Venice, and ordered 3,500 yards. He passed on the commission to local Venetian workmen whom he declared as competent as the highly touted Genoese ones, and much cheaper. 'The goodness of the velvet,' he assured Sarah, 'depends on the quantity of ounces of silk, and one cannot be deceived, as every piece is weighed, and so there must be that number of ounces as is agreed on.' Sarah ordered royal crimson for the Grand Cabinet windows, blue with a gold border for one of the staterooms, bright scarlet for bed-hangings ('I like it better for a bed than crimson, being less common') and yards and yards of yellow and green. The four young ladies swirled and rustled in their trains like gaily plumaged birds. Miss Mary Cairns, a London merchant's daughter whose common sense Sarah approved of, played Serapion the High Priest, wearing a Dresden-worked surplice destined for Blenheim's chapel. She too was living at Blenheim under Sarah's thumb, and being educated by Miss La Vie, governess to all four girls, who played Alexas.

The role of Mark Antony was taken by Captain Humphrey Fish, one of the Duke's loyal officers who had begun as Sarah's page and who would, by his own polished boot-straps, eventually pull himself up to the rank of lieutenant-colonel. He clanked about, there in the Bow-window Room, wearing the diamond-hilted sword given to the Duke by Emperor Leopold I of Austria. Its huge rose-cut diamonds, more than two dozen of them, twinkled and tempted in the candlelight. The Duchess had cautioned him to keep its point well clear of the silks. When his advances to Cleopatra grew slightly amorous, but not nearly as amorous as Dryden had intended, for Sarah's censoring pencil had been at work, Sir Richard Steele began to snigger. 'I doubt this Fish is Flesh,' he whispered to Bishop Hoadly beside him. The Bishop shushed him, with an eye on the Duke.

The Duke, however, had stopped listening and was letting his mind stray into former fields of glory. He was looking at the 'Battle of Blenheim' tapestry, which hung in the Bow-window Room. Sarah had objected; it was far too big, being 14 feet high and 25 feet wide, but the Duke had prevailed, and had it hung on the long south wall. It belonged there in the Bow-window Room, near Blenheim's foundation-stone, for the tapestry was, in a sense, the house's birth certificate, its *raison d'être*.

The Duke never tired of looking at it, for there, woven for all time in rich colours that would never fade, was his finest hour, when he had savaged the French and, as it turned out, spawned a house. In the background, thousands of French soldiers are being driven into the cold blue Danube; in the middle ground, the little German village of Blenheim fills with smoke from burning water-mills. In the right foreground, mounted on his white charger, splendid in scarlet uniform and blue Garter ribbon, the heroic Duke of Marlborough is accepting the surrender of Marshal Tallard and preparing to bundle him and two other French generals into his coach. The Duke had been seventeen hours in the saddle that day, 13 August 1704, galloping along the lines, calm and decisive and daring. In the lower left foreground, a red-coated British grenadier holds the captured French standard, and guards a huge pile of booty, for the booty captured at Blenheim – cannon, ammunition, kettle-drums – was considerable, and for the acquisitive Duke who was the victor the spoils of the actual day were only the beginning of a long and fruitful flow.

While still in the saddle on that glorious day, Marlborough had borrowed a colonel's wine bill and scribbled a pencilled note to Sarah on its back: 'I have not time to say more but to beg you will give my duty to the Queen and let her know her army has had a Glorious Victory.' Then the dusty soldier, Parke, had galloped off to deliver it, dropping exhausted, some days later, at Queen Anne's feet as she sat in the bow-window of

---

OPPOSITE: 'Battle of Blenheim' tapestry.
Detail showing Marshal Tallard surrendering to Marlborough

Windsor Castle's long gallery playing one of her interminable games of dominoes. The Queen and the nation were jubilant. England had welcomed the War of the Spanish Succession, being greedy for more colonies and richer trade; France and Spain stood in her way and owned territory in the New World which England coveted. When Marlborough dealt the French such a decisive blow at Blenheim, the English went mad with hero-worship. Medals were struck bearing the Duke's profile, bonfires flared on every hill, and Britain, bucked up by Blenheim and the taking of Gibraltar in the same month, began her steady march towards imperialist supremacy. On 3 January 1705, the captured standards which would end in Blenheim Palace's Great Hall were paraded through the London streets from the Tower to Westminster with Marlborough at the head of a vast procession of cavalry, infantry and pikemen. Cannons and crowds roared out their welcome and Queen Anne, smiling from her palace window, determined to give the good-looking Duke riding at the head of his guards some stupendous reward commensurate with his service to his country.

In February, she told Parliament what it would be. She would give the Duke the royal manor of Woodstock, a wilderness of 15,000 acres in Oxfordshire, and would build on it, at government expense, 'the Castle of Blenheim'. Within a month the necessary Act of Parliament had been passed. Shortly thereafter the proud Duke had gone to Brussels to see Judocus de Vos, the most skilled tapestry-maker of the day and commissioned the 'Battle of Blenheim' tapestry. Nine others commemorating his further victories would follow, all of them designed by Lambert de Hondt, with wide borders of martial trophies. Louis XIV had glorified his military achievements in the *Histoire du Roi* tapestries. The Duke of Marlborough would follow suit. For ten years the shuttles flew, under de Vos's direction, weaving the bright wools back and forth, transforming the carnage of war into great art, and canny Jack Churchill into a great British hero.

The house hugged its battle tapestry tight across its heart while Marlborough counted his victories and Dryden's verse ricocheted off the walls. Two blue-liveried footmen, both six feet tall, broad-shouldered and as perfectly matched as book-ends, stood stiffly on either side of the door. They felt as if they were standing at the very edge of a tropical island. In front of them, the young ladies rustled and flitted like scarlet and green parrots. But all life stopped suddenly at the door. Behind them stretched the flat, grey-marbled silent sea of Blenheim Palace. Occasionally, one of the footmen glanced fearfully over his shoulder, as if feeling a cold slither on his neck. When he did so, he could see all along the house's main axial vista, through corridor, Great Hall, corridor and Long Gallery, a distance of 320 feet if one measured from eastern bow-window to matching western bow-window in the Gallery. And in all that long expanse, nothing stirred, nothing careened out of line to spoil Blenheim's awesome symmetry and order.

There was plenty of clatter and clutter, however, in the south-west corner of the east court, where the kitchen was situated. The kitchen was a large room 50 by 28 feet wide and 32 feet high. At its long central table, the cook was preparing a battalia pie for the supper which would be served to guests in the Saloon at ten o'clock. The Duchess paid her cook £50 a year but she didn't allow him the usual perquisite of selling the kitchen fat. He had to give it to the chandler in exchange for the tallow candles used in Blenheim's inferior rooms, rather than wax ones. The usual ragged collection of scullions and turnspits (£2 or less a year) scurried about the kitchen like so many rats, trying to keep one step ahead of the cook's sudden clouts. There were also several little boys forever in the way, who got crusts and a sack to sleep on, but no wages. The Duchess showed her modernity by employing one kitchen-maid, who received £6 a year. The kitchen had traditionally been an all-male preserve, presided over by the clerk of the kitchen, but times were changing, and in another hundred years, it would be all-female.

The kitchen-maid was standing at the table next to the cook. She had just finished quartering chickens, pounding their bones, and sprinkling them with nutmeg. Now she was rolling sausage balls in spinach. As fast as they came from the maid's red, glistening hands, the cook placed both chickens and sausage balls into the battalia pie. Whole larks and pickled oysters and lemon slices went in next. His fingers, none too clean but surprisingly deft, seemed to be everywhere at once. The room was hot from the open fire, smoky from the tallow candles, and pungent with the smells of food and unwashed bodies. Everyone was shriller, faster than usual, getting Blenheim ready for its first party. From time to time a gust of revelry blew in the door, a sudden guffaw coming down the long corridor from the servants' hall. There, the groom of the horse and the other stablemen, in blue coats and buckskin breeches with a whiff of manure, were drinking ale with the visiting coachmen and postilions who had brought their masters to Blenheim. But all that gusto of living was a long way off from the silent reaches of the main pile with its one little blossoming island.

The island was about to shift downstream, for *All for Love* had just ended, to polite handclapping and much bowing from the players. The two footmen at the door were leading the guests back down the corridor, then through the Great Hall's south doorway into the Saloon beyond.

Marlborough's bust in white marble looked down from the doorway as the guests passed through, while the flesh-and-blood Duke, his face almost as white, shuffled slowly forward at a much less elevated height.

Vanbrugh had given the Saloon a height of forty feet and elaborate white marble door-cases. A rusticated dado in red and white marble ran round the room; above it was a similar panel painted to resemble marble, so that the genuine and the fake existed side by side. The walls and ceiling had been painted by the artist Louis Laguerre that very summer. He had been born, fittingly enough, at Versailles, and had come to England in 1683, painting his way from one stately home to another, including the magnificent Chatsworth. Sarah considered him a great bargain compared to Thornhill, for Laguerre had painted the Saloon ceiling and the four walls down to the real-marble dado for £500. Around the walls he had painted an open arcade of Corinthian columns rising to a frieze of martial trophies. (By this time, the guests were beginning to feel satiated, nay suffocated, by martial trophies.) Peering through the openings of the fake columns was a motley assortment of Spaniards, Moors, Chinese, Turks … and Dean Barzillai Jones, a Fellow of All Souls, Oxford, whose rotund figure in the flesh could be seen entering the Saloon last, as befitted the Marlboroughs' domestic chaplain. Sarah kept him on the premises, not because she had any religious leanings but because his wit kept the morose Duke amused. Like the Saloon itself, the Dean's talk mixed the spurious and the true, for he had a bad habit of lying, causing a friend of Sarah's to remark that it would be as hard to make his inside fair as to make his outside clean. His protruding paunch, and his plain brown waistcoat, both testified to years of good eating. The Dean would play a prominent role in Blenheim's life-story, but not for many years yet.

The guests paraded round the room, feeling as stiff as its columns. Above them on the ceiling, the illustrious Duke in armour and plumed helmet raced ahead with rearing steeds towards his cold ambitions over the bodies of fallen, fainter-hearted warriors. It was not a scene that encouraged light-hearted banter. According to the fashion of the time, the twenty chairs were all ranged formally round the walls, not dotted about in little islands geared to gossip and confidences. The Duchess was momentarily ignoring her guests, and appraising the marble dado to see if the new housemaid had cleaned it properly that morning, using the special mixture which Sarah had had the housekeeper mix up in the still-room: bullock's gall, soap, turpentine and pipe clay. There was a great deal of marble to be

---

OPPOSITE: In the Saloon, looking north-east

cleaned at Blenheim; the housemaid would get £6 a year, and hands permanently sore and chafed from the turpentine.

Now Hodges the house steward was carrying in the battalia pie, followed by the butler and footmen with other lukewarm dishes. The distance from kitchen to Saloon was too far to keep food really hot. Hodges hated having to always carry in the meat; he was, after all, top servant and chief administrator, in charge of all the house servants, but the Duchess insisted, and for £40 a year he did as he was told.

As soon as politeness allowed, the guests departed, fleeing to their cosy inglenooks and low-beamed ceilings. Bishop Hoadly and Sir Richard Steele were given lighted candles by the groom of the chambers, said their goodnights, and climbed the stone stairs beyond the Hall's arches to their modest bedrooms above. The Duke and Duchess went off to their bedchambers in the eastern wing, to be ministered to by valets and lady's maid respectively. The butler tiptoed through the brooding house, locking its many doors. As each bolt in the huge brass locks slammed home, it pierced the silence like a rifle shot.

Through the long, dark night, the house clutched the tinsel-ends of its one night of youthful frolic, but too much of the ferocity and stress of the second battle of Blenheim had seeped into its stones, and stayed. For fourteen years it had been All for War, and on that August night, while its inhabitants slept, the house still felt its wounds. As cold dawn light crept in through Blenheim's eastern bow-window, the thin little memory of this coming-out party faded, then all but disappeared among the wisps of smoke curling upwards, in finely woven wools, from the first battle of Blenheim.

IN THOSE BREATHLESS DAYS OF 1705, WHEN THE DUKE HAD WON THE battle of Blenheim and been given a castle as reward, the Marlboroughs stood triumphant on the pinnacle of power. 'And Blenheim's Tower shall triumph o'er Whitehall,' scribbled one pamphleteer. When she came to the throne in 1702, Queen Anne had made Sarah Groom of the Stole, Keeper of the Privy Purse, a most apt appointment, and Mistress of the Robes. (Another pamphleteer reckoned the Marlborough Crown emoluments at this time at £65,000 a year.) Queen Anne was timid, morose and usually ill, with a perpetual frown on her sallow face as she tried, with her weak eyes and weaker brain, to see what was going on in her court and her kingdom. She needed Sarah's bright fire and steel, and loved her with a weird, obsessive, erotic love. When the map of Europe and the constitution of England were in the making, Sarah Churchill was the power behind the throne. 'And Anne shall wear the Crown, but Sarah reign,' declared one broadsheet. Statesmen and diplomats rushed to open doors for her; great ladies waited for hours to have a word with her as she sailed through the drawing-rooms of Kensington Palace and Windsor Castle. Everyone seeking preferment – and who wasn't? – had to do it through the proud Duchess of Marlborough. It was a heady time for Sarah, one which sowed the seeds of her subsequent overbearing attitude to the house which a grateful Queen, in the full flush of her dependence, had given to the Marlboroughs.

So the Castle of Blenheim was engendered by one great battle, and one great impulse. The Queen left the Duke free to choose his own architect, but of course expected him to do it within Her Majesty's Office of Works. Sarah plumped for Christopher Wren, who was Surveyor, knowing he would design a neat, no-nonsense dwelling on strictly classical lines. When the Duke overruled her and chose the Comptroller, Vanbrugh, one of his cronies in the convivial Kit-Kat Club, Sarah sulked and bided her time, and kept an eye on Wren. The Duke had heard his Kit-Kat chum Lord Carlisle praising Vanbrugh, whom the Earl had commissioned to build Castle Howard, just then rising to its magnificent dome in the Yorkshire dales. The Duke accordingly went round to the modest house which Vanbrugh had claimed for himself from the ruins of Whitehall Palace, and which his waggish friends christened 'Goose-Pie House' because of its homely roof-line. It was typical of Vanbrugh's panache that he grabbed his pencil, drew Blenheim's grandiose outline with a few sweeping gestures, and talked the Duke into accepting his design – all before he had even gone down to Woodstock to see the site! Later, he had a wooden model made up and placed in Kensington Palace so that Queen Anne could admire and approve.

Vanbrugh's self-assurance was as gargantuan as the houses he designed. He had had no formal architectural training, but he was full of daring and ideas, and he liked to think big. Castle Howard had been his very first house, and he had been only thirty-five when in 1699 he'd taken that spectacular leap into an unknown field, causing his friend Jonathan Swift to quip: 'Van's genius, without thought or lecture, / Is hugely turn'd to architecture.' Born in 1664 to a father of Dutch origin and an English mother, Vanbrugh had grown up amid Chester's medieval towers and Roman walls. He had come to London at twenty-six, when his father died, with a legacy in his pocket. A year later, in 1690, he was arrested in Paris for travelling without a proper passport, and since France was then at war with England, Vanbrugh found himself clapped into the Bastille; its fortified masses would overshadow his own later work in stone. He inched himself into playwriting with more caution than into house-designing, by beginning with translations from the French. One play called *The Country House* deals with the comic misfortunes of a *nouveau riche* who buys a portico to give himself the kind of status that a Rolls-Royce confers today. On Boxing Day 1696, Vanbrugh's first original comedy, *The Relapse*, was performed at the Theatre Royal in Drury Lane and when he heard the audience's loud laughter, Van knew he had arrived. His prescription for comedy was to mix 'Rape, Bawdy and Intrigue' and let the lewd wit flow. In 1702, he was appointed Comptroller in Queen Anne's Office of Works, and henceforth constructed plays and houses with equal verve. He wrote 'Finis', however, only on his plays; once he persuaded some well-heeled client to let him exercise his fertile imagination in stone, Van saw to it that the house was never completed. Castle Howard would keep him as busy after twenty-two years as Seaton Delaval after three. Blenheim and only Blenheim would prove Van's stumbling-block. He was a man of immense good nature, ebullient, high-spirited, always optimistic. The world amused him mightily, and he amused the world, always ready with a witty sally or a ribald joke. For the contest with Blenheim he would need all his confidence and all his humour.

The Duke and Van, with many a jest en route, rattled over the rough roads to Woodstock in the Duke's coach, in February 1705, to see what the Queen's gift amounted to, and to choose the house site. So rich in history was the ground on which the Castle of Blenheim would be built that one could say it would rise in the very citadel of English life and lore. This fact delighted the romantic Vanbrugh and the self-aggrandizing Duke. What neither of them took into account was that much of the history of the site was tragic. Among the oak trees of Woodstock Park's 1,800 acres lurked as many ghosts and ill omens as deer. The history of Woodstock Park – its name compounded from the Anglo-Saxon *wudu* (woods) and *stoc* (main trunk) – begins with the history of England. A Roman road, paved with cobble-stones, passed through the park, and along it Roman generals built their winter villas. In Saxon times the kingdoms of Wessex and Mercia met near by. Alfred the Great and Ethelred the Unready hunted in its thick woods. When the Domesday survey was made in 1086, the little town of Woodstock was already there just beyond the park. When Henry I came to the throne in 1100, he built a great wall around the forest and stocked it with lions and leopards. By that time, there was a manor-house on the steep ridge overlooking the marshy valley where the little Glyme river flowed. Henry II often held his court at the manor-house, and dallied with 'Fair Rosamond' (Clifford) whose skin was so translucent the besotted king could see the blood sliding through her veins. It stopped sliding on the day an incensed Queen Eleanor followed a silken thread clinging to

Sir John Vanbrugh. Portrait attributed to Thomas Murray

Henry's spur to where Fair Rosamond sat humming and stitching in her bower. Rosamond – so the legend goes – was poisoned by the Queen, but the waters of the well named after her kept bubbling forth. It was in Woodstock Park that Henry III, in 1238, narrowly escaped assassination by a person named Ribbaud. John Hastings, Earl of Pembroke, was slain at a Christmas festivity there in the reign of Richard II, and later William Morisco tried to do away with Henry VIII. Princess Elizabeth was imprisoned in the gatehouse from May 1554 to April 1555, and England's future queen scratched on the window-pane: 'Much suspected of me, nothing proved can be.' Charles I spent an anxious night in the manor, hoping Cromwell's men wouldn't find him and had Rosamond's Bower destroyed in case they sought shelter there. Charles II appointed his wicked friend the Earl of Rochester Ranger of Woodstock Park. In that profligate court, Rochester led the way; in the course of five years, so they said, he was never sober and never without a wench. Prematurely aged and no doubt exhausted, he retreated to High Lodge, another building in the park, and died there on 26 July 1680, aged thirty-two.

On that chill, grey February day, however, as the Duke and Vanbrugh tramped over the park, they thought only of its long parade of kings and didn't detect that miasma of misfortune which hung in the damp air. Vanbrugh staked out the site on a broad tableland at the southern end of the park, beyond the little Glyme in its valley and the ruined manor-house on its ridge. He boldly placed the main axis of the whole design so that a three-mile line drawn from Ditchley Gate on the northern boundary would pass through the centre of the castle and end in the tower of Bladon church.

On 31 March Marlborough left England for The Hague to help the Dutch and Germans carry on the war against France and Bavaria. By mid-April, Henry Wise's men were already cutting down trees, and digging a huge cavity in the ground, while in Rotterdam the Duke bought twenty-eight paintings for Blenheim's walls from Madame Schepers, including a Claude Lorrain, a Salvator Rosa and a Veronese. 'Pray press on my house and gardens,' he scribbled to Sarah on 18 June, while marching in heavy rain with English and Dutch troops along the Moselle river to the relief of Overkirk. What he didn't know was that even as he wrote, Blenheim's foundation stone was being laid beneath the future bow-window – and that one hundred and ten years later to the day, another clever Duke would take the field at Waterloo.

Blenheim's entry into the world began about six o'clock on that Monday evening, 18 June. Vanbrugh was present, and Nicholas Hawksmoor, the skilled architect who would assist him as Blenheim grew, giving it much of its beauty of cornice and door-case. With a light heart, Vanbrugh positioned the foundation stone in the ground, a highly polished square, inlaid in pewter with the words: 'In memory of the battle of Blenheim, June 18th, 1705, Anna Regina.' Then Van and Hawksmoor and five distinguished Woodstock gentlemen each tapped the stone with a hammer, and threw down a guinea. 'Several sorts of music' followed and three morris dances: one of young men, one of maidens, and one of 'old beldames'. Then all the villagers who had gathered for the fun fell on the prodigal spread laid out on trestle tables: 'a hundred buckets, bowls and pans, filled with wine, punch, cakes and ale' as one replete participant recorded in his diary. There were plenty of coarse jokes about Van's new child. 'I pretend to no more merit than a midwife,' he was to write later, 'who helps to bring a fine child into the world, out of bushes, bogs and briars.' Whereas Vanbrugh thought of himself as Blenheim's midwife, or, in his less modest moods, as its father, Hawksmoor would be its nurse. He spoke of his 'concern for that building, like a loving nurse that almost thinks the child her own'. It was a warm welcome for tiny Blenheim, that kindly disposed group of midwife, nurse and assorted maids and maidens, dancing and swigging as they watched the sky turn golden, and trying, in their tipsy state, not to fall into Henry Wise's holes. But the darkness came all too soon, and for Blenheim twenty-eight years of traumatic growing pains followed.

It seems significant, in view of her subsequent attitude to the house, that the Duchess of Marlborough didn't attend that 18 June festivity. 'By your saying nothing to me of your going to Woodstock, I find your heart is not set on that place as I could wish,' chided the Duke from the Low Countries. 'I mortally hate all Grandeur and Architecture,' Sarah would later declare; when it came to Blenheim, her antagonism had already begun. And she was, as Dr Samuel Johnson would observe, 'a good hater'. 'I hope some time this summer,' the Duke wrote from Meldert on 3 August, 'you will go down to Woodstock for three or four days.'

If Sarah stayed away from Blenheim, the rest of the world came to gape. Lady Wentworth wrote breathlessly in May of 'the finest house at Woodstock that ever was seen; threescore rooms of a floor'. Then, with the winter chill, Blenheim's bad luck began. Frost cracked its stones and some walls had to be rebuilt. 'The flying of the stone has made a great noise,' Vanbrugh admitted. The bad stone had come from the park quarry; since it had proved inferior, all the stone henceforth would have to be brought from farther away. In the spring of 1706 'some ill person unknown' came in the night when Blenheim was unguarded and broke the bases of several pilasters. The house, it seems, was already breeding anger in hearts other than Sarah's.

That summer 'near a thousand' workmen were busy on the site. Skilled craftsmen from miles around had converged on Blenheim and presented themselves at the makeshift office. Some were hired directly; others signed a subcontract. Vanbrugh as Surveyor came and went, joshing the workmen, waving his arms excitedly to indicate vast heights and sweeping arcs. He got £400 a year, and another £200 riding charges. Nicholas Hawksmoor acted as assistant surveyor for £300 a year. Under them were the two Blenheim comptrollers: William Boulter and Henry Joynes. 'Honest Harry' Joynes was only twenty-one when he came to Blenheim. He was a nervous, earnest, meticulous young man doing his best for £200 a year, inscribing all the costs, in his neat hand, into a giant ledger. Chief masons were the Edward Strongs, father and son, who had helped Wren build St Paul's Cathedral; they worked on Blenheim's main pile. John Townsend from Oxford was responsible for the clock-tower in the east court and Henry Banks for the colonnades leading from the main pile to the east (kitchen) and west (stable) courts. At the end of a hard day's work, the workmen all repaired to the King's Arms in Woodstock to drink deep of the cool ale and to boast to Jockey Green, the owner, that it was nothing to them if some French blighter put a bullet through Marlborough's heart; the Crown itself was paying them for this job. 'Here's to the Queen!' they shouted, and raised their foaming glasses high.

The system devised by the Crown for paying the workmen seemed simple enough: the Treasury paid Samuel Travers who was acting as Blenheim's Surveyor-General in the Office of Works in London; Travers paid his deputy, Taylor; Taylor paid Joynes and Boulter, on the site at Blenheim, and they paid the labourers' accounts. But the flow of money, alas, would prove to be as erratic as the flow of water in the Glyme river north of the house, which alternately gushed and dribbled across the marshy meadows.

Slowly, day by day, the house got bigger, its thousand workmen scurrying about like ants, its noise and confusion equalling the Tower of Babel. Supplies of stone arrived daily from twenty-four different quarries. One hundred and thirty-six carters brought stone from Burford and Taynton alone. To drag the largest blocks up the steep hill from Taynton quarries to the Burford road, an agonizing three-quarters of a mile, they used a specially built wagon drawn by twenty-one horses. The carters cursed and sweated as traces broke and wheels flew off or sank out of sight in mud. It was impossible to haul when it rained, and sometimes it rained for days at a time. Blenheim was proving to be a demanding child. Its walls rose painfully slowly, one giant yellow stone upon another, while all the while wagons came and went, dropping their loads of marble, slate, gravel, lime, bricks, lead and timber, before creaking off again, whips cracking on the sweating backs of tired horses, for yet another load. The timber of choice was oak. Trees of sufficient girth were marked in Whittlewood Forest, in Sir Richard Temple's park at Stowe and in Esquire Holt's at Stoak. Big John Russell lopped and unknotted them where they stood, and then loaded them on to wagons and sent them on their way to Matthew Banks and John Barton, Blenheim's master carpenters.

The Duke, still campaigning in the Low Countries, fretted at being so far from where his dream-house was taking shape; he could do nothing except fill his letters to Sarah with detailed instructions and, whenever he had a quiet moment, buy up paintings and tapestries and furniture for Blenheim's lofty spaces. Sarah, meanwhile, was growing bored attending the Queen, bored with Her Majesty's endless prattle of the cut of a mantle or the condition of her bowels. Sarah came to hate Anne's gouty body and her offensive smells. Once, by mistake, Sarah had put on a pair of the Queen's gloves; upon learning whose they were she had torn them off, exclaiming: 'Oh! have I put on anything that has touched the odious hands of that disagreeable woman!' Sarah yawned over the whist table at Kensington, inched her chair away, and escaped, more and more frequently, to Blenheim, to see what fresh mischief Vanbrugh was up to. At court she was expected to be subservient to her Queen; at Blenheim, she could swagger about, poking and prodding, barking out orders to anyone within earshot. She liked things done in an orderly fashion, neatly and properly, one thing at a time. It drove her wild the way Vanbrugh had started projects in every direction instead of concentrating on the main pile. There was Bartholomew Peisley building a ridiculous bridge, a great big monstrous expensive useless bridge, leading from nothing to nothing, over the tiny little Glyme. There was Henry Wise, already laying out the Great Parterre – coloured sands and dwarf evergreens and raised walks and lime alleys – before the south front of the house, when the house didn't even have a south front yet. Sarah railed at 'the madness of the whole design' at Blenheim, her ideal home being 'a clean, sweet house and garden, though ever so small', but she aimed most of her fusillades at Vanbrugh's shocking extravagance.

'Is not that, sevenpence-halfpenny per bushel, a very high price, when they had the advantage of making it in the park?' she scrawled across a contract for lime. Vanbrugh began to groan when he saw My Lady Duchess's green coach approaching, and behind her back called her 'stupid and troublesome' and 'the old bitch'. 'There's no more money ordered yet, though we are in daily expectation of it,' Van told William Boulter on 7 March 1706. Referring to the Duke, then in England for a few days, Van added: 'And I hope [he] will so adjust things with my Lord Treasurer before he leaves me, that we may begin our campaign at least as soon as he does his.' The canny Duke was staying well behind the front lines when it came to money for Blenheim; he never issued orders except through Treasury channels.

By May, the western bow-window was up to thirteen feet when My Lady Duchess ordered the Strongs to tear it down and rebuild it so as to let in more light. It was disheartening for the two Edward Strongs to have to destroy their own good work, done with such care and skill. Some of their work at Blenheim was done over and over, twice or even thrice, until the very stones beneath their hands seemed to mock and menace.

On 23 May 1706 the Duke won the battle of Ramillies, another stunning victory – and another de Vos tapestry for Blenheim's walls. The battle of Blenheim had cost France all the country between the Danube and the Rhine, and had cost Bavaria all its kingdom. Now, with Ramillies, all Flanders was lost. It took the defeated Marshal Villeroy five days to get up enough courage to tell King Louis at Versailles. The English Parliament thanked the Duke of Marlborough for 'a victory so great and glorious in its consequences that no age can equal it', and the Treasury flow of funds to Blenheim ran in fresh spate. On 18 June, Blenheim's first birthday, the workmen took time off to celebrate, and Harry Joynes's clerk Jefferson recorded the cost of 'six hogsheads of ale' at the top of the day's entries in the accounts ledger, which included 'eight loads of clean horse dung for pargetting chimney funnels' (16s.) and, for his own labours, 'three and a half quarts of ink, three sticks of sealing-wax and a box of sand', some of which still glints today on the page where he sprinkled it to dry his ink. 'I find your heart is not set on that place [Blenheim] as I could wish,' sighed the Duke to Sarah on 8 July. He fretted even more when his staunch friend and ally, the Lord Treasurer, Godolphin, wrote on 25 September to report that 'My Lady Marlborough is extremely prying into ... I am apt to think she has made Mr Vanbrugh a little cross.'

The Duke accelerated his buying spree, needing tangible artefacts that he could see and touch to keep his dream alive. 'I expect every day to hear of three looking-glasses I have bought in Paris that have cost me 300 pistoles,' he informed Sarah on 26 June. Vanbrugh, for his part, was intent on raising Blenheim to his image of what it should be: a monument to John Vanbrugh as well as to John Churchill. He had designed a new kind of window-sash, guaranteed to last for centuries, 'all solid, without anything glued, and the frames are obliged to be very much larger than usual and all of oak.' The Strongs were in despair and doubled their intake of ale at Jockey Green's, for Vanbrugh had ordered them to raise the whole main block of the house another six feet in height and to change the order of capitals from Doric to Corinthian. Yards of good stonework had to be pulled down and all the window levels altered. The cursing carters and their straining horses were having to bring fresh stone from farther and farther afield. When work stopped for the winter, the Hall and Saloon were still unroofed. Blenheim stood bereft and vulnerable through the long, dark twilights and shocking snow.

Sarah was having her own problems at court. It gradually dawned on her that she had been replaced as Queen's favourite by that red-nosed poor relation of hers, Abigail Hill, just become Mrs Masham. Sarah herself had got Abigail a job at court and the 'shuffling little wretch' had somehow wormed her way into the very citadel of the Queen's affections, while Sarah stood aghast, beyond locked gates, with little hope of re-entry. Sarah vented her spleen on Blenheim, protesting to the Duke that it was far too large and far too grand. 'I could have agreed with you in wishing the house had been lesser so that it might have been sooner finished,' he replied on 23 October, 'but as it will be a monument of the Queen's favour and approbation of my services to posterity, I can't disapprove of the model.' 'The Queen's favour ...'; Sarah crumpled the letter into a ball and hurled it across the room.

When the sanguine Duke came home in the spring of 1708, he rushed down to Blenheim and, amidst its dirt and confusion, signed his name on the first page of the huge red leather Visitors' Book which he had bought. Blenheim had a steady stream of uninvited visitors, coming from near and far to view the astounding castle, moving warily among the giant blocks of stone, some already carved into lions, warriors or other fantastic shapes. They gaped upward as a huge statue of some goddess, a colossus on the ground, was hoisted aloft, with Grinling Gibbons shouting orders from below and running back and forth to gauge the effect. The statue got smaller as it flew aloft, and then settled into the weird company of actors frozen for ever on the roof. The sightseers' eyes grew even rounder on the day Aldersea's engine hove into sight and, as word of its arrival spread through Woodstock's taverns, the villagers flocked to see it. The ingenious Mr Aldersea had invented an engine to pump water at the rate of five tons an hour from Fair Rosamond's Well to a cistern on top of the arch leading into the east (kitchen) court, a lift of one hundred and twenty feet. Its pipes were all made of oak and it would keep all the eastern half of the palace supplied with water. Only the richest families in England enjoyed the luxury of piped water. A backstairs with a delicate iron-work handrail led from My Lady Duchess's bedroom down to a plunge-pool of hot water in the undercroft. A marvel indeed! If Blenheim was a trial to its midwife and its parents as it grew, it afforded constant amusement to the Woodstock villagers. Life was dull; roads were too rough to allow much travelling; poor people stayed put, or went only as far as the nearest market village. Now, right in their midst, they had a captive monster which changed daily. It was better than any side-show. Over their ale, they listened to the Strongs bewailing Blenheim's bewitched stones which moved restlessly about looking for a final resting-place. 'She be a tartar,' they agreed. The locals had long since decided on the castle's gender.

'I am advised by everybody to have the portico, so that I have writ to Vanbrugh,' the Duke told Sarah. Van must have chuckled to himself. He'd known full well, recalling his play *The Country House*, that the Duke was enough of a parvenu to want a portico. He would give My Lord the grandest portico ever. My Lady Duchess, on the other hand, was growing ever more recalcitrant. She was 'determined not to raise the price of the carriage of the stone' as a harassed Vanbrugh told Harry Joynes on 24 June. 'So that you must acquaint those who go with the carriages,' Van continued, 'that there is positive orders rather to let the work stand still than to give anything more than six pence a foot; they must bring in the great stones for that price as well as the small ones.' With his usual hyperbole, Van eulogized his own vigilant thriftiness, which made him 'avoid all company and haunt the building like a ghost from the time the workmen leave off at six o'clock till 'tis quite dark ... studying how to make this the cheapest, as well as the best house in Europe which I think My Lord Duke's services highly deserve'. On 11 July, the Duke grew even more deserving by winning another great victory at Oudenarde; the Marlborough myth was growing apace with Blenheim's walls. 'It will be as impossible for his enemies to hurt him, as for the wind to blow down Mr Vanbrugh's thick walls,' wrote her secretary, Maynwaring, to Sarah that July. A great Thanksgiving Service for Oudenarde was held at St Paul's. The Queen had refused to wear the jewels Sarah had chosen for her. On the steps coming out of the cathedral, the Queen and her Mistress of the Robes hurled bitter, angry words at each other. Sarah's fury went too far: she ordered the Queen to be silent, lest the people hear her. The gulf between the two women grew wider than ever.

On 14 September, Vanbrugh wrote to Marlborough, telling him, as always, exactly what he knew My Lord Duke wanted to hear. Vanbrugh genuinely admired Marlborough, and liked to keep his hero happy. 'I dare answer for it,' he wrote, 'that all shall be covered in two summers more', with the exception, he continued, of the Long Gallery, the Chapel and a few rooms at the western end of the house. (No house Van designed ever got finished at its western extremity but the Duke didn't know that.) 'And as to the expense,' Van soothed, 'it will appear at last that there has been such husbandry in the design (which is the Chief Concern) as well as in the execution, that the whole will by all people be judged to have cost full twice as much as will be paid for it.' Cunning Van, not for nothing was he a playwright before he turned architect. His letters to the Marlboroughs show him to be as keen a judge of character as of metaphor. Blenheim aroused in My Lady Duchess her pragmatic bent and her habits of parsimony, just as the castle aroused in My Lord Duke his hunger for fame and his love of ostentation. So to My Lady Duchess Van talked of linen cupboards and sixpences saved; to My Lord Duke he spoke feelingly of posterity and porticos.

As Blenheim's growing pains continued, its martial origins were somehow, in a strange teleological way, dictating its life pattern. Was peace never going to come? Vanbrugh and the two Marlboroughs, each under a different standard, were tossing its stones about and laying siege to its soul.

Even its name was caught in the cross-fire. Was it a 'castle' or a 'house'? The 1705 Parliamentary edict stating Queen Anne's intent called it 'the Castle of Blenheim'. The word 'castle' derives from the Latin *castellum*, a diminutive of *castrum*, which means fortified camp, and every Norman baron in England built one to keep rival Normans or rebellious Saxons at bay. The last overtly military castle was built at Thornbury in Gloucestershire during the reign of Henry VIII by Edward Stafford; he never finished it for the simple reason that he lost his head. When the English nobility no longer needed fortified 'castles' they built 'houses' instead. There is no equivalent in English for the French *château* or the Italian *palazzo*. In the eighteenth century, no matter how large or how grand, the English usually called their home a 'house'. The *Gentleman's Magazine* in 1774 refers to 'Blenheim-house', which is what the public commonly called it in the eighteenth century, particularly from 1750 on. Not until the nineteenth century did the name 'Blenheim Palace' become the accepted one.

Vanbrugh and the Duke both took their cue from Queen Anne; they looked back at Britain's illustrious past and yearned for a 'castle', but beyond that their attitudes to Blenheim were very different. In designing Blenheim, Vanbrugh more or less ignored the 'house' tradition of Palladian simplicity and classicism already established by Inigo Jones and continued by Christopher Wren and others. Van looked to the sixteenth and seventeenth centuries and came up with his own original concept of fortified baroque. He would build a 'castle' that was unique, colossal, wondrous, embedded in romantic myth, and designed by the only man with a creative libido big enough to pull it off.

The Duke also wanted a 'castle' that would advertise one man's worth. But instead of an imaginative *coup de main*, the Duke would make a direct assault on history. Blenheim would anchor him in time and place, giving him both a historical context and a power base. Its bulk and bold façade would trumpet to the world that here lived a man who had enormous power and who knew how to keep it – power over a vast network of tenant-farmers paying him rent, and constituents voting for whomever the Duke chose for Woodstock's parliamentary seat. In Blenheim's stately rooms, vassals would pay homage; lords would confer; kings would deign to visit. Blenheim would be first of all a show-place; comfort didn't count. He approved of Vanbrugh's priorities in design – 'State, Beauty and Convenience', as Van put it; convenience trailed a long way behind. But Blenheim would also be the Duke's reward: his haven and final port, his heaven on earth. He would walk from room to room to taste his glory, and to gloat.

The Duchess was not a reactionary like Vanbrugh and the Duke and had not one shred of idealism anywhere in her make-up. She was thoroughly modern and practical, and looked to the future, not the past. Blenheim would be a 'house', not a 'castle', a comfortable, convenient home, not a show-place. 'I never liked any building so much for the show and vanity, as for its usefulness and convenience,' she declared. She shared Alexander Pope's view of Blenheim, whose naughty verse was on everyone's lips:

> 'See, sir, here's the grand approach,
> This way is for his Grace's coach;
> There lies the bridge and here's the clock,
> Observe the lion and the cock,
> The spacious court, the colonnade,
> And mark how wide the hall is made!
> The chimneys are so well design'd
> They never smoke in any wind.
> This gallery's contrived for walking.
> The windows to retire and talk in;
> The council chamber for debate,
> And all the rest are rooms of state!'
>
> 'Thanks, sir,' cried I, ''tis very fine,
> But where d'ye sleep, or where d'ye dine?
> I find by all you have been telling
> That 'tis a house, but not a dwelling.'

Sarah's taste was to have 'everything that is useful and mighty clean and cheerful to live in a comfortable way', as she told her granddaughter Diana.

The idea of 'comfort' in a house showed Sarah's forward-thinking, for it was a concept new to the Dutch *bourgeois* of the seventeenth century and only recently brought to England. Not until the end of the eighteenth century would Georgian house owners opt for beauty and comfort combined.

So the battle raged in and around and through Blenheim, with Vanbrugh and the Duke ranged not too far apart on one side and the Duchess a long way off on the other. Castle or house; traditional or modern; symbolic or pragmatic; the battle lines were clearly drawn. Take, for example, that matter of oak window-sashes. Vanbrugh wanted them to last and to look original; the Duke wanted them to last and to look impressive; the Duchess wanted them to keep the cold out and to look neat. It was as if every piece of wood and marble and stone that went into the shaping of Blenheim was pulled three ways.

In the spring of 1709, the Duchess left Blenheim's battlefield temporarily and flounced off to confer with Sir Christopher Wren. *She* would show Vanbrugh and her husband how to build a house! She told Sir Christopher to build her something 'strong, plain and convenient', and the simple classical façade of London's Marlborough House began to rise overlooking St James's Park. (Sarah later fought with Wren, fired him and finished the house handily herself within two years.) 'I do wish you all happiness and speed with your building at London,' wrote the Duke to Sarah from Rotterdam on 9 June, 'but beg that may not hinder you from pressing forward the building of Blenheim.'

He needn't have worried; Sarah soon missed her skirmishing with Vanbrugh and started a fresh battle over the fate of the ancient manor-house still standing on its ridge north of Blenheim where so many kings had supped and wenched and foundered. The romantic Vanbrugh, of course, wanted to preserve it. The practical Sarah – what possible use was it? – was all for tearing such an eyesore down and the sooner the better. The Duke agreed with Sarah. Blenheim would bear the imprint only of the Marlboroughs, not of former kings. Vanbrugh gave in graciously – whatever My Lord Duke and My Lady Duchess commanded would be done, yes, yes ... but that was not the end of it.

It was the Duke's golden vision of Blenheim which drove him forward on the real battlefield abroad. On 11 September, he won another great victory at Malplaquet. 'I am so persuaded that this campaign will bring us a good peace, that I beg of you to do all you can that the house at Woodstock may be carried up as much as possible,' he had written to Sarah, 'that I may have a prospect of living in it.' Long before it was finished, the Castle of Blenheim was already a formidable enough presence to affect the course of history. It made a strange counterpoint for the Duke:

the carnage of one bloody battle after another, interspersed, for so many years, with the fingering of velvets and the selection of mirror mouldings. 'There are seventeen pieces of the enclosed pattern,' he told Sarah on 19 March 1710. 'I desire you will let me know what use you can make of this velvet.' Excellent quality, excellent value, he assured her, in prim, housewifely tone, only 'one hundred and nineteen pounds'. 'Three or four of the pieces are damaged, however they will not sell them, unless they be all bought.'

On 6 April Sarah confronted the Queen in her small, dark closet at Kensington. Queen Anne had become, as Sarah put it, 'exceeding gross and corpulent', her face red and puffy from her excessive drinking. Why had the Queen withdrawn her favour? Why had Her Majesty countenanced all the vicious rumours about her loyal Mistress of the Robes that her enemies were spreading? Sarah grew more and more heated but no matter how many times she rapped out her questions, the phlegmatic Queen refused to answer. Then Sarah lost her temper, screamed out 'the most disrespectful thing I ever spoke to the Queen', as she later confessed, without being more specific. This time Sarah had really gone too far. The Queen dismissed her at once, and Sarah never spoke to her again. On 7 August, the Queen removed the Marlboroughs' ally, Lord Godolphin, from his post as Lord Treasurer.

Now Blenheim was in real trouble. Godolphin had signed the warrants empowering Blenheim's two comptrollers to pay the workmen, and had kept funds flowing. In that sere autumn of 1710, Marlborough's sworn enemies, Harley and St John (afterwards Viscount Bolingbroke), became Chancellor of the Exchequer and Secretary of State respectively, and the Tories were swept into office. The Marlboroughs hadn't a single friend left in high places and Blenheim's fate had never looked darker. The workmen's hammers felt heavy in their hands; would they ever be paid?

The sudden arrival one misty August morning of four great copper balls in the courtyard took their minds off their troubles, if only for a moment. They circled the giant balls warily, touched them here and there with a hammer. They gave off a deep, gloomy note. Were they balls for the world's biggest cannon or – as one wag put it – the balls of the devil himself? To much hooting and laughter, two balls were hoisted aloft on to central pinnacles above the portico; the other two were destined for the towers in the east and west courts. John Smith sent in his bill from London for £325 3s. 6d., and Honest Harry placed it neatly atop the growing and worrisome pile on his desk.

Canon William Stratford, of Christ Church, Oxford, wrote to Harley on 21 August to tell him how desperate the situation was:

The debt to the workmen at Blenheim that is known is above £60,000. They owe to Strong the mason for his share £10,500. It will go hard with many in this town and the country who have contracted with them. Their creditors begin to call on them and they can get no money at Blenheim. One poor fellow, who has £600 owing to him for lime and brick, came on Saturday to Tom Rowney [Member of Parliament for Oxford] to ask for a little money he owed him. Tom paid him immediately. It was about £5. The fellow thanked him with tears, and said that money for the present would save him from gaol.

On 30 September, Vanbrugh wrote to Harley begging for enough money to make Blenheim fast for the coming winter, telling him 'that the credit is extended beyond even the power of getting in a little lime and bricks. I cannot help looking on this building,' he continued, 'with the tenderness of a sort of child of my own, and therefore hope you will forgive my troubling you for its preservation.'

Then, as autumn winds tore the leaves from the fruit trees Henry Wise had planted, Blenheim was dealt a sudden, savage blow which left the workmen reeling. On 3 October, the Duchess of Marlborough sent word to Blenheim that all work was to stop immediately, 'not suffering one man to be employed a day longer', as Vanbrugh wrote pitifully to the distant Duke. If the labourers stopped at once, without covering in for the winter, Vanbrugh continued, it would expose 'the whole summer's work to unspeakable mischief'. And the angry, unpaid workmen could well become violent, so that 'the building might feel the effects of it'. Sitting in his dripping tent near Aire, the Duke read Vanbrugh's letter, felt a headache like a thunderclap, and a sudden attack of 'spleen', as he told Godolphin on 25 October. He wrote at once to Sarah, cursing the slowness of the Dutch post and sending his letter via Ostend to hasten it. Beyond the vexations of his dream crumbling and the prospect of his own purse being depleted was the frustration of being so far away. The Duke implored Godolphin to reason with Sarah.

The worst misery, however, was at Blenheim. The carters were literally starving and the desperate masons plotting revenge. 'Our distant carters that fetch stone fourteen, fifteen and some twenty miles from Woodstock,' Harry Joynes told Henry Wise on 24 October, 'lie out with cattle at inns and without supply of money in reasonable time they can't hold out.' Harry, with shaking hand, also wrote to Sam Travers who held the government purse-strings in London: 'If the masons stop and I have no money to pay them … [they] will cause a great murmur in the country, besides the afflictions to the poor wretches. They have begun their pranks already in breaking some of the capitals of the columns.' In addition to its three main contenders in the battle, its midwife and parents, Blenheim now faced a frightening mutiny, a fresh battery of abuse from the calloused hands supposed to be nurturing its growth.

Sam Travers immediately took coach to Blenheim and, out of his own pocket, paid £300 to the most destitute workmen. He asked Vanbrugh how much was needed to secure the ill-fated palace against the winter. Eight thousand pounds, Van told him. The Treasury grudgingly sent down £7,000 to Joynes; to date they had doled out £200,000 for Blenheim and there seemed no end in sight.

Sarah felt not a tinge of sympathy for the starving workmen and Blenheim's threatened stones. She had tears of pity only for herself, so blameless, so unjustly persecuted by her Queen. 'As the building will never be finished at Blenheim,' she wrote to a relative in December, 'it can never be any advantage or pleasure to My Lord Marlborough or his family, but will remain now as a monument of ingratitude instead of what was once intended.' Let it stand, mute testimony to an ungrateful monarch's treatment of her devoted subjects, the Duke and Duchess of Marlborough. Let it stand, derelict and deformed, for ever, its hard stone a match for the Queen's heart. Sarah had never wanted to live there anyway.

For his part, Vanbrugh shrugged, heaved one mighty sigh for his crippled child, recovered his equanimity almost at once, and went blithely off to build Kings Weston for Sir Edward Southwell in Gloucestershire, taking the master-mason Townsend with him.

When the Duke of Marlborough got back to England in January 1711, he went straight to Queen Anne. He talked of his devotion, his war record, gave her an abject letter from Sarah asking for reconciliation, smiled and cajoled and charmed. But Queen Anne looked sour and unmoved and demanded that within two days Sarah's gold key be returned, thus signifying her formal dismissal from her offices as Mistress of the Robes, Groom of the Stole and – unkindest cut of all – from Keeper of the Privy Purse. When John told Sarah, she flung the key across the room and screamed a few choice oaths. And so it happened that Sarah, first Duchess of Marlborough, fell precipitately from her pinnacle of power, and Blenheim's foundations shook alarmingly with the force of her fall.

In London, the political campaign against Marlborough grew hotter that year. The Tories, still in power, had an expert pamphleteer on their side: Jonathan Swift drew on his considerable powers of irony and invective to write *The Conduct of the Allies*, attacking Marlborough for prolonging the war with France, saying he had done so to keep money flowing into his own pocket. On 31 December, Queen Anne, goaded by St John and Harley, now Earl of Oxford, dismissed Marlborough from all his employments. Then, on 7 June 1712, she issued explicit orders that no further funds should be handed out for Blenheim Castle. Her wrath continued to smoulder and spread, for in April of the following year she dismissed Vanbrugh from his lucrative sinecure in the Office of Works.

Stripped of their offices and stung by public abuse, the disgraced Duke and Duchess of Marlborough decided to go abroad for an indefinite stay. In August, the Duke bade a sad goodbye to Blenheim, his dreams broken into rubble at his feet. Real power was gone; only the icon remained, standing jagged and lopsided against a leaden sky. He committed the keys to Harry Joynes and left the castle in his keeping. With dragging feet, the Duke headed, yet again, for the Continent. Sarah followed with forty manteaux, seven leopard-skin muffs, thirty-two of the paintings John had collected and seventeen wall-hangings. The Marlboroughs settled, with a fine show of opulence, into a large house in Antwerp for their exile.

Blenheim was left to its fitful dreams. Before the summer was gone, the mice had begun to play. Harry Joynes went fishing where the Glyme was deepest, and caught two fourteen-inch trout, one chub and eight dace. Tilleman Bobart, who had been left in charge of the grounds, began making hay for his own use. Nicholas Hawksmoor wrote from London to Honest Harry, asking him to 'make inquiry concerning the state of the venison at Woodstock' and to send up 'a good fat buck and send it away fresh, by the Woodstock carrier, and leave it for me at the Dog at the Gravel Pits [in Kensington] but pray give me notice when you send it, that it may not lie at the Dog, and be spoiled, as it did last summer. Be sure to direct it for me, on a piece of vellum and give strict charge to the carrier about it.' But these were small perquisites. With his usual panache, the inimitable Van outdid them all. Instead of tearing down the ancient manor-house, as My Lady Duchess had ordered many months earlier, he had been quietly repairing it, making it fit for habitation. As soon as the Marlboroughs had sailed away, with a jaunty step and a wide smile, Van moved in, lock, stock and burgundy, and made himself cosily, contentedly, at home.

The real war and the Blenheim war came to a halt about the same time. In March 1713 the Treaty of Utrecht was signed, ending the War of the Spanish Succession. Louis XIV had done very well for France at the bargaining table and magnanimously sent tipsy Queen Anne two thousand bottles of champagne to keep her that way. The war had begun, ostensibly, to keep Louis's grandson Philip off the Spanish throne. That he subsequently reigned as Philip V bothered Britain not at all, since her aims all along had been colonial and commercial. By the Treaty she secured Gibraltar, Minorca, Nova Scotia and St Kitts, and the right to ship slaves to the Spanish colonies. With two ports in the Mediterranean, two colonies in the New World, and a lucrative trading privilege, Britain came out of the war bigger and stronger than ever, whereas Blenheim's cease-fire had left her in a most pitiful condition, looking unsightly and despairing of any future growth.

Then, suddenly, on 1 August 1714, the house's fortunes changed for the better. On that day, Queen Anne, who had been comatose for some time, finally died. One day later, the jubilant Marlboroughs landed at Dover, and on 5 August drove in their glass coach, escorted by a great retinue of gentlemen on horseback protesting their devotion, towards Marlborough House. Crowds lining the route cried 'Long live the Duke of Marlborough!' and 'Long live King George!' in a ratio of about three to one. The new king, George I, fifty-four years old, was short, shy and rather stupid, with bulbous blue eyes, brusque manners and a weird taste in mistresses, for the two he brought with him from Germany, one fat, one thin, were both excessively ugly. With all his faults, he had one shining virtue: he was kindly disposed to the Marlboroughs. A former soldier himself, he knew a good one when he saw one and immediately restored the Duke to his post as captain-general of the land forces and master-general of the ordnance, telling him in his halting French, for he spoke not one word of English: 'My Lord Duke, I hope your troubles are now all over.'

The Duke hoped so, too, and looked forward to some peaceful days in beloved Blenheim. He was sixty-four and sick to death of battles. He and Sarah went to Woodstock for three days at the end of August, putting up at High Lodge, where Rochester had died. A cocky Sir John Vanbrugh, newly knighted by King George on a quiet word from Marlborough, escorted him round the half-formed castle, but kept him well away from the old manor-house. The Duke told Van that 'when the government took care to discharge him from the claim of the workmen for the debt in the Queen's time, he intended to finish the building at his own expense'. Sir John thought he could finish it to His Grace's high standards for £54,000. The Duke henceforth would have to dig, ever so reluctantly, into his own pocket.

And so, equally reluctantly, the workmen came back to the ill-omened palace and picked up their tools for the final campaign. Grinling Gibbons was not among them. When the work had stopped in 1712, he was owed £1,117 18s. 4d. (He would later recover only a third of this.) He sent word from his narrow house in London's Bow Street, Covent Garden, that he'd had quite enough of Blenheim. The labourers and craftsmen who did return were full of anxiety, and still unpaid, for Marlborough steadfastly refused to pay one penny of back wages; that was the Crown's responsibility. One can still read the pathetic petitions to His or Her Grace, in faded brown ink, of the disillusioned but still deferential workmen. One such is the 1716 'humble petition' of Joshua Fletcher and Christopher Cash, so ironically named, which

> humbly showeth that they agreed and articled with Sir John Vanbrugh by Your Grace's order in behalf of His Grace the Duke of Marlborough for the finishing the south-west, north-west and chimney towers at very reasonable rates, that your petitioners were very unwilling to undertake the said work at such prices they have agreed to, but were induced to it by Sir John's promising they should have money – whenever they desired it, and that as soon as they had begun they should have some to enable 'em to carry on the work. Upon this encouragement they ventured to come as low as possible and proceeded with vigour. But contrary to their articles, encouragement, or expectations, they have not yet received one penny towards the said towers, two of which are now done, and amount to near eleven hundred pounds. Your petitioners think they have very hard usage having faithfully performed their part of the articles in doing their work in good and workmanlike manner.

Kit Cash had whistled merrily as he'd worked, first on the towers, then on Blenheim's floors, placing black-diamond insets so proudly and precisely into the corners of the white Portland stone. 'She be a tartar,' the workmen sighed, listening to the details of Kit's 'hard usage' as they swigged their beer at Jockey Green's. There were no jokes now, no jaunty toasts, and Jockey had to give them credit, for their pockets were empty.

Meanwhile, Sarah peered and poked among Blenheim's scaffolding. 'All without doors,' she complained to a friend, 'is a chaos that turns one's brains but to think of it; and it will cost an immense sum to complete the causeway, and that ridiculous bridge in which I counted thirty-three rooms.' Vanbrugh told My Lady Duchess that she could sit in their cool recesses on a sweltering day, and listen to the coaches rumbling over her hot head. Then he walked away from her scolding towards his Homeric bridge, and quietly incised a huge V above a window in one of its thirty-three completely useless rooms. The local people sneered and snickered every time they looked at that bridge, which could handily span the mouth of the Thames, rearing its hump over the tiny trickling Glyme. One clever wag came up with an epigram on Marlborough: 'The lofty arch his high ambition shows, / The stream an emblem of his bounty flows.'

In the spring of 1716, Vanbrugh told the Duke cheerfully that 'the house painter has made a great progress' and that the chimney-pieces 'should be put in hand'. Then, knowing how much the disorder of Blenheim's awkward age vexed her, he reported it to My Lady Duchess in great detail, concluding that 'it makes all look in a most disagreeable confusion'.

In April, the Edward Strongs walked off the job and subsequently sued the Marlboroughs for their huge arrears of pay. In September, Henry Wise withdrew all his workmen and Harry Joynes, with great relief, gave up the struggle and became Clerk of the Works to Kensington Palace.

On 28 May, one of Blenheim's principal assailants involuntarily defected. Marlborough had a stroke which left him partially paralysed; he was very weak and unwell all that summer of 1716, thereby leaving the field to Vanbrugh and Sarah. She saw to it that by mid-July the kitchen, scullery, pantry, larders, dairy, housekeeper's room and servants' hall were all completed in the east court. The orangery there was still unfinished, yet Vanbrugh was already waving his arms and talking of a grander one in the western court. She scotched that idea soon enough. Vanbrugh assured her, tongue-in-cheek, that he would 'have the homely simplicity of the ancient manor in my constant thoughts for a guide in what remains to be done'.

Not until 18 October was the Duke well enough to go down to Blenheim, where Vanbrugh and Hawksmoor escorted the Marlboroughs round. While the Duke shuffled and mumbled, Sarah's sharp eye took in everything. The private apartments in the eastern wing were still not habitable; the workmen were proceeding so slowly westward that they were only now beginning on the first stateroom west of the Saloon. The bridge, on the other hand, looked finished enough. But worst of all was the manor-house. Vanbrugh had not only had the gall, the effrontery, the wickedness, to disobey her orders to tear it down. The detestable man was actually *living in it*! Vanbrugh had to go.

Sarah wrote all her grievances down, her quill pen scoring the paper, covering many sheets. 'These papers, madam,' wrote a venomous Vanbrugh to the Duchess,

> are so full of far-fetched, laboured accusations, mistaken facts, wrong inferences, groundless jealousies, and strained constructions that I should put a very great affront upon your understanding if I supposed it possible you could mean anything in earnest by them but to put a stop to my troubling you any more. You have your end, Madam, for I will never trouble you more unless the Duke of Marlborough recovers so far, to shelter me from such intolerable treatment.

So Vanbrugh resigned, turned on his heel and walked away from his fond creation. It looked as if the Duchess had won the day. At High Lodge, two days after Vanbrugh sent in his resignation, the distraught Duke had his second stroke. This one severely impaired his speech, and sapped his remaining strength. If his days on earth were numbered, he wanted only to spend them at Blenheim. To Sarah, the monstrous house was 'a chaos which nobody but God Almighty could finish' but for beloved John's sake, she squared her shoulders and prepared to battle it out with the house in hand-to-hand combat, one Amazon against the other. Her needle flew as she began making up into bed-hangings and curtains the velvets which John had so carefully chosen. They would soften Blenheim's angularity, and keep out draughts. She was, she boasted to a friend, a better 'upholsterer' than most professionals, and every stitch she took saved money. She wrote to a London relative who helped her with household matters:

> I shall want a vast number of feather beds and quilts. I wish you would take this opportunity to know the prices of all such things as will be wanted in that wild unmerciful house, for the man you go to is famous for low prices. I would have some of the feather beds swansdown, all good and sweet feathers.

As Sarah went ahead with her preparations, trying to make Blenheim comfortable, 'the wild unmerciful house' began draining her of all energy, and depressing her spirits utterly. She found it 'so vast a place that it tires one almost to death' and dreaded the day when she would have to move in and actually live there. 'It is impossible for me to be at this place,' she wrote to her son-in-law in 1717,

> without being very melancholy, which has already cost £315,000 [a gross exaggeration] without one room in a condition to put a bed in; the vast bridge in the air, without so much as a possibility to have water, and the prodigious cavities which all the hills in the park cannot fill up, is such a picture of madness and folly as no person can describe.

Folly it might be, but Blenheim was also an island of affluence in a surrounding sea of poverty; it had to be properly protected. Sarah gave orders to have the windows fitted with strong bars and two huge locks fixed 'to the iron gates in the grand court to keep all others out'.

The public began to hate Blenheim as much as the Duchess did. 'A sad, irregular, confused piece of work' was one Oxford diarist's assessment. Alexander Pope toured the palace in September, 1717, and reported to a friend:

> I never saw so great a thing with so much littleness in it. I think the architect built it entirely in compliance to the taste of its owners; for it is the most inhospitable thing imaginable, and the most selfish; it has, like their own hearts, no room for strangers … It is a house of entries and passages among which there are three vistas through the whole, very uselessly handsome … In a word, the whole is a most expensive absurdity, and the Duke of Shrewsbury gave a true character of it, when he said, it was a great Quarry of Stones above ground.

Even Vanbrugh was feeling less than charitable towards his abandoned child. He was still owed £6,000 'for many years' service, plague and trouble at Blenheim'. He was busy building himself a 'castle' at Blackheath with round towers and castellations, and on 14 January 1719, fifty-four-year-old Van, a confirmed homosexual, had married Henrietta Yarburgh of Heslington Hall, near York, a fine red-brick Elizabethan manor. When his first actual child arrived, a friend wrote to Sarah: 'I hear his child is the biggest that ever was seen. I think you may the easier forgive him his vast designs at Blenheim since it appears to be so much the tendency of his nature.' Vanbrugh now felt only cool detachment, and even a hint of repugnance, towards his former offspring, Castle Blenheim, which he had once regarded 'with the tenderness of a sort of child of my own'. Certainly, he would never, ever want to *live* there. 'One may find a great deal of pleasure, in building a palace for another,' he told his friend and confidante, Jacob Tonson, 'when one should find very little, in living in it oneself.' When, in the July of 1719, he did go to visit Blenheim, he went, as he told Jacob, 'not with any affection, for I am thoroughly weaned, but some curiosity. The Duchess of Marlborough having taken a run at last to finish in earnest, which (though in no good or graceful manner) she has advanced so far that in less than a month it will be fit to receive the Duke.'

Blenheim waited for the Marlboroughs to move in that August of 1719 with much trepidation. Its midwife had turned indifferent and gone elsewhere; its female parent was whipping it into shape grimly, with only hatred in her heart; only its father still felt fond and indulgent, but the Duke, alas, was very much on the sidelines. Still, the palace looked forward to some happy times. It looked most particularly to those four young ladies, the Marlborough granddaughters and Mary Cairns, to spread some sunshine through its wistful rooms.

At last the great day came, and the palace warmed its stones in the August sun and opened its doors wide to receive its family. Slowly the entourage approached across the bridge and into the courtyard. The menservants came on horseback. The steward, Hodges, and the groom of the horse had packed up all the furniture, plate and bedding, while the clerk of the kitchen saw to the provisions. All this paraphernalia arrived piled up in wagons, with the two housemaids and the kitchen-maid perched on top keeping a close eye on the china and other breakables. The family arrived last, in two coaches that also carried the Duchess's personal maid and Miss La Vie, the governess. Sarah's lace and jewels and collection of snuff-boxes were stowed in cloth parcels under the seats.

The house enjoyed that initial clutter of bolsters and bedding piling up in the Hall and of soup tureens hiding behind the pillars. Then came a great scrubbing and polishing, the second one. The first had been done by Woodstock women under the housekeeper's eye before the family moved in, but the Duchess had pronounced it inadequate, and ordered a second one which would get at the dirt, so to speak, beneath the nails. After that the rooms began to come alive, with crackling log fires and candle-glow and the smells of lavender and roast pork and clouds of hair-powder and the Duchess's snuff – the excitement of it all coalescing, finally, in the diamond-sparkle of *All for Love*.

The morning after the theatrical party, as soon as breakfast was over, Sir Richard Steele and Bishop Hoadly prepared to depart. According to the usual custom, they found all the menservants lined up in the Great Hall, palms extended, waiting for their 'vails' (tips). 'Must one give money to all these fine fellows?' a flustered Sir Richard inquired of Little Ben, trotting by his side. 'No doubt,' he replied. 'But I haven't enough,' the embarrassed Steele muttered. Then inspiration struck. He made the servants a velvety speech, telling them that since they were all 'men of taste', they were invited to Drury Lane, where he held shares in the patent, to see whatever play they cared to bespeak. Then, to general acclamation, he waved his arm and made a dignified and graceful exit.

After Blenheim's coming-out party, the Duke settled down to enjoy his dream-house. He liked to wander about, to contemplate Blenheim's long vistas, its fine symmetry of rooms, its French and Italian furniture, all gilded, all imported (English was still second-best). He liked to count those treasures given to him by grateful cities – Brussels, Antwerp, Ghent, so many others – or by emperors and princes, whose names he couldn't remember. There were richly glowing paintings by Rubens and Titian, Raphael and Van Dyck, silver-gilt basins three feet across, a mammoth centre-piece, all solid silver, of himself on horseback scribbling his famous Blenheim note to Sarah. The Duke caressed a bronze Venus, ran his hand down a silk velvet curtain, breathed in gratefully the incense of great wealth and great acclaim.

After a few weeks, however, an insidious change took place. Blenheim was no longer a marvel; the castle began to mock him. He had failed it, and its sardonic walls reproached him. He couldn't take up the challenge of those lofty rooms. He was weary and ill and helpless; he wanted only a comfortable old chair by the fire and a bowl of gruel in the evenings. Blenheim demanded someone active and powerful and commanding who could stand tall and thunder through its rooms. Blenheim cried out for the ritual of great ceremonies, and for stately, plotted manoeuvres of knight and bishop and pawn. But most of all, Blenheim pleaded and begged, every stone of it, for a monarch.

When Blenheim came into being in 1705, absolute monarchy had reached its zenith. Society believed in hierarchical order – God, King, Nobles, Commoners – 'All served, all serving, nothing stands alone. / The chain

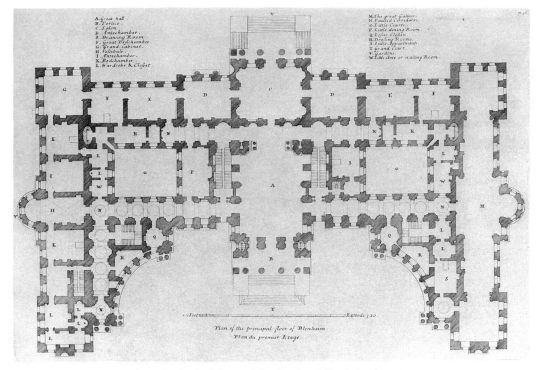

Plan of principal floor of the Castle of Blenheim (1717)

holds on, and where it ends, unknown,' as Alexander Pope put it. Blenheim's room plan translated the Great Chain of Being into stone and timber, into wainscot and deal: servants far removed in the east court; tenant-farmers and other lowly suppliants received in the Great Hall; lords and gentry ushered through to the Saloon beyond; and only the country's sovereign escorted eastward along the south front, through antechamber, state drawing-room and state bedchamber to the Holy of Holies, the Duke's inner sanctum, the Grand Cabinet in the south-east corner. How far the Superior Being would progress along the axis, and how far the Inferior Being could entice him, was the name of the power game. West of the Saloon was an identical suite of three staterooms, ending in the immensity of the Long Gallery where the monarch could parade up and down when the weather was inclement. Blenheim, as Pope realized, had few rooms for ordinary mortals, but it could house, in luxurious self-containment, *two* kings at a time.

The Duke of Marlborough, alone and unattended, walked along the regal route. There above the Saloon was the gallery where musicians could play sweet airs while the king dined; there in the state bedchamber were the crimson damask bed-hangings 'bound with rich bold stiff galoon', the arms of King William and Queen Anne emblazoned on tester and head-cloth. There in the Grand Cabinet were the Duke's fondest possessions: a horde of medals, bronzes, paintings, coins, chosen to charm a kingly connoisseur. Everything was swept and squared and polished, as Blenheim waited to receive and bed its king.

Alas, the only regal head which lay at Blenheim was Louis XIV's: Louis in a vast curling wig, with a sunburst medallion on his chest, Louis in stone, captured by the Duke at Tournay, and waiting to be placed in the exact centre of the south front where he could gaze down on Wise's Great Parterre and pronounce it vastly inferior to Le Nôtre's at Versailles.

To be sure, there were plenty of kings and queens on Blenheim's damask walls. There was Van Dyck's Charles I on horseback, in full armour, hatchet-faced and red-bearded, with his equerry, Sir Thomas Norton, in deferential crouch, handing him up his helmet. There was Edward Lilly's Queen Anne, in ample purple and ermine, her crown resting on a Bible to underline the Divine Right of Kings. There were lesser monarchs, too: Van Dyck's Marie de Medici, wife of France's Henry IV, Rubens's Anne of Austria, wife of Louis XIII, and Van Dyck's Henrietta Maria, wife of Charles I. They stared stonily at the Duke as he passed by, and they, too, seemed to mock and sneer.

Then all the mighty Dukes of Marlborough joined in: the white marble Duke above the Hall doorway, the blue-togaed Duke on the Hall ceiling, the chariot-driving Duke above the Saloon's marble wastes. And in the many great gilded mirrors which he had bought with such delight and anticipation was the real Duke, bowed and wan and wistful, appearing again and again down the long vistas. Once he took a long look at Kneller's portrait of handsome John Churchill in his prime, life-size in armour, the Garter on his knee, a crimson and ermine mantle on his left arm. 'That was once a man!' the Duke mumbled softly to the empty room, and tears streamed down his wasted cheeks.

No crowned heads; no cowed vassals; only empty spaces – and mountains of bills. Shortly after he'd moved into the castle, the Court of Exchequer gave their verdict on the back pay, thousands and thousands of pounds, owing to the workmen. The debts were the Duke's and not the Crown's. To the Edward Strongs alone he had to dole out £12,000.

Blenheim towered and taunted until, to the overwrought Duke, the rooms seemed to sway with hollow laughter. Fortunately, he had other more comfortable, less demanding houses, such as Windsor Lodge and Holywell House where he could live out his last days. Shortly after that happy evening when *All for Love*'s stirring defence of valour and honour wove its music through the Battle of Blenheim tapestry, John, first Duke of Marlborough, left Blenheim Castle never to return. It was only then that he remembered the subtitle of Dryden's play: 'The World Well Lost'. Blenheim had defeated him, the conquering hero, the victorious Duke. That was the final irony. It was the only battle he ever lost. He turned his back on his nightmare castle, and beat a hasty retreat.

The house's life and bustle went with him. The Duchess departed, taking the four gay-spirited young ladies with her, and all the servants except the housekeeper, the porter, Tom Jenner, and the watchman, John Tompkins. Blenheim's family piled into wagons and coaches and rattled away, farther and farther, until they were tiny moths on the horizon, and then they disappeared from view.

On a bleak autumn day in 1720, Minerva, the Warrior-Goddess, clutching her javelin in one hand and her shield in the other, toppled from her perch atop the great north-front portico, and crashed on the roof. Richard Paine did his best to mend her, and sent in his bill for £1 10s. 0d. but Minerva never really recovered from her fall from the heights.

In June 1722 the Duke lay in a coma at Windsor Lodge and died in the grey dawn of 16 June, in his seventy-third year. He lay in state at Marlborough House and was buried, with fine military pomp, in Westminster Abbey, but his restless bones had not yet found their final haven. 'There were in the procession,' complains an invoice endorsement in Sarah's bold scrawl, 'only seventeen trumpeters, and yet there are twenty-four in the bill.' 'Mr Harris has had 48 yards of black cloth to line and cover the mourning coach and six for harness,' she noted elsewhere, 'which is enough to cover my garden; and I have upon inquiry found that several coachmakers have offered to do it with 35 yards.'

The Marlboroughs had no living son to inherit the dukedom so, according to an earlier Act of Parliament which had broadened the descent to include females, it passed to Henrietta, Countess of Godolphin, the elder of the two daughters still living. The new Duchess of Marlborough did not inherit Blenheim, which was Sarah's for her lifetime, nor did Henrietta ever live there. She and her mother were not on speaking terms. She lived modestly in Bath with her playwright-lover Congreve, bore him a daughter in 1723, to their mutual surprise, for she was forty-two, and died ten years later.

The Duke's estate amounted to well over £2m, including 'his mortgages upon many a distressed estate, and besides what God Almighty knows of in foreign banks,' as Vanbrugh told Jacob Tonson, 'and yet, this man would neither pay his workmen their bills nor his architect his salary'.

Van's quill pen bit deep: the Duke 'has given his widow (may a Scotch ensign get her) £10,000 a year to spoil Blenheim her own way, £12,000 a year to keep herself clean, and go to law.' Sarah was now the richest woman in England. She would finish the hated Blenheim 'her own way', haggling over every penny and turning what had never been a home into a mausoleum honouring the heroic exploits of the dead Duke. He had left her £50,000 earmarked for Blenheim. The Keeper of the Puny Purse, however, when she finally finished the house in 1733, was thrilled to find that she had paid out only £25,315 17s. 5d. (This brought the grand total of Blenheim's cost to £300,000, of which the Marlboroughs had paid £60,000 and the munificent nation the rest.)

The Triumphal Arch, Woodstock

Sarah finished the Long Gallery first. She had to pay Nicholas Hawksmoor £2,800 to gild its ceiling. On the other hand, Henry Hawke worked every day for a month carting rubbish and scaffolding from the Long Gallery and the stable court and his total bill came to £1 3s. 0d. James Hearn worked for fifteen days cleaning the roof gutters and got 15s. for his pains. When Sarah finally got around to paying these bills and others, she routinely paid a shilling or two less than requested.

She had a huge Triumphal Arch erected at the Woodstock entrance to Blenheim, which proclaims in Latin: 'This gate was built the year after the death of the most illustrious John Duke of Marlborough by order of Sarah his most beloved wife to whom he left the sole directory of the many things that remained unfinished', an inscription neatly coupling John's fame and his wife's power.

In September 1728 Sarah stayed at Blenheim only long enough to supervise the erection of a Column of Victory on a northern mound in the park. A twenty-five-foot Duke in Roman armour, atop a 130-foot pillar, holds a Victory figure aloft for all the world to see. Sarah suffered a bad attack of gout and blamed it on 'the coldness of this stone house'.

By 1731 the Chapel was finished, and was duly consecrated by the Bishop of Oxford on 4 September. Scripture readings began with 1 Kings viii, 22–62, in which King Solomon dedicates his house to God. Verse 27 rang out with particular resonance: 'But will God indeed dwell on the earth? Behold, the heaven and heaven of heavens cannot contain thee; how much less this house that I have builded?' The Dowager Duchess, wearing all her lace and embroidery and jewels, then listened to the Bishop reading John ii, 13–17, in which Christ drives the money-lenders from the temple. 'Take these things hence; make not my Father's house an house of merchandise,' the Bishop declaimed, while Sarah caught the words, but not the irony.

Two years later, Sarah paid Rysbrack £2,400 to erect, in white and two shades of purplish-grey marble, an immense monument to Marlborough on the Chapel's east wall. The Duke appears armour-clad yet again, and Fame and History are in close attendance.

Occasionally, the deserted palace got a livelier human form inside it. Daniel Defoe, creator of Moll Flanders and Robinson Crusoe and other social outcasts, came in 1724 to assess Blenheim's wonders. 'A palace too big for any British subject to fill, if he lives at his own expense,' was his depressing verdict, and he made Blenheim's future look particularly bleak: ''Tis yet a house unfurnished, and it can only be properly said *what it is to be, not what it is*. As the Duke is dead, the Duchess old, and the heir abroad, when and how it shall be all performed, requires more of the gift of prophecy than I am master of.' But if Blenheim's real outline was still blurred, its mythic one was firmly etched in the British imagination: 'The magnificence of the building,' Defoe decided, 'represents the bounty and the gratitude of the English nation, to the man whom they delighted to honour.'

In June 1725, Vanbrugh felt a sudden urge to see his gargantuan child again. In company with his wife Henrietta, Lord Carlisle and others, Vanbrugh applied to the porter at Blenheim's gate, only to have his request to tour the castle rudely refused. There was 'an order to the servants, under

OPPOSITE: The Rysbrack monument in the Chapel

Her Grace's own hand, not to let me enter anywhere,' he fumed to Tonson, 'and lest that should not mortify me enough, she having somehow learned that my wife was of the company, sent an express the night before we came there with orders ... the servants should not suffer her to see either house, gardens, or even to enter the park, which was obeyed accordingly, and she was forced to sit all day and keep me company at the inn'. The London wits chuckled when they heard the story: 'The Dutchman may not visit his own child, who, however he may appear a mere lump and misshapen to others, may seem beautiful in his eyes that begot him.' Van vented his wrath on My Lady Duchess, the instrument of his humiliation. 'Being forced into chancery,' he complained to Jacob, 'by the B.B.B.B. old B. the Duchess of Marlborough,' who was claiming that 'I never was employed by the Duke of Marlborough and therefore had no demand upon his estate for my services at Blenheim'. 'I wonder her family don't agree to lock her up,' expostulated Van to Lord Carlisle. Van finally collected what the B.B.B.B. Duchess owed him and died on 26 March 1726, 'of a quinsy', aged sixty-two. He was greatly mourned.

The year 1727 saw the coronation of George II and Queen Caroline, whose skirt was so weighted with £100,000 worth of jewels that it had to be drawn up, as Horace Walpole gleefully reported, 'with pullies like a little curtain' so that she could kneel and receive the sacrament. The Dowager Duchess of Marlborough invited her new sovereigns to visit Blenheim, but they graciously declined. Blenheim did, however, get a noteworthy visitor that year. Young Voltaire, released from the Bastille on 2 May on condition that he would exile himself to England, came to see the palace. '*Que c'était une grosse masse de pierre, sans agrément et sans goût,*' was his terse assessment.

One of England's most assiduous aesthetes, Horace Walpole, then a slim, foppish undergraduate at Cambridge, dropped in on Blenheim in 1736. He saw 'nothing but a cross housekeeper and an impertinent porter, except a few pictures, a quarry of stone that looked at a distance like a great house, and about this quarry quantities of inscriptions in honour of the Duke of Marlborough, and of Her Grace, too – she herself mentioned as putting 'em up, in almost all of them'. Blenheim's self-esteem sank towards its cellars as visitors came and went, hurling their brick-bats of criticism.

Its mistress was rarely there; Sarah was too busy waging war on everyone around her, and it was partly Blenheim which had made her battle-stance habitual. When her daughters inconsiderately died, she vented her spleen on her grandchildren, including Lady Anne Spencer, who had acted so prettily in the Blenheim theatricals. Sarah blackened her portrait, and wrote underneath: 'She is more black within.' She was particularly venomous towards her grandson Charles Spencer, brother of Diana and Anne, who had inherited the dukedom in 1733. He was the first of a long line of spendthrift Marlboroughs, and had already gone through half a million pounds.

Sarah waged legal battles with everyone concerned with the building of Blenheim, and when the principals died, she fought with their executors or assigns. In addition to her martial propensities, Blenheim had given the Duchess a passion for building, and turned her into a zealous amateur architect, a thoroughly modern one who believed that form follows function. Her letters are full of directions to friends and relations on how to build or renovate. She told her granddaughter Diana, who had married the Duke of Bedford, exactly how to remodel London's Bedford House; and Sarah herself designed a no-nonsense brick house at Wimbledon, and eighteen almshouses at St Albans.

Only when she had to supervise some work or cleaning – what a burden the house was! – did she come to Blenheim in her final years. She was a 'perfect cripple' with gout and lived there in one small room. Occasionally, when she wanted to harangue some workman, she was wrapped in flannel, slung into a pole-chair and jolted through the empty rooms by two footmen, past the marble Dukes and door-cases and the marble slab in the Chapel waiting to get her underneath its eternal chill.

She came to Blenheim briefly to supervise the placement of a life-size statue of Queen Anne at the north end of the Long Gallery. If Sarah couldn't have a real queen at Blenheim, she would make do with a marble one. Queen Anne, looking positively benevolent, was sculpted by Rysbrack in 1735, and Sarah finally got him down to £300 for his fee. 'I never design to see Blenheim again,' she wrote in 1736. At Holywell House or Windsor Lodge she had 'everything convenient' and pronounced Windsor Lodge 'a thousand times more agreeable' than Blenheim's cold acres.

When her thoughts did occasionally turn to Blenheim, it was to recall her possessions there. She sat up in bed making a detailed inventory in 1740, covering twenty pages closely written, of household goods which she hadn't seen for four years, but of which she had total recall. She knew that she had exactly 809 damask napkins and 91 tablecloths 'of the best sort'. She remembered that her water-closet contained a cabinet, chest and folding dressing-table, all in walnut, as well as two wainscot stands, and that in the Chapel were 'a great many Common Prayer books' and 'one large Bible'.

On 18 October 1744, at Marlborough House, London, Sarah, Dowager Duchess of Marlborough, died in her eighty-fifth year. She left behind no one to mourn her passing, but a great deal of money, and a great deal of land, including more than thirty separate estates. Her will, which had kept her busy down the years, took up sixteen skins of parchment, and eight more for the codicil. When it was printed in three instalments in the *London Magazine* it covered twenty-eight pages, and everyone in that materialistic age read it with as much interest as if it had been a Grub Street scandal sheet. Sarah left to her grandson Charles Spencer, third Duke of Marlborough, 'all my furniture, pictures, etc., which shall be in Blenheim-house, in Oxfordshire, at the time of my deccase'. (It is worth noting that she calls it 'house', not 'castle'.) 'My will and desire,' she continued, 'is that I may be buried at Blenheim, near the body of my dear husband John late Duke of Marlborough, and if I die before his body is removed thither, I desire Francis Earl of Godolphin to direct the same to be removed to Blenheim aforesaid, as was always intended.'

The conquering Duke and the commanding Duchess came home together, on an autumn day when Blenheim crouched in the long meadow-grass, stalking the dark, scudding clouds. The house bore its master and mistress along its vaulted corridors, suffered them to lie beneath its Chapel floor and gathered them, without much enthusiasm, to its veined-marble heart.

The battle was finally over. Three egos had struggled to raise Blenheim in their own image: one impulsive midwife and two authoritarian parents embroiled in the Forty Years' War. All three were gone now, and out of that violent, bitter conflict had emerged the most tyrannical ego of them all. Blenheim Palace stood, strong and solitary, against a clearing sky.

2
GOLDEN YOUTH

Surely among a rich man's flowering lawns,
Amid the rustle of his planted hills,
Life overflows without ambitious pains;
And rains down life until the basin spills,
And mounts more dizzy high the more it rains
As though to choose whatever shape it wills
And never stoop to a mechanical
Or servile shape, at others' beck and call.

W.B. Yeats, 'Ancestral Houses'

BLENHEIM-HOUSE RECLINED DREAMILY ON A LARGE EMERALD velvet cushion, for greensward now encircled it. The paved courtyard on the north side had been grassed over; the iron clang of horses' hooves had given way to the feather-stitch of peacocks' feet. The Great Parterre on the south side had also been grassed over, its battalion of stiff, identical yews replaced by a thousand sheep wandering at will, and by plump pheasants who had to walk only as far as the outstretched hand of their feeder. (They didn't know that they were fattening for the 4th Duke of Marlborough's table.) At the far edge of the south lawn, a girdle of beech trees had been so skilfully placed that it concealed all disagreeable sights beyond and, here and there, unbuttoned just enough foliage to reveal a Bladon tower or two. Beyond the towers, round violet hills spilled out on to the (almost) limitless horizon.

The palace's stones were golden as the sun set on that Friday, 19 October 1787. There were two palaces now: a rigid one against the sky, a rippling one in the waters of the lake. The lake was quite in scale with massive Blenheim, for it covered eight acres; the little Glyme river had been dammed and cajoled until it had spread out into two blue satin ribbon loops with Vanbrugh's nonsensical bridge forming the perfect bow-knot between. Reflected in the lake was a beautiful, beguiling Blenheim, wearing a topaz necklace of windows glinting in the sun, and a diadem of roof-statues resting on a peruke of clouds. Blenheim awaited the usual confetti of compliments as a hired post-chaise with three young men talking excitedly inside rattled over Vanbrugh's bridge. The desultory chat changed to exclamations of delight as the idyllic scene burst upon them. Swans and wild geese glided about the lake; the Duke's pleasure-boat, launched that very summer and christened *The Sovereign*, was moored to a rustic landing-stage. Beeches and Lombardy poplars on the lawn stood about in tight little circles, ladies-in-waiting to the palace, whispering gossip behind their leaves, breathing the air and consuming the soil like true aristocrats, knowing that air and soil were theirs by right to enjoy in full liberty and luxuriance. Their tresses were bedecked with 'variegated lamps hung in the most tasteful devices', as the actor-playwright Frederick Reynolds, one

View of the lake showing Vanbrugh's bridge

of the three raucous young men in the chaise, would describe them. He and his two companions, fellow actor-dramatists Joseph Holman and Miles Peter Andrews, tumbled out of the carriage with much joshing and shoving, waved their tickets of invitation in the face of the porter guarding the gate, and disappeared inside the eastern court.

The pulse of life was quickening in the house's eastern arm. A few servants and visiting coachmen were sitting idly round the table in the servants' hall on which, from morning to night, beer and tea and cold meats were laid out. Many more servants were bustling about the kitchen which was, as always, full of gross smells and offal and curses. The kitchen activity was a necessary adjunct of good living, but one best ignored, as a gentlewoman ignores her stomach rumblings. In the orangery which occupied the south side of the eastern court, however, was a much more agreeable perfume and propriety.

Blenheim-house could faintly recall that evening in August 1719 when *All for Love* had been performed in the Bow-window Room. How very gauche and makeshift that production had been! Screens for scenery and curtains for costumes! Tonight's theatricals would be quite a different affair. All the best houses had private theatres now – the Dukes of Richmond and Ancaster had led the fashion – and Blenheim's own beloved Duke had recently given orders for its orangery to be made into a proper theatre. Tonight was the gala première, and five more evening performances would follow, with a repertoire of no fewer than four plays.

The orangery walls had been painted a soft dove-grey, with white pilasters and garlands set against pale blue niches and friezes, the tints as delicate as birds' eggs. The stage was at the western end, with the motto 'Laugh where you may, be candid where you can' ribboned above. Everything was 'fitted up in a style of peculiar elegance', with 'appendages correspondent to the munificence and fortune of the owner', according to the Revd William Fordyce Mavor, Woodstock's rector, schoolmaster and sometime mayor, whose *New Description of Blenheim* was just about to appear on bookstalls. Mavor was Blenheim's very own Mr Collins, quite as brimming with obsequious praise for Duke and palace as that reverend gentleman was for Lady Catherine de Burgh and Rosings in Jane Austen's *Pride and Prejudice*. From time to time the Revd Mavor's adulation cascaded forth in ode form; he was even now seated in a back row of the audience mentally composing 'On Converting the Greenhouse into a Private Theatre'. The 'easy and commodious' seats around him, 'capable of accommodating two hundred persons without including the side-boxes' were filling up with neighbouring gentry and the Corporations of Woodstock and Oxford. The three London playwrights in their crumpled cravats with greasy collar-lines sat down in one of the side-boxes with a good deal of commotion, while the more elegant members of the audience rustled their silks and bowed to each other and read their large vellum programmes. They were to be treated to a double bill: Kelly's comedy, *False Delicacy*, followed by Mrs Cowley's *Who's the Dupe?*

The audience hushed as the Hon. Richard Edgecumbe, a family friend of the Marlboroughs, recited a prologue written by William Cole, the Duke's former chaplain. Then the velvet curtains parted to reveal a beautiful garden scene painted by Michael Angelo Rooker, chief scene-painter at London's Haymarket Theatre, whose name clearly proclaimed the artistic heights to which he aspired in that highly cultured age.

False Delicacy was a piece of froth in which three pairs of lovers chased and lost and misunderstood and finally found each other. Members of the press were in the audience, and since this was a peer-ful production, they were predisposed to praise. 'Never before had such an assemblage of rank and beauty and elegance,' *Town and Country Magazine* gushed, 'graced the stage.' The actors included a brother and nephew of the Duke, a brother of the Duchess, and their son, Lord Henry, aged sixteen. The actresses included three of the Duke's daughters: Lady Caroline, who would turn twenty-four the following week, Lady Elizabeth, twenty-three, and Lady Charlotte, celebrating her eighteenth birthday that very day. The palace remembered the three Marlborough granddaughters who had performed in *All for Love*. How much more elegant these three young ladies looked!

The costumes were indeed splendid. Lady Caroline played Miss Marchmont in pink bodice, gauze petticoat and plumed hat. 'The mental powers of this lady,' declared *Town and Country*, 'give the highest brilliancy to her personal charms.' Lady Elizabeth as Lady Betty Lampton 'gave the most striking proofs of a refined taste, not only in the elegance of her dress, but in the display of her manners'. Lady Charlotte, named for her godmother, George III's wife, played Miss Theodora Rivers, dressed *à la bergère* – shepherdesses being the latest French craze – in a Devonshire brown dress and white petticoat. Charlotte was the Duke's favourite daughter. He had commissioned James Roberts of Oxford to paint her in her costume; the original would be hung at Blenheim, reproduced the following year by J. Jones in mezzotint and bought up quickly by a ducal-mad public. Charlotte was beautiful, clever and supremely good. It was as if the porcelain smoothness of Blenheim, its patina of satinwood and silver, had distilled themselves in Charlotte. Blenheim had been a fine governess; raised in that sweetness-and-light setting where sheep may safely graze and 'life overflows without ambitious pains', Charlotte never spoke a harsh word or had an unkind thought. 'The juvenility and beauty of this lady,' *Town and Country* noted, 'were most happily adapted to the character she represented.'

Most happily adapted indeed, as another ten years would show. Miss Theodora Rivers is persuaded by Sir Harry Newburgh to elope with him behind her father's back. 'When he sees we are inseparately united,' boasts Sir Harry to Theodora, 'a little time will necessarily make us friends, and I have great hopes that before the end of three months we shall be the favourites of the whole family.' But Theodora's father, Colonel Rivers, remains unmoved: 'By and by, I shall have this fellow at my feet,' he declares, 'entreating my forgiveness, and the world will think me an unfeeling monster if I don't give him my estate as a reward for having blasted my dearest expectations.' He thereupon throws his daughter's dowry at her: 'Here then in this pocket-book are notes for that sum [£20,000]. Take it – but never see me more.'

'Never see me more . . .' The words crawled into the dove-grey walls of Blenheim's theatre and stayed there, biding their time.

If the costumes were sophisticated, so was the lighting – large 'reverberators' (lenses and reflectors) placed at either side of the stage – and the machinery, ingeniously contrived by 'Austin of Woodstock'. Mr Talbot led the orchestra of professional musicians, and Lady Elizabeth sang an Italian air, '*Non dubitari*', which bore no relevance to the play but which amply demonstrated how attentive she had been over the years to her music-master. The ladies in the cast all carried small bouquets, moved with studied deportment, and performed a dance at the end of *False Delicacy* without a single wrong move.

Plenty of art and artifice, but the veneer of false delicacy was all there was. No life, no passion pulsed underneath. *Town and Country*'s flowery encomiums carefully skirted the truth, the truth being that not one player could act and not one word could be heard.

The three dramatists in the audience, who stood lowest on the social ladder but highest on the creative one, fidgeted and fumed and felt ready to explode. There was far more energy and feeling in their side-box than on the stage. Frederick Reynolds has left his account of that evening:

> Being myself unable to hear one line out of twenty, which these *really private* actors uttered, I expressed a wish that some friendly person would hint to them, that the entertainment of their audience would not be diminished, if they would condescend to speak audibly.

Miles Andrews assured Frederick that '*not* to hear them is our only chance of getting through this tiresome evening', for 'we have no hope of seeing even one good performer here'. At that precise moment, the Duke's porter appeared on stage (the servant players were not listed in the programme) and delivered his only line: 'A letter, Sir Harry!' in such a 'strong, natural, audible tone of voice' that the three actors in the side-box applauded him loudly, while the Duke frowned and pouted in a petulant way and the Duchess fanned herself and raised her chin another six inches.

At the end of the second act, the ten Blenheim footmen brought in trays of tea, coffee, ices and orgeat (a cooling drink of almonds and orange-water). The bumpkin plainness of liveries in mean old Duchess Sarah's time had given way to liveries elaborately laced and gold-braided with crimson cloth coats, buff waistcoats and crimson shag breeches. The present Duke 'took on himself', as Reynolds reports, 'the office of grand sur-intendant of the whole proceedings', and saw to it that within his fairy-tale palace, every wish would be instantly gratified, with one wave of the ducal wand:

> No host, perhaps, was ever more attentive to his guests. Soon after the third act had commenced, His Grace, hearing the clattering of cups, and a loud

whispering, arising from that part of the theatre where the aldermen and other electors of the city of Oxford, together with their wives and children, were seated, His Grace naturally concluded, from his knowledge of the civic character, that the afore-mentioned noise was a hint for additional refreshments. During the serious love scene, between Sir Harry Newburgh and Miss Rivers, one of His Grace's suite hastily arose, and (at the very moment Sir Harry was on the point of rushing into the heroine's arms) addressing himself to the noble performers, he thus most energetically exclaimed: 'Stop – some of the company want more tea.' Then, turning towards the body corporate, he added, 'Ladies and Gentlemen, you shall be served immediately.'

At long last, the play ended, the players bowed and curtseyed to generous applause, and Miss Peshall, another family friend, daughter of Sir John Peshall, in a pink-bound, rose-wreathed, cinnamon-bodiced gauze gown, inaudibly spoke the epilogue, much to the frustration of John Randolph, Oxford Professor of Poetry, who was waiting expectantly in the audience to hear the honeyed words he had so painstakingly composed.

Who's the Dupe? was greeted with genteel laughter, and Michael Angelo the Second's set, which depicted Marlborough House and St James's Park, was much admired. As soon as the performance ended, the Duke and Duchess had the three actor-playwrights brought to them to be presented. The Marlboroughs received them graciously, then waited expectantly for the petal-shower of plaudits and compliments sure to settle round them. But not for nothing had Miles Peter Andrews been staring for three hours at the motto above the stage: 'Be candid where you can.' 'For your own sakes, I speak my mind,' he declared boldly. 'Your theatre is too cold, and you have chosen a dull, obsolete play. Even real sterling talent could have done nothing with it.' The ducal party frowned or fanned furiously, depending on their sex, and stalked off without inviting the three young upstarts to supper, which was about to be served in the dining-room. Nor were they invited to the public breakfast to be held next morning. The chosen few, all of whom told the Duke and Duchess exactly what they wanted to hear, strolled across the greensward, admired the twinkling lanterns in the trees, and entered the Great Hall.

The groom of the chambers, William Tibbett, (salary £60 per year) received them at the door and directed them to the dining-room. 'Tibby', as the family called him, had been with them for many years, beginning as boy-fiddler and footman. He still played his violin whenever the Marlboroughs wanted to hear that new composer, Mozart, but Tibby's main kingdom now comprised all the reception rooms. Three times a day he went round to see that all writing-tables were stocked with crested notepaper and sharpened quill-pens. He also supervised the frequent cleaning of the silver, which was done by the footmen using a mixture of Spanish white (powdered chalk) and ammonia, followed by rouge (powdered ferric oxide) applied with a chamois, followed by a final rub with a soft woollen brush. The footmen had learned to do a thorough job, for his Tibbs could see a pin-dot of tarnish from a hundred feet away. Tibby ushered the guests past the antique statue of Diana gambolling with her dog, placed on a marble slab in the Hall, into the Saloon where a large 'Sleeping Venus and Cleopatra with her Asp' reclined on two more marble slabs. The guests proceeded through the Saloon to the dining-room just east of it. The three rooms between Saloon and Grand Cabinet were no longer a formal suite waiting for a monarch, but rather the much-used communal rooms of a couple with eight children. Monarchs had slipped a little in status; George III ruled by consent rather than divine right and his powers were more restricted than Queen Anne's had been. The property-owning aristocracy, still the country's most powerful élite, were busy building country houses where they could enjoy themselves, not entertain a king. Formal houses such as Blenheim, with a rigid hierarchy of rooms and long axial vistas, were out of fashion. Reception rooms in the newest houses spread out in egalitarian arcs, or moved up one flight to the top of an impressive circular staircase sweeping through the hall.

The Marlboroughs were stuck with their formal house, but had done what they could. The eastern antechamber, drawing-room and bedchamber fit for a king were now the family's dining-room, winter drawing-room and summer drawing-room.

The wainscot panels in the twenty-eight-foot square dining-room were painted white, and the white chimney-piece was delicately sculpted with lyres and scallop-shells. In the middle of the mantel rested an elegant clock which not only gave the time but also registered the current state of Empire: a large bronze elephant reassured viewers that in India Britain's trade and territory were expanding, and a much smaller bronze North-American Indian reminded them that at the battle of Yorktown six years before, Britain, most regrettably, had lost the continent's southern half. Above the mantel was Rubens's painting of 'The Three Graces'. Their beauty of face and pose, the Duke never tired of saying as he looked up each evening from his bottle of port (1,400 more in his cellar), reminded him of his own three Graces: Caroline, Elizabeth and Charlotte. Those in the painting were gathering fruit just as their real-life counterparts did, metaphorically speaking, from Blenheim's rich cultural store.

The painting which dominated the dining-room, however, was the large family portrait of the present Duke and Duchess with six of their children. Francis and Amelia, now aged eight and two, had been born since it was painted, ten years previously, by Sir Joshua Reynolds, for £700. The Duchess sits in the exact centre of the canvas, under a Blenheim arch, dominating the scene, and laying a directing hand on the Duke's arm. He extends one relaxed white-stockinged leg to show the fine curve of his calf, and beside him, in red velvet, stands his eldest son and heir, the Marquis of Blandford, who has the same indecisive chin as his father. Both of them hold antique gems from the Duke's fine collection, while the Duke's sword lies abandoned on a nearby chair. The other bland-faced children cluster round, and in the upper right corner looms the hard stone form of John Churchill, 1st Duke of Marlborough, seemingly transported from the top of his Victory Column in the park, and looking remarkably out of place amid all that limp-wristed insouciance. The only really passionate participants in the scene are the dogs, two spaniels and a whippet, who tense with fear and cringe from the frightening mask which little Charlotte holds before her face.

Sir Joshua's portrait of Blenheim's current family, all of them so refined, so accomplished, rested on its soft damask wall like a large cameo. The company were now seating themselves around the long mahogany table which was laid for supper with the Duke's set of two dozen gold knives, forks and spoons engraved with his coat of arms. He had bought them impulsively some years before – the Duke stinted himself on nothing – and the Bond Street goldsmith's bill, which included 'adding festoons to a large tureen and gilding two ice pails' came to £332 5s. 7d. The china at each place was part of the hundred-piece Meissen set given to the present Duke's father by the King of Poland in exchange for a pack of stag-hounds. Sprinkled on a white ground were tulips, roses and daffodils, with thin lemon-slice finials on the covered dishes. The finials were the only astringent note in all that cloying sweetness.

The guests arranged themselves according to the new fashion for 'promiscuous seating' of gentleman alternating with lady; earlier in the century, females had ranged themselves on one side of the table with men on the other. The Duke and Duchess had seated themselves at head and foot with their children very evenly and tactfully interspersed along the two sides. 'The Duke and Duchess,' reported *Town and Country*, 'conducted themselves with a dignified, yet amiable condescension to their visitors.' Dignity was the Duchess's prerogative; amiability, the Duke's.

He spoke in a soft drawl, and pressed food upon his guests at the end of every sentence. George Spencer, 4th Duke of Marlborough, was forty-eight years old, and the handsome, clear-cut features of his youth were beginning to soften and spread, like an over-ripe pear. George had been born with one of his gold spoons already in his mouth on 26 January 1739,

DUKE of MARLBOROUGH · Caroline D⁹ of MARLBOROUGH · George MARQUESS of BLANDFORD · LORD Henry Spencer · LADY Caroline Spencer · LADY Eliz⁹ Spencer · LADY Charlotte Spencer · LADY Anne Spencer

George, 4th Duke of Marlborough and his family.
Portrait by Sir Joshua Reynolds

at Langley Park, a sprawling house in Buckinghamshire which his father Charles Spencer, 3rd Duke of Marlborough, had bought the previous year from the widower of Abigail Hill Masham, the 'shuffling little wretch' who had stolen Queen Anne's love from Sarah. Charles Spencer, who had become 3rd Duke in 1733 upon Henrietta Churchill's death, always preferred Langley to Blenheim, which became his when Sarah died in 1744. His son George, on the other hand, had given his heart to Blenheim by the time he was eight. 'Pray answer this letter,' he wrote to sister Betty from Eton on 7 October 1747, 'and tell me when I shall come to Blenheim. Pray tell Papa I shall circumcaricumfricate him, if he does not send for us soon, for I know he will say we shall come presently, and presently, till at last it will be too late.' 'I forgot to tell you the canary-bird desires his love to his brother,' little George scrawled at the bottom of his letter, 'pray mine to Mama and Papa and sister Di and brother Robert.' From this affectionate beginning, George grew into a sensitive, highly strung young man who hated his army service in the Coldstream Guards and was overjoyed to leave when, on 20 October 1758, his father died suddenly of dysentery in Germany and George found himself, at nineteen, in the best of all possible worlds with the best of all possible titles. The new Duke of Marlborough inherited £500,000 capital, a rent-roll income of £70,000 a year and all the treasures of Blenheim which were his to love and to cherish till death. Thanks to his ruthless, hard-hitting great-grandfather, John Churchill, George could afford to be relaxed and refined; all he had to do was move into Blenheim and enjoy the fruits.

All the single young ladies in England's titled families were eager to share them with him, for George was the country's most eligible bachelor, with 'fortune, title, figure,' as one young lady put it, giving the precise order of importance, 'just what one could wish'. In spite of his good looks and gold-plated position, however, George was timid, nervous and very, very shy. Once, playing at quinze, he had thrown his cards into a heap, knowing that he was about to make a hundred pounds on the next move. He couldn't have borne all those people crowding round and clapping him on the back had he won. (How great-grandfather John must have squirmed in his grave, at a descendant of his voluntarily passing up a hundred pounds!) If he wanted something, however, George Spencer had learned early to indulge himself, and he was a very sensual young man. 'He is excessively wild and given to women, as was his poor father before him,' sighed one young lady. Another reported, in February 1760, that the Duke of Marlborough was 'so entirely given up to women that it's quite dreadful, for he has a terrible disorder that hinders him dancing'. England's match-making mammas agreed that what the wild young Duke needed was a wife, and those with unattached daughters were soon in full cry after him. Leading the pack was Gertrude, Duchess of Bedford, second wife of the 4th Duke of Bedford, whose first wife had been Diana Spencer, Sarah's beloved granddaughter and actress in Blenheim's 1719 theatricals. The Duchess of Bedford resorted to all sorts of 'mean and unbecoming artifices which she had so little pride as to use in public' to secure the highly eligible George for her daughter Caroline. The Duchess appeared nightly at Ranelagh's pleasure gardens with Caroline in tow, and planted her squarely in the Duke of Marlborough's primrose path. 'Eight and forty hours after His Grace declared himself a lover', according to one gossip, the Duchess of Bedford had George and Caroline already at the altar, and the pleased Duke of Bedford 'never despatched a matter quicker than this', by giving Caroline £50,000 dowry with as much to follow on his death. On Monday, 23 August 1762, George Spencer and Caroline Russell said their marriage vows in the chapel of London's Bedford House, which Sarah had helped granddaughter Diana redesign in the 1730s. Caroline would prove, in the beginning, to be one of George's treasures. He was a veritable Hamlet of indecision on all matters large and small. He could wander back and forth in his mind's corridors for hours, days even, in a dreamy, shilly-shally way. He needed Caroline to point him in the right direction or nail him into a corner. In the first fifteen years of their marriage, she did it with dispatch. Then the weight of Blenheim, and other factors, worked a radical change on the sprightly, strong-willed Caroline.

The house congratulated itself on the company which ringed its dining-table like a rainbow-feathered boa. The men wore velvet coats in rich colours of plum and russet; the ladies wore silk gowns in delicate shades of lavender and sea-green, with creamy lace dripping from their elbows, and diamonds filling in their low décolletages. The food was sumptuous, too: two removes of sixteen dishes each: beef, mutton, pork, veal, boiled tongue, chickens, ducks, geese. The head cook, James Beckley, who earned £73 yearly and the kitchen-maid, Mary Corner, who earned £7, had taken all afternoon to make the dessert. James had baked a large cake in the new cast-iron kitchen range which had recently replaced the old brick wall-oven for baking. The kitchen-maid had whisked twenty-four egg whites for a full three hours with a birch-twig whisk to make the icing; then the cook had swirled it on to the cake in beautiful patterns using a bunch of feathers. There would be apple pie and plum pudding as well; very sweet desserts were popular in that ambrosial age. Mountney the butler, who earned £45 a year, was already pulling the new bell-rope just installed beside the sideboard, which rang a bell labelled 'dining-room' on the board outside the servants' hall, and John Wheeler, head footman (£30 per annum), brought in the cake on one of John Churchill's huge silver-gilt plates, and the guests sighed in a pleasantly satiated way, and the Duchess smiled on them with just the right blend of hauteur and graciousness.

At forty-three, the Duchess of Marlborough was still lovely, with a conventional, even-featured beauty, although she had an affected way of making up her mouth, and a queer, unattractive voice. Her resident French hairdresser (£80 a year) had piled her light brown hair up into elaborate puffs and curls, but it was less elevated than in the Reynolds portrait behind her, where it was more than two feet high. 'Lady Car is as beautiful as an angel,' one Countess had written when Car Russell was only twelve, but until she married at nineteen, she had been rather a hoyden, with speech too shrill and petticoats too muddy and ankles too much in evidence. The dignity and weight of Blenheim had quickly tamed her. Lady Sarah Lennox, who had hoped to snare the Duke herself, commented on Caroline's 'improved state' to a friend, 'for you may remember the great difference between the bouncing Lady Car Russell and the gentle Duchess of Marlborough. In the latter state she is very winning in her manners.' If Blenheim made her proper, it also made her insufferably proud. The Duchess had grown up at Woburn Abbey where the footmen wore rose-coloured coats and white breeches, where two complete sets of rooms allowed alternative summer and winter living quarters, where there were four pioneer water-closets and a hot bath quite as grand as the one in Blenheim's undercroft, where earthenware stoves imported from France relieved the chill of staircases and passages. Caroline had never felt intimidated by Blenheim's grandeur. But the combination of Woburn and Blenheim, magnificence squared so to speak, had made her, according to Queen Charlotte, one of the two 'haughtiest and proudest women in England', the other being Lady Carlisle, who swished her silken trains through Castle Howard, Vanbrugh's other masterpiece of megalomania.

The Duchess spread her condescension round the table like silver gauze; the claret flowed, the gold forks clinked against the Meissen, the compliments fluttered above the food like butterflies. How blessed were the Duke and Duchess of Marlborough, in their Spenserian – or rather, Spencerian – Bower of Bliss with their beautiful house, and garden, and children. Every person in the room, except the servants, felt a ballooning envy as they raised their glasses, and drank silent toasts to Blenheim, a veritable Eden.

It was only after the guests had departed and the tired residents were sleeping soundly on their swansdown pillows that the house allowed itself, in the darkness and gloom of 4 a.m., to stare starkly at the truth. All was not well at Blenheim. The Duke had had one of his 'deaf-mute' spells at dinner when he suddenly, like a snail, withdrew his soft presence into a shell of silence and incomprehension. The Duchess, and the five older children, seemed to be drifting, quite rudderless, towards apathy and stasis. Relations between the Marquis of Blandford and his parents were severely strained. Blenheim's next master, impulsive and headstrong but always so alive, hardly ever came to Blenheim nor communicated with his parents. His sisters often wept softly at their dressing-tables; they longed for London balls and ridottos where they could look for husbands, not home-grown theatricals attended by fat Oxford aldermen; but their parents wouldn't budge from Blenheim.

An owl's hollow cry sounded from the black cedars on the lawn; floorboards creaked in the attic; the moon went behind a cloud and the palace brooded on its past. From cold palace of art it had been transformed, when the 4th Duke came, to warm house of life. Now its pulse and passion were weakening day by day. What had gone wrong? When had the deep draughts of living and loving in its golden youth begun to drain away, leaving only this saccharine sediment?

FIRST HAD COME THOSE LONG YEARS OF EMPTINESS, BEGINNING with the 1st Duke's ignominious retreat in 1720 and lasting until the present Duke had married in 1762 and come to live permanently at Blenheim, its very first resident Duke. In between had come Dowager Duchess Sarah's hard-hitting forays, followed by occasional visits from the 3rd Duke, Charles Spencer, bringing little George and his other children to romp through the halls. After he succeeded in 1758, George would sometimes come and tut-tut his way from room to dusty room, and then stand, slim and handsome, at a cobwebbed window looking out on unkempt meadow and marsh. And all that time Blenheim sat hunched and bedraggled, like Cinderella in her rags and ashes.

Horace Walpole came to scoff in July 1760: 'We went to Blenheim,' he told a friend,

> and saw all the old flock chairs, wainscot tables and gowns and petticoats of Queen Anne that old Sarah could crowd among blocks of marble. It looks like the palace of an auctioneer, who has been chosen King of Poland, and furnished his apartments with obsolete trophies, rubbish that nobody bid for, and a dozen pictures that he had stolen from the inventories of different families. The place is as ugly as the house, and the bridge, like the beggars at the old Duchess's gate, begs for a drop of water, and is refused.

The cold palace waited for its prince to come and animate it, but when newly-weds George and Caroline moved in, late in the summer of 1762, the castle was still ignored. The ducal pair cooed like turtle doves and had eyes only for each other. 'Lady S. Keppel says that it does her good to see two people so fond of one another as their Graces of Marlborough; she has been at Blenheim,' wrote Lady Sarah Lennox Bunbury to the Marchioness of Kildare on 7 November. When he wasn't billing and cooing at Blenheim, the Duke was active in the larger world, doing his duty as a good peer should. He had become Lord-Lieutenant of Oxford two years before and now became Lord Chamberlain and Member of the Privy Council. In April 1763, he became Lord Privy Seal, and in October, the Duke and Duchess's first child was born. Alas, the baby was a mere girl, not the longed-for heir; her parents named her Caroline after her mother. Baby Elizabeth arrived one year later, so that Blenheim's pink-ribboned nursery was enlivened with rosy-cheeked little faces and delightful gurgles and nursemaids bustling in and out with piles of fresh-smelling linen.

By 1764, the Duke and Duchess had stopped gazing at each other long enough to take a hard look at their house's interior and realized that there was plenty of room for improvement. The miracles which would change Blenheim from cold, ugly castle to vibrant, beautiful home began. First came a great deal of refurbishing of window curtains and wall-coverings. The needles of upholsterer Charles Arbuckle flew as the Duchess dictated her choices and invoices piled up on Her Grace's writing-table. A typical one for 24 June 1764, lists 'six draw-up curtains lined and fringed, with arched heads' and '357 feet of *papier mâché* border in burnished gold to resemble large nails'. Dark-coloured draperies gave way to spring-like shades of primrose and periwinkle and celadon-green, with plenty of white woodwork.

Sarah's old 'flock chairs' and 'wainscot tables' with their huge lion's paw feet were banished to the attic. They were replaced by Chippendale mahogany chairs whose delicate ribbon-carved backs the housemaids dusted daily with a paint-brush, and by card-tables with urn-and-swag inlays in ochre and olive and russet-coloured woods. Cabinets appeared with golden pagodas and friendly dragons and bent little mandarins wandering over their shining black-lacquer surfaces. Chairs and tables no longer stood, like soldiers on sentinel duty, round the walls; lighter in weight now, they could be moved about on whim to form cosy little groupings in the middle of a room. The rigidity of the first half of the eighteenth century had given way to the fluidity of the second half; the Age of Reason had become the Age of Sensibility, and furniture followed suit. In Blenheim's drawing-rooms were several of the new Pembroke tables whose leaves flew up or down depending on how flamboyant or restrained its owners felt. Ladies of hartshorn-and-handkerchief sensibility, given to fainting fits and tears, couldn't sit bolt upright; they had to recline, so Sarah's high-back chairs and hard day-beds gave way to upholstered sofas. 'Elegant and useful' were Thomas Chippendale's twin ideals, according to his 1754 book of furniture designs, the first pattern-book to be published by a practising cabinet-maker. Sofas had elegant curves of back and arm, but they also, for the first time, had springs, so that one's artistic eye and one's backside were equally accommodated. (Even in furniture, art married nature.) How Sarah had longed for comfort at Blenheim without ever finding it! Now it was there in abundance, for just as the Marlboroughs started their redecorating, England began to concentrate on 'comfort' as a domestic ideal destined for a long reign. 'I sing the Sofa,' begins William Cowper's long poem *The Task* (1785) and several pages of blank verse extol the comfort of 'that soft settee'.

The Duke had now turned his full attention on Blenheim. After the first fine careless raptures of his marriage, he began looking about for a new lover who would inspire him, as the perpetually pregnant Caroline couldn't, to fresh passion and new ecstasies. He didn't have far to look. The ideal mistress – one who would never disagree or defect – was already enfolding him, and George for the rest of his life would remain loyal – to Blenheim, his first and last love. On Blenheim he would lavish all his cosseting and most of his wealth, in the form of extravagant draperies,

Engraving of the north front of Blenheim Palace, *c.* 1745, before the forecourt was grassed over

gemstones and a spectacular new setting. If the 1st Duke of Marlborough had seen Blenheim as a propaganda piece where he could show off his wealth and fame, the 4th Duke saw it as a pleasure-garden where he could indulge his senses, particularly his sense of sight. George prided himself on his superb taste, even though he was handicapped by one tiny flaw: he was colour blind. George III had confided the sad fact to Fanny Burney, the popular novelist who served his wife as second Keeper of the Robes: 'The Duke of Marlborough actually cannot tell scarlet from green!' exclaimed the King. 'How unfortunate,' replied Fanny, 'that such an eye should possess objects worthy the most discerning – the treasures of Blenheim!' Fortunately, the Duke could afford expert advisers who *could* tell red from green to help him deck out his chosen one.

Certainly the Duke was wonderfully inventive in the variety of his expenditures. He woke each morning with the thought: 'Now how to amuse me today?' and often by sundown he had conjured up some fresh delight for house or grounds. One June morning in 1763, the Duke helped himself to a sheet of gilt-edged ivory notepaper from the pile on his desk which, miraculously, never got any lower, and scribbled a note to Lancelot 'Capability' Brown, the most fashionable landscape-architect of the day. The Duke told Capability that he wanted to make 'expensive alterations' to Blenheim's dishevelled grounds. 'I have a notion I shall begin here immediately so that the sooner you come the better,' the Duke wrote in the peremptory tone which he used towards underlings.

Lancelot Brown's career, at forty-seven, was just then at its peak. He had started humbly as a boy in Northumberland by tending the vegetable garden at Kirkharle Hall. In 1741, when he was twenty-five, Brown became gardener to Lord Cobham of Stowe, who had served with the 1st Duke of Marlborough in his Netherlands campaigns. Brown worked for nine years as apprentice to William Kent, who taught him everything he knew about making gardens look natural and uncontrived. By 1750, Capability had eclipsed Kent as England's most sought-after gardener. Before he turned his attentions to Blenheim, he had already beautified the grounds of Petworth House in Sussex, Chatsworth in Derbyshire and Alnwick Castle in Northumberland. Brown was one of that growing group of middle-class artisans who served the nobility with distinction, and kept their eye on the main chance. He himself would end as High Sheriff of Huntingdonshire and father-in-law to Lord Holland. When he came to Blenheim to work his magic, he had just enrolled his eldest child at Eton, been appointed Master Gardener at Hampton Court and moved into Wilderness House in its grounds. It was a snug brick house of the late seventeenth century with four elegant panelled rooms on the main floor, in one of which Brown,

Lancelot 'Capability' Brown. Portrait by Nathaniel Dance

during the autumn of 1763, worked long hours drawing his Blenheim designs. His house's only defect was that often, while he was working on his plans for Blenheim's wide waters and wondrous cascades, his cellar-kitchen, in a remarkable act of empathy, was quietly filling up with water.

Brown's philosophy of landscape gardening was based on the premise that nature was rather a careless strumpet and needed art's helping hand to look her best. Like a clever couturier, he could assess 'capabilities' at a glance, and knew, after one quick tour of an estate, exactly where to accentuate a curve, or disguise a defect with a belt of trees, doing it all in a way that never looked too artificial or constrained. When Brown 'improved' Nuneham for Lord Harcourt, the Duke of Marlborough's mentor, friend and neighbour, a minor poet called Whitehead, dashed off a witty verse in which Brown addresses Nature:

> Observe all these changes, and candidly own
> I have clothed you when naked, and when overdrest
> I have stripped you again to your bodice and veil;
> Concealed every blemish, each beauty displayed,
> As Reynolds would picture some exquisite maid.

For the next ten years, Brown applied his expertise to Blenheim. He was frequently to be seen tramping about in his dark green coat and neatly rolled bob wig, the cheeks of his egg-shaped face as red as crab-apples, waving his arms in sweeping arcs only a little less flamboyant than Vanbrugh's. Surrounded on all sides by dirt piles, giant holes and armies of workmen, Blenheim seemed to be slated for another siege of physical and financial stress as in the days of its building. However, the work went forward smoothly enough, and the Duke paid Brown amounts varying from £500 to £1,200 without a single qualm or quibble until finally £21,500 had changed hands.

To create the lake, a hefty dam was made near Bladon and two causeways were cut through so that the Glyme could spread out on either side of Vanbrugh's bridge. A Grand Cascade was made at the lake's western end so that, with silver plume and spray, its waters could sweep on to join the river Evenlode. The Great Parterre and north courtyard were replaced by grass; girdles of beech trees were draped seductively round the periphery of the park; clumps of cedars were placed here and there like filigree brooches on the wide velvet lawn.

As Blenheim grew more comely, Capability's self-esteem soared. 'Thames will never forgive me,' he declared proudly as the lake got wider and wider, and he haughtily informed his bank manager, in the spring of 1765, that henceforth 'Mr Lancelot Brown' was to be addressed only as

'Lancelot Brown, Esq.' Indeed, Brown grew a little too cocky, or at least Horace Walpole thought so. The aristocratic Horace disapproved of Brown's 'impertinence to the Duke of Marlborough. The moment a fashionable artist, singer or actor is insolent,' wrote Horace, perceiving the first tiny tubers of middle-class rebellion, 'his success is sure. The first peer that experiences it, laughs to conceal his being angry, the next flatters him for fear of being treated familiarly, and ten more bear it because it is *so like Brown*.' It was in the cultural flowering of those mid-eighteenth-century years that the status of England's artists grew higher than ever before or since. Society revered them, and they puffed out their chests and sauced their social superiors.

While Capability was waiting for the lake to fill, for it took a very long time, he built a Gothic-fronted granary in the grounds and a menagerie to keep the Duke's growing family amused. Then he added Gothic crenellations to High Lodge where John and Sarah had sometimes stayed, and where Rochester's tipsy ghost still staggered about, finding it hard, now, to recognize its home.

The Duke resigned as Lord Privy Seal in 1765, and when George III offered him the post of Master of the Horse he turned it down and hardly took an instant to decide; he was having far too much fun at Blenheim. From this point on, the 4th Duke of Marlborough turned his back on public duty and settled down in Blenheim-house to live the blissful life of country squire. On 3 March 1766, just as the first daffodils opened, his longed-for heir was born and christened George after his father, who had high hopes for the new Marquis of Blandford and future 5th Duke of Marlborough.

Both inside and out, Blenheim's beautifying went on apace. Following on Brown's heels, in 1769, came William Chambers, England's most fashionable architect, who had 'improved' Woburn Abbey and Castle Howard and Horace Walpole's more modest Gothic confection, Strawberry Hill. In his youth, Chambers had sailed to China in a ship of the Swedish East India Company and some years later had helped spark England's chinoiserie craze with his *Designs of Chinese Buildings, Furniture, Dresses, Machines and Utensils* (1757). He had studied architecture in Italy for ten years and returned to England in 1755 to begin his career, bringing a headful of Palladian concepts, an Italian wife, and a trunkful of elegant coats, including one custom-made in Paris which had interlaced palm-leaves in bright gold on a dull gold background, with flowers between and buttons to match. Buttons were no longer just a status symbol, as they had been earlier in the century; whether they were made of diamonds or horn was less important now than whether they complemented the garment in an aesthetically pleasing way. In 1756, Chambers designed a summerhouse and pagoda at Kew for the Dowager Princess of Wales and became architectural tutor to her son, who would become George III four years later. Chambers was a kindly, even-tempered man with a rollicking sense of fun. 'My wife and daughters thank you for your kind invitation,' he once wrote to Oliver Goldsmith, 'but they have seen your play twice, and laughed so immoderately both times that they dare not venture upon a third, for fear of the hysterics.' The 4th Duke would prove a trial to Chambers, and Blenheim's wanton luxuriance always made him feel uncomfortable, for he had been raised in a plain Scottish merchant's house.

He worked at Blenheim-house off and on from 1769 to 1775, at which time he heaved a great sigh of relief and went off to London to design its largest building to date and his greatest achievement: Somerset House in the Strand. 'I cannot tell when I shall be at Blenheim,' he wrote in July 1772 to his friend the Revd Weston, who lived near by in Witney. 'The transition from a palace to a cot, as you call your habitation, is more agreeable to me than you can well imagine. I shall enter your door with a jovial heart,' wrote Chambers in his elegant script, 'which I seldom have in the mansions of the Great. With you I shall consider myself as a welcome guest. With them I am like the Egyptian bird who picks the teeth of the crocodile, admitted and cherished while there is any work to be done, but when that is over the doors are shut and the farce is at an end.'

Like Brown, Chambers refused to feel intimidated by the Duke of Marlborough. He sent off a bold letter to the Duke on 23 May 1771, protesting His Grace's callous treatment of a workman. 'Wilson the slater laments with great grief his loss of the Duke's business,' wrote Chambers.

> I really wish the poor man was reinstated. His fault seems to me a trifling one. He refused to give half a guinea towards a feast when he had not half a guinea to give and declined going to a merry-making because he was just a-going into a gaol. I think I should have acted as he did under similar circumstances, and should have thought myself very hardly used if I had been so severely punished.

Chambers also resented his peremptory summonses to Blenheim. 'Please to present my most humble respects to His Grace,' Chambers told Charles Turner, the Duke's steward, on 26 May 1772, 'and acquaint him that I am very sorry I cannot come to Blenheim this week for I have engagements every day till Friday upon business of different kinds.'

The Duke was over-fussy and fastidious and changed his mind a dozen times with each new project. The first one was for some new chimney-pieces to be sculpted with classical motifs. 'Herewith I send Your Grace a drawing for the Duchess's dressing-room chimney-pieces,' wrote Chambers

LEFT: The state bed designed by Chambers
RIGHT: Mirror and console table in the Grand Cabinet designed by Chambers

on 2 July 1772. 'The frieze and panels of the pilasters may be of any other colour as green or red. If there are any objections,' continued the wily Chambers, 'I should be glad to know them now that I may alter the drawing or make a new one.' In April 1773, Chambers designed a base for Alexander the Great's marble head. 'Finding that Your Grace did not like the shape of the therm', Chambers was quite willing to alter it, but the colours of the new and old bits wouldn't match, so that 'the whole from being a very neat piece of workmanship will become a slovenly piece of work'. He was, he continued, gritting his teeth, 'ready to do it whenever Your Grace pleases to command'. The first design for a new bedstead and hangings for the state bedchamber in the western suite of rooms didn't

The garden tripod designed by Chambers and sculpted by Wilton

please His Grace, so Chambers did a second one, and sent off a full-size sketch to the Duke. 'It may be cut out and put up to see the effect,' Chambers told him on 14 August 1773. The finished bed had plumed casques at its four corners with a frieze of delicate gold acanthus leaves carved on a cream background all round the top. The bed and its blue silk hangings were made in London by Ince and Mayhew. Mr Mayhew had written *Universal System of Household Furniture 1759–63*, and cleverly ensured the Duke's continuing patronage by dedicating it to His Grace, 'a patron ever willing to promote and encourage Industry and Ingenuity'.

The Grand Cabinet came next. The Duke thought he might like arched gilt cornices above the three windows, and, between them, pier-glasses with something suitable – shells would be nice – carved on top, and matching console tables underneath, but nothing too heavy-looking. Chambers drew, and drew again, and finally the approved designs went off to Mr Ansell in London. Ansell agreed to make mirrors and tables for £200 after the Duke had objected to £240, which, Ansell claimed, would allow him to 'do them in the highest perfection' in two colours of gold. The Duke stood firm at £200 and one colour of gold, and Ansell replied that 'he would do the work well at any rate for his own credit'. Six weeks later, Ansell himself came down to Blenheim to supervise the placement of mirrors and tables. 'As they are oil gold and fresh done,' wrote Chambers to the Duke, 'care must be taken not to handle them upon the gilt part as for some time every touch will make a mark.' That should keep the Duke from shifting them about on the walls. The windows were hung with new red silk damask curtains (or were they green?) and the Grand Cabinet was pronounced fit for a Duke with exquisite taste.

'Chambers, I should like...' The Duke moved on to the grounds. Chambers built him a Temple of Flora. *And* a Temple of Diana inscribed with verses from the *Hippolytus* of Euripides. Then he laid out an oval flower garden south-west of the house with a porphyry obelisk and four white marble vases finally placed, after much ducal dithering, in exactly the right spots. Just beyond the flower garden, the Duke thought a tripod might be nice. Chambers designed one with large satyrs and small cupids and plenty of garlands and swags, all of it blending the sensual and the seemly in the best neo-classical style. It was sculpted by Joseph Wilton and the Duke was very, very pleased. Then one day the Duke took a hard look at the eastern gate which housed the cistern, and shuddered. Something would have to be done. 'Chambers, I should like...' Chambers cut panels in the too-plain pilasters and tricked them out with little statues and rope-like swags, which the Duke thought 'very handsome'. 'The only parts we wish to have altered in your drawing,' the Duke told Chambers, 'are the

UNDER THE AUSPICES OF A MUNIFICENT SOVEREIGN THIS HOUSE
WAS BUILT FOR JOHN DUKE OF MARLBOROUGH. AND HIS DUCHESS
SARAH, BY SIR J. VANBRUGH BETWEEN THE YEARS 1705 AND 1722.
AND THIS ROYAL MANOR OF WOODSTOCK, TOGETHER WITH A
GRANT OF £ 240,000, TOWARDS THE BUILDING OF BLENHEIM
WAS GIVEN BY HER MAJESTY QUEEN ANNE AND CONFIRMED
BY ACT OF PARLIAMENT (3.&4. ANNE C.4) TO THE SAID JOHN
DUKE OF MARLBOROUGH AND TO ALL HIS ISSUE MALE AND
FEMALE LINEALLY DESCENDING.

trophies under the cornices; we think the lions' heads in your first sketch looked better than the trophies.' Blenheim had, in the opinion of its peace-loving 4th Duke, more than enough martial trophies as it was.

On 31 January 1774, the Duke began fussing about a fountain and told Chambers to come to Blenheim at once, where the parts of the fountain to be erected would be laid out awaiting his inspection. Chambers didn't know whether to laugh or cry. It was well below zero with snow on the ground and the Duke had nothing more pressing on his mind than fountains! Chambers told His Grace, with admirable courtesy and calm, that he would come down in the spring when the weather warmed up, and give his full attention to the fountain.

When spring came, the Duke grew even more restless and querulous. 'I think I shall like to build a villa,' he wrote to Chambers on 20 June 1774, 'if I can find a pretty spot of ground with a few old trees. I don't want it very large, a good drawing-room, a good dining-room, a few good bedrooms, not a great quantity of stabling.' The Duke was obviously enjoying his dreaming.

> I hate a brick house but I think it may be whitened to look like stone, and there must be a stone staircase. I should think I might build a villa of this sort for £6,000. I think I had rather build than buy a villa ready built, as I shall enjoy the building and making a place very much, but if I do build it certainly shall be on a dry healthy spot. I don't mean that you should make a plan, but I wish you would send me a little thing scratched out upon a bit of paper with the sum or nearly the sum of what it will cost. I should likewise wish to know when the house may be lived in, if it is begun next spring. We mean to have it furnished quite plain, but I should wish to have it all in taste.

Oh, it was a merry thing, thought Chambers, as he tossed the gilt-edged letter on to the work-table in his cramped Berners Street house, and got on with the strenuous task of earning his living, a merry thing indeed to be a duke!

Brown finished his transformations at Blenheim in 1774, and Chambers one year later. By then the Duke was more enamoured of his *favorita* than ever, and Blenheim's richest, happiest years began. One dew-filled morning when the lake, at long last, was full, the miracle occurred. Below the actual house, which, though lively enough within, still presented a solemn, static façade to the world, appeared another house with quite a different mien. There, in the waters of the lake, Blenheim's hard stones were swaying and

---

OPPOSITE: Entrance gateway to east court decorated by Chambers

rippling in the breeze, its rigid chimneys were dancing in the blue and its bellicose roof-statues were leaping and cavorting on the fluffy clouds. The Blenheim in the mirror was full of variety and movement, and the palace, seeing its entrancing image in the lake, had never felt so vibrantly alive. On that wondrous day, Blenheim came of age and took possession, finally and fully, of its golden youth, and of its golden mean, when it was perfectly balanced between art and nature. In the halcyon days that followed, Eros reigned: the kind of Eros Plato talks about in the *Symposium*, where love of the sensual is lifted up, one step at a time, until it becomes love of the spiritual, and body and soul are joined, as they were joined on the chimney-piece plaque in the winter drawing-room, designed by Chambers from a gemstone in the Duke's collection. The plaque depicted, in high relief and great beauty, Cupid's marriage to Psyche. The wise Greeks got it right; according to their legends, Cupid and Psyche produced a daughter, and her name was Pleasure.

Ever since the 4th Duke had moved in, Blenheim had gradually been changing from cool detachment and torpor to warm commitment and abundant vitality. John Churchill, its first Duke, had imported paintings, sculpture, tapestries and furniture from France and Holland, Belgium and Italy. The creativity that sparked them and gave them life was foreign, and far away from Blenheim. These imports were lifeless artefacts, and the Blenheim rooms that housed them were mere containers, larger than the ones the treasures had been shipped in, but still boxes. Not until the 4th Duke succeeded to the title did Blenheim begin to get its own strong, indigenous, creative pulse, bringing its rooms to life. Brown and Chambers, Reynolds and Romney, took their inspiration from house and countryside, worked on the spot, rooted their artistic flowering firmly in that particular soil. The occupants of Blenheim added their own more modest contributions to Blenheim's artistic life. Elizabeth and Blandford were both musically gifted; she played the harp; Caroline could draw; Charlotte, born in 1769, would soon begin the piano and prove a talented painter, as was the Duke's sister Diana, who often came on visits. Between its professionals and its amateurs, Blenheim buzzed with cross-fertilization and artistic growth.

Blenheim's rich flowering at this time reflected what had been happening to Britain as a whole during the previous two decades. Both economically and culturally, it was becoming the envy of the world. In 1757, Robert Clive had defeated the Nabob of Bengal and secured that vast province, the first of many territorial acquisitions in India that would give Britain rich trade in indigo, cotton, silk and spices, and provide her with a large market for her own manufactured goods. Two years later, Wolfe defeated the French General, Montcalm, in Quebec, and added Canada to the Empire, plus a lucrative trade in furs and lumber. Blenheim's estate holdings were growing, too – rather more modestly, of course, than the Empire's – and included Cornbury in Wychwood Forest and more land in the next parish of Wootton. (Later, the 4th Duke would add Dornford and Hordley farms to his land holdings.) Trade goods poured into Britain in a rich stream, just as the Duke's income from his tenant-farmers, with even less effort, kept coming in year after year in a most gratifying way. Just about the time Blenheim's lake filled up, Britain's home manufactures in iron, cloth and shipbuilding had risen to impressive heights. Iron-masters had learnt to use coal instead of charcoal for smelting; Hargreaves and Cartwright had invented the spinning-jenny and the power-loom; James Watt had dreamed up the steam-engine in 1763. China and glass, silver and furniture were being produced with pride and great artistry in Britain's small factories and workshops. No wonder that when George II had dropped dead of his exertions at his close-stool one October morning in 1760, and George III succeeded, he told the Lords and Commons, in his first speech from the throne, that he 'gloried in the name of Briton'.

The peers in his audience gloried, too, for society still recognized their right to all the plums of wealth and privilege, and the middle-class industrialists, who were even then beginning to pile up thick bank-rolls, had not yet become strong or numerous enough to seize the reins of power from those flaccid white hands. The future dukes and lords of England, in that Golden Age, made the Grand Tour of Europe for several years to turn themselves into Men of Taste and amass artistic treasures, succeeded on their fathers' deaths to beautiful houses in which to display them, collected their rent-rolls in thousands of pounds and doled out a goodly number of them to the country's fine painters and sculptors and artisans.

The 4th Duke of Marlborough patronized the arts and gratified his senses all under his own roof, and as art flourished at Blenheim, so did nature. The nursery walls resounded merrily with the increased squeals and giggles within. Henry was born in 1770, and Anne in 1773, so that by then there were six little Spencers making the house quicken. Within doors, Blenheim developed an intense, centripetal life which got its impulse and inspiration from within its own walls. Blenheim became a tight little island complete unto itself, offering a great variety of pleasures. For the adults, there were card-games and modest gambling, billiards for the men, embroidery and novel-reading for the women. For the children, there were plenty of riotous games and dressing-up larks and charades; once the Duke hired 'a Giant', so described in Blenheim's household account books, for one of the children's parties.

Blenheim had plenty of bounce, bucolic fun and innocent merriment. One day, the beautiful, witty Lady Craven, who was a frequent visitor, brought the Duc de Guisnes to see Blenheim. While the company were sitting in the summer drawing-room after the usual large 5 p.m. dinner, the Duchess had a sudden hankering for a syllabub. She sent word to the confectionery maid, Mary Meredith (£6 per annum wages), to make one up using warm milk from one of the cows. Mary measured three pints and whipped it with a pint of Rhine wine, half a pint of sherry, the juice of three lemons and a pound of double-refined sugar. The syllabub duly arrived in the drawing-room, carried in by a footman on a silver tray. The Duc de Guisnes tasted it, screwed up his Gallic features and exclaimed: '*Madame la Duchesse, mais je n'aime point votre sillybum.*' The Duke laughed so hard he had to leave the room and the Duchess was 'unable to speak' and took refuge behind her fan.

There were plenty of guests at Blenheim in the 1770s, and the dining-room walls from 5 to 9 p.m. fairly perspired with conviviality. Until the dinner hour, everyone had gone their separate ways, in search of amusement. They had breakfasted at 10; the women appeared in morning gowns with their hair already dressed, and the men in riding-boots and shabby coats. There was no chat; guests sat anywhere, acted as if they were alone, drank their tea or coffee or chocolate, ate their bread and butter, and read the newspapers. But dinner was a very different affair, with formal seating and everyone in evening dress. There was a great deal of lively conversation, and a great deal of food. After several hours, finger-bowls appeared and one rinsed out one's mouth and spat into the bowl, or merely dipped the fingers, depending on whether one was reactionary or avant-garde. Then the ladies withdrew and the gentlemen sat for two more hours over their claret and port, drinking toasts to King and Queen and wife and lady-love and country and consuming two or even three bottles each. They got up and relieved themselves into the chamber-pot kept in a lower cupboard at one end of the long, elegant mahogany sideboard, with its brass rail, and knife-boxes ranged on top. Valets got used to picking their masters up off the dining-room floor at the end of it all. Those who could still stand wove their way towards the drawing-room where the ladies waited anxiously behind the coffee urns to see which gentlemen were still on their feet. A few games of whist followed, with a light supper brought in at eleven, just before everyone toddled off to bed. And the next day the ritual would begin all over again.

When the Duke's sister Diana and her new husband came to Blenheim for Christmas, 1772, the house found itself filled with a greater variety of life than usual. Diana had recently divorced Viscount Bolingbroke, nephew of John Churchill's sworn enemy, and married Topham Beauclerk, a witty, penniless man-about-town. The ladies' hair-dos that year had almost reached their maximum height, and it took the resident hairdresser hours to draw the hair up over a wire frame, secure it with 'double pins' (hairpins), add a few artificial curls and then cover the whole magnificent creation with pomatum and white powder. The ladies left their hair up for many days at a stretch; on every dressing-table lay a long stick with little ivory claws at one end, used to relieve the itching caused by accumulated powder. After Topham's arrival, the ladies scratched ever more frantically, for he had brought lice to elegant Blenheim. One of the gentlemen took Topham aside and 'began delicately hinting how much the ladies had been inconvenienced'. 'What!' exclaimed Topham, 'are they so nice as that comes to? I have enough [lice] to stock a parish!' Lady Diana tried to make amends to the Duke for her husband's solecism by painting on the gilt edges of a vellum copy of Virgil printed by Baskerville, a 'view of Blenheim which disappears altogether when the volume is closed'. The Duke particularly liked that shimmering Blenheim which came and went as quickly as his dreams.

The idyllic days unrolled like a satin ribbon, every day different and every day the same. When the sun shone, and the lake sparkled, everyone moved outdoors. The children raced about the lawns and played hide-and-seek among the mossy stone blocks hauled fifty years before to finish the western quadrangle, and still lying abandoned in the grass. Mrs Reeves, the governess, and Mrs Pope, head nanny, scolded their charges for getting too near the slippery edges of the lake, and ran after them with jackets and scarves in case they got over-heated. Sometimes the Duke and Duchess and children and guests toured their Garden of Eden in a waske, a long, topless carriage which held fifteen people and was pulled by six horses. From time to time, the Duke plunged a line into the well-stocked lake and pulled it up almost at once with a gasping perch or pike or carp on the other end.

On 1 September the shooting began. Shots rang out in the crisp, still air of the oak woods and copses, and pheasants and partridges thudded to the damp earth. Occasionally, the Duke went further afield in search of sport. He attended the four-day Burford race-meet every year, where the main event was a stag hunt. A buck was loosed each morning on the downs, with the Duke's splendid pack of forty hounds in close pursuit. The Duke employed a female servant whose job it was to boil the dogs' meat, served hot and fresh to them each morning. His Grace recorded all his hounds' names in a ledger, from 'Blaster' and 'Darling' to 'Welcome'.

One day when the Duke was feeling rather at a loose end, he organized a race long remembered and talked about in sporting circles: the running footman race. The running footman, for £20 a year, dressed in cutaway coat and knee-length, gold-fringed silk petticoat-breeches, always ran in front of His Grace's carriage to let people know that a great man was approaching. The footman carried a long staff with a silver ball-shaped container at the top holding white wine mixed with egg from which he sipped occasionally to keep himself going for the sixty miles he was expected to cover, running at a steady pace of seven miles per hour. The Duke wagered that he could get from London to Windsor in his phaeton and four quicker than his running footman could, both to start at the same time. The Duke won; what capital fun it was! The footman collapsed from his tremendous exertions, and died.

Then there was the day the tiger arrived. The children were ecstatic. Lord Clive, the wealthiest English nabob in India, had sent it for the Blenheim menagerie, one small item in that long, rich stream of imperial plunder making its way from India to England. The clerk of the kitchen, Henry Turner, son of Charles, the steward, ordered the tiger's daily ration of beef, and the butcher sent his bill: 'Meat for the tiger: 24 lb of beef delivered every 2 or 3 days, at 3s. a time, with sometimes a head 4d.' In three spring months, the tiger consumed £4 4s. 2d. worth of beef; in the previous January, on the other hand, the six poorest families in Hensington, just beyond Blenheim's gates, had been given 12 loaves of bread and 52 lb of meat by their benevolent Duke, at a total cost to him of £1 3s. 4d.

Blenheim's cup of life in the seventies splashed high and overflowed. In those blissful eighteenth-century years when Britain's aristocrats had not yet been frightened by the French Revolution nor reformed by Evangelical zeal, they felt 'la douceur de vivre', Talleyrand's phrase for that very special sweetness of living. Blessed and cosseted by Blenheim-house, the lucky 4th Duke of Marlborough drank in the sweetness that John, 1st Duke, had 'longed for night and day', the gentleness missing from his bitter, violent age.

For many years to come, everyone beyond the gates of Blenheim saw it as a paradise where nature and art freely wandered hand in hand. John Byng, later 5th Viscount Torrington, sums up the prevailing opinion in his diary. One day when rambling through Blenheim Park, he could hear hounds in full cry in the greening woods, and two French horns being played in the house. The Duke 'lives the life of a quiet domestic gentleman, surrounded by his children,' wrote the envious Byng, 'in which truly happy and glorious situation, I espied him in the gardens. I really felt myself when in the flower-garden,' sighed Byng, 'to have a conception of paradise.'

Those who could afford to do so came to Blenheim in ever greater numbers. One diarist returning from Blenheim to the Woodstock Inn, reported that 'a world of high dress'd heads went by in coaches and chaises, to the public day at Blenheim, which is on every Tuesday'. A coach called 'The Blenheim' went from London to Woodstock three times a week.

When the writer and lexicographer Samuel Johnson arrived in 1776 with Boswell, fresh from their Hebridean tour, Johnson didn't bother to tour the house – the strictly classical taste of the time had turned against the house, which everyone thought far too baroque and ornamented and ponderous – but approved of the grounds. 'You and I, sir,' Johnson exclaimed to Boswell, 'have, I think, seen together the extremes of what can be seen in Great Britain – the wild rough island of Mull and Blenheim Park.'

Beyond Blenheim's gates, however, was a very different world. The mass of the people were either unemployed or poorly paid, all of them uneducated and undernourished, trying to cope with dirt and disease in small cottages or mud-and-straw hovels. The better cottages could boast as furniture a rough deal table, a straw mattress, a broken chair, blocks of wood for the children to sit on, a few old pots and pans. A few lucky Woodstock residents found work in the village's two industries. Those who made steel utensils earned from 15s. to 2 guineas per week; those who made leather gloves got 8 or 9s. They lived on cheese, bread and tea rather than on two dinner courses of sixteen dishes each. Many of the poor were stuffed into the Oxford gaol awaiting deportation to Australia for stealing a piece of meat much smaller than those fed to Blenheim's hounds and tiger. If Blenheim was heaven, hell was never far away.

Within Blenheim, in any case, all was not quite as Arcadian as it appeared. The Duke was growing ever more silent and neurotic. 'The Duchess is in hopes,' wrote one London society matron to another in 1777, 'to bring the Duke into such company next winter [in London] in hopes to make him speak.' By 1778, the Duke could hardly steel himself sufficiently to review the local militia. Their loyal friend and adviser John Moore, then Dean of Canterbury and soon to become Archbishop, wrote to the Marlboroughs: 'I have seen with pain how much Your Graces have both withdrawn yourselves from the world of late, and I have feared it would grow upon you.' The Duke would be a happier man, Moore told him, if he could banish 'that emphatical word Fuss' and have 'the thing itself turned out of the doors of Blenheim'. 'I much fear that both Your Graces would look upon it as a distress,' Moore chided in another letter, 'if four or five of the best friends you have in the world should be announced to you unexpectedly any day in the week.' 'Your oyster uncle and my

oyster brother-in-law,' wrote Lord Pembroke to his son, referring to the
Duke of Marlborough, 'will hardly stir any more. He is so benothinged,
and so beset ... that His Grace's oysterical apathy is baneful to all near
him as well as to himself.'

The Duke and Duchess were both sinking farther and farther into the
swansdown pillows of Blenheim, with no hint of struggle or resistance.
The Duchess had good reason to feel drained. In the first eleven years of her
marriage she had produced six children and suffered several miscarriages as
well. Two more babies were to come: Francis in 1779 and Amelia in
1785, when the Duchess was forty-two. In addition, the very weight and
responsibility of Blenheim was flattening her. It was all a bit much – eighty-
eight servants to supervise and 187 rooms more or less – she had once
inquired of the servants, but none of them seemed to know just how many
rooms Blenheim contained, or whether one should include the ones in the
bridge ... but it really was of no particular consequence ... Blenheim's
thick paddings of tufted silk and respectful footmen were gradually mass-
aging the former Car Russell into torpidity. With all these factors working
against her, Caroline had lost her sense of direction and was drifting
through her days. She had none of Sarah's relentless iron, hardly even a
shred of whalebone left, and her indecision grew as maddening to others
as the Duke's. 'The week before last I met the Marlboroughs at Lady Di's,'
Horace Walpole scribbled to Miss Berry. 'The Duchess desired to come
and see Strawberry again [Strawberry Hill, his house]. I proposed the next
morning; no, she could not. In Her Grace's dawdling way, she could fix
no time, and so on Friday, at half an hour after seven, they arrived, and
the sun being setting, and the moon not risen, you may judge how much
they could see through all the painted glass by twilight.'

It was not surprising that the children were growing spoiled and headstrong. They needed firm handling and got none from their parents. The
Marquis of Blandford's screaming fits grew so horrific that his personal
servants demanded higher wages and his tutor, Mr Coxe, resigned in
despair. One day in 1775, when Lady Craven was visiting, two-year-old
Anne 'threw herself screaming on the carpet on my entrance, and terrified
the Duchess'. Anne had another tantrum in August 1777, when Sir Joshua
Reynolds came to Blenheim for a fortnight to finish painting his splendid
family portrait. 'I won't be painted!' Anne had screamed and stamped her
little satin foot when Sir Joshua asked her mildly to pose.

Sir Joshua, like Brown and Chambers before him, had enough pride as
artist not to be cowed by Blenheim's splendours, even though his own house
in London's Leicester Fields couldn't compare. One day while he was painting, the Duchess ordered a servant in a peremptory tone to bring a broom

to sweep up the snuff Sir Joshua had dropped on the priceless carpet. In a tone even more peremptory, Sir Joshua ordered him to leave the snuff where it was; he brooked no interruption, and the dust raised by the broom would do far more injury to his canvas than the snuff to the carpet.

The Duke insisted that Reynolds paint him with one of his prized gems in his hand, for by the time Reynolds came to Blenheim the Duke was becoming obsessed with his carved gemstones. He had begun collecting them at the time of his marriage, when he had bought most of the Zanetti collection in Venice. He bought up two subsequent collections, from Lord Arundel and Lord Bessborough, and gathered more gems on his own. At the final count, there were 739 cameos and intaglios, carved on emeralds, sapphires, garnets, amethysts, lapis lazuli, peridots, chalcedony, agate, sardonyx and jasper. There were gems from ancient Greece and imperial Rome and Ptolemaic Egypt, as well as more modern ones. The Duke kept them nestled on velvet, in red morocco cases, and spent many hours totally focused on those very small, very hard, very cold objects. He had commissioned Bartolozzi to do engravings of the hundred choicest stones; *Gemmarum Antiquarum Delectus*, two large folio volumes bound in red leather with the Duke's coat of arms in gold and his portrait as frontispiece, were privately printed in 1780 and 1791. The text, in Latin and French, is printed on thick, creamy paper on the right-hand page, and the engravings, on the left-hand page, are protected by sheets of tissue.

Through the 1780s, the Duke spent long hours in his Grand Cabinet, cradling one gem at a time in his soft white hand, losing himself in each small, perfect world. The cameo head of Apollo – white face, brown ringlets, blue-grey base – was carved on a sardonyx $1\frac{3}{8} \times 1\frac{1}{16}$ in., yet within that circumference, Greek civilization peaked. 'It is by studying little things,' Samuel Johnson said, 'that we attain to the great art of having as little misery and as much happiness as possible.' The Duke wholeheartedly agreed. He was living in a house which he dearly loved, but where everything – stones, golden roof-balls, towers – was Brobdingnagian in scale. The Duke needed his gemstones. Intaglios and cameos had all been cut with diamonds, and the craftsmanship was superb. There were Grecian ladies with elaborate braids and ringlets; Roman heroes in togas, with bulging calves; three relaxed and supine cows; a most elegant hand, holding a dead mouse; Socrates and Plato, face to face; Fortuna with cornucopia in one hand, wheat-ears in the other. When the Duke fingered his gems, the real world disappeared. He gave permission to his friend Josiah Wedgwood, who sometimes came to Blenheim, to make a cast of the Duke's favourite cameo, the marriage of Cupid and Psyche, to be reproduced on Wedgwood ware and distributed round the kingdom.

As the Duke collected gems, so daughter Caroline collected suitors, toying first with one, then another, comparing, weighing, but never quite able to decide which one could best be moulded into a husband. Lady Caroline had been raised in the soft air of a house whose silk walls were gently brushed with silk dusters to clean them, raised by two parents who both ruled with a velvet hand in a velvet glove. Like them, Lady Caroline had lost her will and her way forward. In August 1782, her trousseau had been bought, all the settlements drawn up and her fiancé, Lord Trentham, come to Blenheim to sign them, when Lady Caroline told him that she thought she should not like to marry him after all. Lord Trentham, deeply in love, was devastated; he fled at once to the Continent and stayed away from England for a year, trying to erase from his mind Caroline's haunting face. ('She has the very sweetest countenance that can be,' her aunt had once remarked.)

That same year, the Duke had a rather offputting session with his steward and estate agent. The Duke always tried to walk away from any unpleasantness, but they had him pinned between them at his writing-table, and were flipping through thick ledgers of figures and talking of overdrafts and sinking funds and all those tiresome details which always made the Duke feel dizzy. Since 1763, when Blenheim's beautifying had begun, His Grace, it seemed, had gone through £100,000 of capital. He had indulged himself with such delights as two covered tureens, with ladles and twenty-four matching dishes, all in solid silver (£805 12s.). He had already cut the number of servants from eighty-eight to seventy-five, and some of them, such as James Cowdery the postilion, received only £4 annually. What more could His Grace do? With plenty of urging and helpful hints from his two advisers, the Duke carefully wrote out, in his beautiful script, a neat sheet of possible economies, and hoped that would be the end of it. The Duke had begun his dukedom with a fountain-flow of generosity, settling £2,000 a year on each of his brothers and £1,000 on his former tutor, Jacob Bryant, who had his own room at Blenheim. But the palace had proved a most demanding mistress, and the Duke had grown stingier and more like his great-grandfather John with every passing year. When sister Diana 'had not five guineas', as she put it, he demanded the £50 interest she owed him on a loan, and as her penury continued, the Duke grew frostier in his relations, and stopped inviting her to Blenheim.

Visitors now paid 9 or 10s. to view the house and grounds. The young American lawyer Thomas Jefferson came on 3 April 1786, fresh from the former colony which, five years before, had taken its manifest destiny into its own very practical hands. His diary account of his visit to Blenheim shows him to be, like many of his countrymen, obsessed with figures. He

View of the lake from Fair Rosamond's Well

notes that Blenheim had 2,500 acres, of which 200 were garden, 150 water, 12 kitchen garden and the rest, parkland. Two hundred people were employed to keep it all in order, and the turf was mowed every ten days. Jefferson had designed Monticello, his strictly classical villa in Virginia, by flipping through a book on Palladio, and Blenheim's charms, in comparison, left him unmoved. Apart from the lake, 'the garden has no great beauties; the trees are scattered thinly over the ground ... Art appears too much,' wrote the founding father of America, remembering its wild, untrammelled spaces. Mr Jefferson's stout republican soul refused to be impressed by Blenheim's ducal magnificence.

Four months later, the man who had let America slip through his pudgy fingers, George III, came to see Blenheim. When the sagging Duke and Duchess of Marlborough learned to their utter consternation that King George and Queen Charlotte wanted to pay them a visit, Archbishop Moore tried to put some steel into them. 'Nobody has so fine a family in so fine a place to show,' Moore wrote, 'and My Lord Duke will be amply paid for all his misgivings on the occasion by the reflection that what is done is right and that the omission would scarcely be doing justice to his family or himself ... Long deliberation won't do,' he continued cannily, knowing Their Graces well; 'your first thoughts will deserve to be followed by immediate act.'

Never had so much fuss made its whining, hand-wringing way from room to room at Blenheim as in those August days preceding the royal visit. Of course the Marlboroughs knew Their Majesties well. The Duchess had been a bridesmaid when George III had married Charlotte of Mecklenburg-Strelitz on 22 September 1761. The Duke and the King quite liked each other. They had a great deal in common; they shared an interest in astronomy – the Duke was even then fitting up an observatory in one of Blenheim's towers – and they were both getting queerer by the day, although in opposite directions, for while the King couldn't stop talking, the Duke couldn't seem to start.

The King had already had one severe attack of madness, in which he had volubly lusted after the Duke's sister Betty, Lady Pembroke, then serving as lady-in-waiting to the Queen. The Marlboroughs had by now given up going to Court and, unlike John and Sarah, they had done it quite voluntarily. They never dreamed of their monarch coming to see *them*.

After a sixty-seven-year wait, the house was finally about to get its king! But when the actual day arrived, 17 August, there was little pomp and circumstance; the whole affair was far too *al fresco*.

The King and Queen had been staying at nearby Nuneham with Lord and Lady Harcourt, and arrived at Blenheim at eleven in the morning. Queen Charlotte wore her diamond *parure*, and her gown, as usual, was spotted with snuff. The King insisted on the *parure* to offset his wife's unattractive face, which was so formidably ugly that when King George took her to bed, he had to close his eyes and think of England – which, being a dutiful sovereign, he had done often enough to produce fifteen children. Three of the girls accompanied their parents to Blenheim: Princess Elizabeth, Princess Augusta, the prettiest, and the Princess Royal, who blushed whenever spoken to. A year before, she had sent the Duchess of Marlborough several of her very accomplished etchings, including one of a wood nymph, 'which I feel the more ashamed of,' she declared, 'since Mama has been so good as to indulge me with the sight of some beautiful drawings which Lady Caroline and Lady Elizabeth made her a present of'. The etchings were waiting on the walls of the Bow-window Room for the Princess Royal's pleased glance to light on them, once she had given the Battle of Blenheim tapestry its due.

The royal party included the Harcourts and a suitable complement of equerries and ladies-in-waiting but not, to her chagrin, Fanny Burney, second Keeper of the Robes, who had been left behind at Nuneham because the Marlboroughs felt it quite enough to have to entertain a king and queen without the added trauma of playing host to strangers. Only those attendants whom they already knew were invited to Blenheim, and Fanny, who longed to see it, was left to vent her spleen in her diary: 'In all royal parties, the whole company is always named by the Royals, and the Lords and Ladies of the mansions have no right to invite a guest.'

The Royals were met at Blenheim's north portico by the Duke and Duchess, and escorted through the three staterooms west of the Saloon – through the green damask drawing-room with Romney's portrait of the Duchess above the mantel, through the white damask drawing-room with its white marble mantel with central urn motif, through the blue damask bedchamber with its Chambers-designed state bed empty and drooping – and finally, into the Long Library. The former Gallery, a spectacular room 183 feet long, as in so many other stately homes, had had its portraits replaced by books. Blenheim had been especially blessed, for in 1749 its family had acquired the famous Sunderland Library, collected by Charles, Earl of Sunderland. This magnificent collection of 24,000 volumes was shelved behind elegant gilt-wire lattices along the entire east wall and across the two ends. Queen Anne still stood at the north end where Duchess Sarah had placed her half a century before, and at the south end was Alexander the Great sitting on William Chambers's ram's-head therm.

Breakfast was laid out for the royal party on a Pembroke table, the tea and chocolate in huge ornate silver pots, the bread cut as thin as poppy petals. Above them as they ate, Hawksmoor's beautiful ceiling, one of the greatest delights of the palace, sang its siren song. Isaac Mansfield had stuccoed its flowers and garlands in 1725 under Duchess Sarah's eagle eye. Painted white on a pale apricot ground, they had a lyrical lightness not to be found in the rest of the house. Beyond the bow-window in the centre of the west wall, Capability Brown's lake shimmered in the morning sun and stately swans glided past the royal eyes.

After breakfast, the regal party toured the grounds, and returned to the house for cold meats and fruits. The King was properly impressed, and was heard to exclaim: 'We have nothing equal to this!' His Majesty lived at Buckingham House – on the site of the present Palace – an undistinguished building plainly furnished, which King George had neither remodelled nor refurbished, beyond buying some Canalettos for its walls.

Duchess Caroline wrote a full account of the day for Moore before collapsing that night into her feather-bed:

Considering the shortness of the notice, it all went off very well. Lord and Lady Harcourt told us we were to sit as Lord and Lady of the bedchamber all the time they stayed here; and poor Lord Harcourt seemed quite happy to be able to rest himself, and the Duke of Marlborough found him sitting down behind every door where he could be concealed from royal eyes. We were just an hour going over the principal floor, as they stopped and examined *everything in every room*, and we never sat down during that hour, or indeed, very little but while we were in the carriages, which fatigued me more than anything else, as I was not at all well at the time. Lord Harcourt told the Duke of Marlborough that he had been full-dressed in a bag [wig] and sword every morning since Saturday; but the Duke of Marlborough could not follow his example in that, as he had no dress-coat or sword in the country . . . Nobody could do the thing better or more thoroughly than he did. His eyes are better, and he means soon to bathe, which, I think, will contribute to strengthen them . . . My head is far from clear, and has ached ever since they left us, but I was determined not to put off writing to you the first moment I could.

The King sent the Duke, as a thankyou gift for all his pains, a ten-foot telescope by Dr Herschel for his new observatory. 'I can answer for the excellency of this instrument,' the King told the Duke, 'having twice compared it with the one in my possession.'

So Blenheim got its king, and the Duke got his telescope, and the Revd William Fordyce Mavor got his inspiration and dashed off 'To Their Majesties' Visit to the Duke and Duchess of Marlborough':

> Though Albion's Kings relinquish Woodstock's shades,
> Their partial presence still our spirits glades;
> And George and Charlotte, brightest, happiest pair!
> Have own'd the magic of these objects fair.
> Have felt the charm of Beauty link'd with Taste,
> And Worth congenial to their own embrac'd.

And on and on, in the same vein. Next year, there was talk at shabby Buckingham House of another visit to splendid Blenheim, but the 4th Duke and Duchess of Marlborough had had more than enough of royal favour and sent word to the King and Queen that the Duchess was unwell and that it grieved them deeply to be unable to receive Their Majesties.

It was in that year, 1787, that the Blenheim young people, feeling the growing silence and inertia inside Blenheim-house oppressing them, persuaded their parents to mount some theatricals. The Duke was ready enough to take on a new artistic project and so the orangery became a theatre and *False Delicacy* was the order of the day. There were more theatricals in 1788; the young people got up Colman's *Musical Lady* and Burgoyne's *Maid of the Oaks* and Michael Angelo Rooker painted more scenery, and the productions were quite as luxurious, and quite as lifeless, as before.

In 1789, a new player, who would eventually liven things up considerably, joined the cast. He was a friend of Lord Henry's called Edward Nares, and he was very short and very sprightly, with a large nose, blue eyes and fair, wavy hair. He distinguished himself in *False Appearances*, translated from the French by General Conway who sat, uncritical and beaming, in the front row. 'Those who have been at Blenheim since,' wrote Nares, 'can have no idea how princely the whole establishment was at that time, and yet how little the family mixed with the world at large.' The Duchess, for her part, told Nares that 'it was impossible for her to express how much they appreciated the pleasure of his company, and that the more he could make it convenient to be at Blenheim, the more happy he would make them'. Nares, for *his* part, was more than happy to oblige. On 29 December he played prominent roles in *Cross Purposes* and *The Deaf Lover*.

It was in 1789 that the King recovered from another attack of madness, and the Duke made a rare excursion abroad and visited him at Kew in March, where he was so moved to see His Majesty 'just as I could wish as to health and spirits' that he burst into tears, twice. King George gave the Duke an astronomical watch, and the Duke thought he should like to celebrate the King's recovery by building a Temple of Health at Blenheim, so he got John Yenn, a pupil of Chambers, to design one, and it was duly erected in Blenheim's pleasure-garden. The Duke often sat in it and said a little prayer for continued sanity.

In the 1790s, Blenheim's young people began to marry and take themselves off to smaller domiciles with a less precious air. Lady Elizabeth departed first, in 1790, on the arm of her new husband John Spencer, her first cousin, who had for the past three years shared with her what Jane Austen would, in *Mansfield Park*, disapprovingly call the 'dangerous intimacy' of private theatricals. The Marquis of Blandford married next, on 15 September 1791, a daughter of the Earl of Galloway, but he wasn't missed in the Blenheim circle for the simple reason that he was never there. In March 1792, Lady Caroline finally made her choice, after ten years' dithering, and settled on Henry, Viscount Clifden, but not before encouraging and discouraging the advances of her first cousin, the Earl of Pembroke's heir.

On 8 April 1795, George, Prince of Wales, drunk on brandy, was held upright at the altar long enough to tie him to ugly, unwashed Princess Caroline of Brunswick; Lady Charlotte Spencer, the Duke of Marlborough's cleverest, prettiest daughter, made a winsome bridesmaid, but the

Duke declared himself not nearly strong enough to carry the Sword of State. Then, on 3 July, a cruel shadow fell across pastoral Blenheim. Lord Henry, the Marlboroughs' clever, amiable second son, died suddenly from fever in Berlin where he was pursuing a distinguished diplomatic career. He was only twenty-five. The Duke and Duchess had doted on Henry, particularly when they compared him to Blandford, who was conducting himself in a truly scandalous manner. The lesson the Marquis of Blandford had learned at Blenheim's silken knee was to gratify his every wish, and he had learned it well. He was a terrible spendthrift, deeply in debt to money-lenders, and he shared his father's collecting mania. In addition to exotic plants, some of which cost him £500 each, Blandford collected rare books and common women and was so wild and debauched that he was a great trial to his parents.

If there was a snake in the Garden of Blenheim, its name was self-indulgence. It had already ruined the Marquis of Blandford, and the outgoing passion and engagement of all dwellers remaining therein was gradually curling in on itself, becoming more self-engrossed and narcissistic with every passing day.

Lady Anne, who had more or less stopped having screaming fits and grown quite comely, married the Earl of Shaftesbury's brother, the Hon. Cropley Ashley, on 10 December 1796. Blenheim slipped farther towards cold hibernation. There was, however, one pocket of warmth, a con-flagration sparked by the amatory fires of the theatricals. Little Edward Nares had fallen in love with Charlotte, and she with him. Edward made repeated respectful assaults on the fastness of the Grand Cabinet, and asked the Duke, ever so politely, for his daughter's hand. The Duke, however, had no intention of giving his favourite daughter in marriage to a commoner whose father was a former Oxford MP and whose unpre-tentious home, Warbrook House, at Eversley, Hampshire, would fit into Blenheim's kitchen court, and have room to spare. Since 1794, Nares had been Bursar of Merton College, Oxford, earning far too little to keep the lovely Charlotte in the opulence to which she had become accustomed. If Blenheim had made her placid, with 'a temper so serene that I do not recollect a single instance of its being ruffled', according to the besotted Edward, the house had also made her self-indulgent. Courtship and mar-riage mores, in 1797, were firmly fixed. Either parent or offspring could suggest a match, but both had the power of veto; parents shouldn't force a daughter to marry against her will, nor should a daughter go against her parents' wishes. Filial disobedience was a major sin.

Nevertheless, on 16 April 1797, Nares's widowed sister Mrs Treacher fetched Lady Charlotte from Blenheim in her shabby carriage and whisked her off to Henley, where the Provost of Worcester College forthwith married her to Edward. The next day, Charlotte received a letter from steward Charles Turner stating that His Grace had ordered him to pay her £400 a year, but that she was never to enter Blenheim's gates again. It was the worst punishment her father could have devised. Nares got a living in Kent; Charlotte pined for her beautiful home, developed 'spasmodic rheumatism', and died on 15 January 1802. 'When a woman flies from the protection of a parent who merits the utmost return of her affection,' Charlotte had glibly recited fifteen years before, 'she must be insensible indeed, if she does not feel the sincerest regret.' Charlotte had stood on the orangery's stage on her eighteenth birthday, holding the bright nosegay of 'many happy returns' in both hands, and spoken those haunting words. 'Poor thing!' wrote her impoverished aunt Diana Beauclerk to a friend, herself feeling Blenheim's cold shoulder and the lack of both hospitality and financial help. 'Her parents' hardheartedness helped to break her heart I feel,' continued Lady Diana. 'They really are become callous to all but themselves.'

The Duke was now well into the third and final stage of his relationship to Blenheim, and to the world beyond. In his earliest days in the house, in the 1760s, the Duke had been active outside Blenheim, doing his public duty as a peer of the realm, and also within the house, engaging artists to enhance it, and, through the seventies, feeling passionate about its artistic and its human life. In the second stage of his Blenheim sojourn, through the 1780s, the Duke had withdrawn farther into his oyster shell, relying on the house and its artefacts, not on people, to provide him with mild stimulation. First Blandford, then Diana, then Charlotte had been rejected; the pearly gates had slammed shut at their approach. In 1800 the Duke's youngest son Francis married the daughter of the Duke of Grafton; that left only daughter Amelia and the Duchess to people Blenheim, with the Duke more and more oblivious to their needs, treating them as if they were just irritating grains of sand. Beginning around 1800, the Duke entered his final phase, and began sinking quietly to the bottom of Blenheim's grey marble seas.

When Lord Nelson, accompanied by Sir William and Lady Hamilton, came to see Blenheim on a July day in 1802, the Duke refused to receive him, and sent out refreshments to the grounds, which the indignant hero refused. Sir William, with true magnanimity, considering that Nelson was then bedding down his wife, declared that if the great Marlborough could have risen from his tomb, he would have been eager to do the honours of his house for another great victor such as himself. Emma Hamilton offered even greater balm. If she were a queen, she soothed, as reward for the battle of Aboukir, she would give Nelson such a principality that Blenheim Park would be a kitchen garden in comparison. Nelson's eyes filled with tears, and he was comforted. He climbed back into his coach and left Blenheim as quickly as possible. The palace windows reflected his retreat; he was not the first martial hero to show his backside to Blenheim's glassy, enigmatic stare.

Four years later, in 1806, the Revd William Fordyce Mavor revised his not-so-*New Description of Blenheim* yet again, devoting only fifty-eight pages to the half-alive house and 148 pages to the heavenly grounds. In November 1810, George III went mad for the fourth and final time. After that, the Duke of Marlborough avoided the Temple of Health, whose stones were beginning to crumble.

In the leafless days of October 1811, the Duchess of Marlborough, who had been seriously ill for three months, asked to see her estranged son, Blandford. An express was sent to him at Whiteknights, his luxurious estate near Reading, and he came as swiftly as possible. An affecting scene at his mother's bedside followed, but the Duke sent word that he was 'too nervous' to see his eldest son. After Blandford had been served a 'cold collation', however, the Duke changed his mind. Blandford knelt at his father's knee, and the poor, distraught Duke sobbed and sobbed. On 26 November Caroline, 4th Duchess of Marlborough, died, in her sixty-eighth year. On 2 December, a cloudy day with temperatures just above freezing, the Duchess joined John and Sarah in the vault beneath the chapel. 'The funeral was conducted in as private a manner as consistent with the attention due to Her Grace's distinguished rank,' according to the *Gentleman's Magazine*.

On 22 September of the following year, 1812, the Duke's youngest daughter Amelia married Henry Pynches Boyce, Esq., and bade farewell to Blenheim and her father. After that, Blenheim and the Duke had only each other. The palace enfolded, cosseted, stroked his sensibility, as it always had, but the Duke seemed to grow ever more distant and detached.

The Duke in his slippers wandered through the silent rooms where the ruffles and ringlets of his little daughters had once bounced so high. Sometimes he looked into the orangery, grey and hollow now, where music and laughter and hand-clapping had pushed against the walls like a soft-fleshed pomegranate about to burst. Sometimes he walked through the three staterooms where the silence was piled up like dust-cloths from carpet to ceiling. In the white damask stateroom Romney's life-size, full-length portrait of the Duke in Garter robes, painted in 1779, towered above the mantel. Below it, printed on a white satin firescreen, was a much smaller sepia reproduction of Romney's Duke, not nearly as grand and not nearly as glowing.

Sometimes the Duke spent the whole day in his Grand Cabinet. Above its dark grey marble mantel was a bronze 'Listening Slave' and a bronze 'Reclining Venus', but there was nothing to hear and nothing to love. From time to time, the Duke would stand, like Narcissus, gazing at his reflection: a very pale Duke in William Chambers's pier glass surrounded with large shells in one colour of gold. On days when the Grand Cabinet felt too big, the Duke stayed inside his dressing-room with its straw-coloured, flock-papered walls. Here he kept his choicest gems, and would play with them for hours, sitting in the shadows, holding each one carefully, tracing its outline with a gentle finger. Sappho with deep décolletage; Phryne with voluptuous breasts showing through gossamer drapery; two satyrs supporting a reeling Silenus; a nymph, in highly erotic pose, sacrificing to Priapus and – the stone which the Duke reached for again and again – Cupid marrying Psyche. Each gemstone so small, so circumscribed, a cold pastoral, all passion spent. The Duke bent over them, while Rubens's 'Sleeping Venus' looked down from the wall. Sometimes the Duke raised his head, catching a scent, rich and redolent as pot-pourri, of the palace's gathered memories of its golden days, when artists streamed through its rooms with sketch-pads in hand, when servants piled tables high with fruit and sugar confections, when the summer drawing-room sang a paean to Pan with flutes and horns and Tibby's piercing fiddle.

The palace felt itself slowly slipping back into that horrid, embalmed state which it had experienced between the 1st Duke's retreat and the 4th Duke's marriage. It wanted, so desperately, to hold on to warmth and life. Some of Blenheim Castle's early violence and bitterness still lay coiled, beneath the garlands and the gilding. One day, the house made its silent, swift attack. With one convulsive movement and without a single sound, Blenheim-house opened its beautiful mahogany doors on oiled hinges ... and swallowed the Duke whole.

After that, he never left the house and grounds, and he never spoke. He went three years without uttering a single word. One morning, the silence was suddenly shattered, as if a giant stone had been hurled into the glassy lake. The butler came to tell the Duke that the French writer Madame la Baronne de Staël, whom the poet Lord Byron pronounced 'frightful as a precipice', had arrived to pay His Grace a visit. 'Take me away!' screamed the Duke, to the utter astonishment of his servants, and they did, as quickly as possible. The shock waves subsided, and after that there were no further ripples to disrupt the smoothness and sameness of the house's 'life', if one could call it that.

The loudest sounds in the empty house were the ticking of the French clocks, one in almost every room. Tick, tick, tick, followed by the delicate silver chimes that marked the hours. But the chimes were never, one with another, quite in tune or quite in time. There was always a faint disharmony, a dislocation left hanging in the air, hinting that time was, ever so slightly, out of joint.

The Duke was as still and silent as the walls; the walls were as still and silent as the Duke; house and master seemed to merge.

The Duke's valet, William Bateman, came and went silently too, serving his master as faithfully as he always had, for his £47 yearly wage. He rubbed His Grace's cold, white back with eau-de-cologne if he had ventured outdoors and got caught in the rain, rubbed back and forth, back and forth, with the same patient motion which the housemaid used to polish the white marble wainscot in the Hall. The valet mixed up the Duke's shaving soap just the way he liked it, with fresh lye, lamb suet and olive oil; then he shaved the Duke's sagging chin every morning while the housemaid scraped the ashes from the cold hearth and drew back the curtains on another stale day.

On the morning of Thursday, 29 January 1817, the Duke's valet, who for several years past had slept on a cot in His Grace's bedchamber, found the Duke dead in his bed, with a peaceful expression on his marble-white face. George Spencer, 4th Duke of Marlborough, was seventy-eight years old. On 7 February, he was placed in the vault beneath the chapel, and the palace gave one long, soft, expiring sigh.

3
SMUG
MATURITY

... though now it seems
As if some marvellous empty sea-shell flung
Out of the obscure dark of the rich streams,
And not a fountain, were the symbol which
Shadows the inherited glory of the rich.

W.B. Yeats, 'Ancestral Houses'

WHEN, IN THE 1820S, THE JOURNALIST AND CRITIC WILLIAM Hazlitt described Blenheim as 'a conglomeration of pigeon-houses', he was truly prophetic, for there is no more apt description of Blenheim Palace in its Victorian years. Everything inside Blenheim – rooms, wardrobes, dressing-cases, minds – everything was subdivided and compartmentalized to an astonishing degree. Some of Blenheim's partitions were clearly visible in the form of walls, screens, velvet portières, green baize doors and bandboxes; others were invisible, but quite as firmly placed and quite as effective.

At 5.59 a.m. on Wednesday, 30 November 1859, all the pigeon-holes of Blenheim Palace were still stuffed with blackest night. (No one called it 'Blenheim-house' any more, for it occupied a position far too pivotal in the national scheme of things to be addressed by any name less exalted than 'Palace'.) At exactly 6 a.m. a feeble light – only a few candle-power – appeared in Blenheim's south-east tower. Where George Spencer, 4th Duke of Marlborough, had once gazed absently at the stars through Dr Herschel's telescope, the housemaids now slept, as far away from the bedrooms of male servants as Duchess Fanny, the 7th Duke's wife, could get them. No male at Blenheim – or at least no male of servant status – ever penetrated the chill fastness of Housemaids Heights.

Scullery-maid, dairy-, laundry- and kitchen-maids, housemaids and still-room maid all slept there. Since they formed, in that exact ascendant order, the lower-servant female echelon, they rose at six, an hour before the upper servants had to leave their warm beds. The lowly maids who dwelt, paradoxically, in the Heights, were stashed in rooms so narrow that they might well, some morning, have emerged flattened to two dimensions. Each bedchamber had room only for the iron cots where the girls slept two-to-a-bed, and for their boxes, wherein each maid locked up her individuality, her pathetically meagre arsenal of self-assertion. Imagine the contents of each box: a few carefully folded clothes, three half-crowns in a shabby purse, a silver penny wrapped in paper, an enamel box which proclaimed itself to be 'A Trifle from Margate', three dog-eared badly written letters, and two books, one faded and foxed, one obviously new.

The old one, *Advice to Young Women on Going to Service*, issued in 1835 by the Society for Promoting Christian Knowledge, told its readers to refrain from scratching, coughing, nose-blowing and whistling in the master's presence, and to remain, resigned to their fate, in the lowly station of their birth. 'Had God seen it would have been better for your eternal good that you should be great and rich,' *Advice to Young Women* declared, 'He would have made you so, but He gives to all the places and duties best fitted for them.' The new book, published that very year, offered very different advice. In *Self-Help*, Samuel Smiles told his readers that every man and woman in the kingdom, no matter how low-born, could, by self-discipline and hard work, achieve wealth, property and social position. *Self-Help* sold 20,000 copies in 1859 and 130,000 in the next thirty years. It helped usher in Britain's new competitive society where all the plums no longer dropped automatically into peers' pockets; they were shared among the able and the ambitious. *Self-Help* lay humbly in its green cover in one corner of the housemaid's box, but it was, none the less, a time-bomb within Blenheim, which would eventually alter, radically and per-manently, the palace's neat strata.

At the moment, however, the housemaids had no time for *Self-Help*. Only half awake, they drew their thick cotton stockings, washed once a week, on to feet washed only once a month, for water was hard to come by in Housemaids Heights. Underwear next, then petticoats, print dresses, aprons; boots laced, hair pinned up, caps anchored; their hands fumbled a little, blue with cold. Then down the long winding stairs they flew to their appointed tasks. They would have two hours' work before breakfast.

The lowly scullery-maid crept into the silent kitchen along with the first shafts of grey dawn, and began at once to clean and light the huge kitchen range. Her hands were very red and chafed, for she spent her day scouring pots and pans, or on her knees scrubbing cold floors in scullery, larder, kitchen and servants' hall. She was fifteen years old, a cottager's child who had been in service since she was twelve, and who had advanced from £7 to £10 a year. Her face was pale; almost all the maids looked pasty, for they hardly ever got outdoors. Each maid got a half-day off per month, and a whole day every third month. Only the laundry-maids had rosy cheeks and sparkling eyes, due partly to the steamy atmosphere of the laundry-room and the brisk winds of the drying-yard, and partly to the fact that they worked in the Achilles' heel of Blenheim's Plan for Sexually Segregated Servants. Laundry-room and drying-yard were far too handy to the stables, and the stablemen had an ineradicable habit of straying. At any hour of the day one tended to find in the laundry-room, as soapsuds billowed into rainbows, stablemen teasing and laughing and laundry-maids blushing and saying 'Have done then!' over and over, without ever meaning it.

At 6.15 a.m., the lower housemaids, who earned £12 a year, were going from room to room taking out ashes, and cleaning the fire-irons with a rag dipped in vinegar and ashes, followed by an oily rag, followed by scouring-paper. Then they cleaned the hearths and laid new fires. The middle housemaids, who earned £15 a year, sprinkled damp sand on floors and carpets and swept them clean. The upper housemaids, who got £18 per annum, dusted and tidied – no sinecure, considering the quantity of bric-à-brac. All the main-floor rooms had to be cleaned before the family came down to breakfast.

The still-room maid, who got £20 a year, laid and lit the fire in her domain, the still-room, which boasted a large zinc-lined sink and three walls of cupboards and shelves. She had to prepare the early-morning-tea trays for family and guests – twenty-four to do this morning. As soon as she had set them out and cut the bread and butter, she moved on to the housekeeper's sitting-room to lay and light the fire and to sweep and dust. Its walls were lined with china cupboards and linen presses, but it still managed to be a homey room, one of the cosiest in Blenheim, with a drugget carpet, a plumply upholstered easy chair and footstool, a round skirted table, a perpetually purring cat, and a neat row of daguerreotypes and funeral cards on the mantelshelf.

At 7 a.m. more candles and gas-lamps were lit in Blenheim and more heads left their pillows. House steward, groom of the chambers, butler, housekeeper, cook, footmen, governess and nanny, ladies' maids and valets, both resident and visiting, were now rising and dressing. The housekeeper, like her easy chair, footstool, pillows, cat, and indeed, almost everything else inside Blenheim, was fat – fat with the upholstery of righteous living. She put on her black silk dress, black apron and white net cap with ribbon quillings, and hooked her symbol of high office, her chatelaine of jangling keys, at whose approach all housemaids trembled, securely round her thick waist. She got £50 a year, and complete control of all china, linen, preserves and groceries. Now she unlocked the china and linen cupboards, took out plates and cups and the linen cut-work cloth and napkins needed for the family's breakfast, and then relocked the cupboards.

By 7.20, the still-room maid was in the steward's room setting the table for the upper servants' breakfast. The footmen were 'powdering' in their special powdering room, fitted along one side with mirrors and wash-basins. They hung their coats on hooks, put towels round their shoulders, dunked their heads in water, rubbed soap into a stiff lather over their hair, combed it through so that the tooth marks showed in even rows, then powdered each other, using huge puffs and flour. England's richest peers supplied their footmen with violet powder, but the 7th Duke of Marlborough, with only £40,000 per annum, settled for ordinary flour. He did, however, boast an even dozen footmen, all programmed to move, when on display in the family rooms, in perfect unison, two by two, like well-oiled robots.

At 8 a.m. the upper servants assembled in the steward's room for breakfast, augmented by the visiting valets and ladies' maids and waited on by a footman. The house steward sat smugly at the table's head and controlled the conversation quite as firmly as, for £100 a year, he controlled the household accounts and hirings. The visiting valets and ladies' maids were addressed only by their employers' names, and as they ate their eggs and kippers, gossip flowed from 'Portarlington' to 'Macclesfield' in a steady, subdued stream, like treacle.

At 8 a.m. the rest of the servants, with the exception of the nursery staff, who ate in their own domain, had seated themselves at the long table in the servants' hall, a room sparsely furnished with pin rails for hats, a jack towel-roller and a small shelf of books placed there by the 7th Duke of Marlborough, their pious master, including Doddridge's *Rise and Progress of Religion in the Soul*, Biddulph's *Prayers for the Morning and Evening of Every Day Through the Week*, Scott's *Sermon on the Fatal Consequences of Licentiousness* and similar improving works, all of which looked remarkably pristine and unspotted. Seated at the table's head, the cook poured the steaming tea and cut up the cold meat pie which constituted breakfast. What really nourished everyone at table, however, was the delicious gossip passing freely up and down. Servants' lives were mundane and monotonous, with the same daily grind repeated over and over and few forays into the wider world. Those elevated enough in the hierarchy to get beyond kitchen court and stable into family rooms, brought back, like industrious squirrels, tasty bits of conversation and correspondence for everyone to share. To be sure the pickings at Blenheim were leaner than at some great houses; its family were so very tight-lipped and taciturn.

At 8.25 a.m. the butler was in his pantry earning his £45 a year by ironing *The Times*, which, since its 1785 founding by John Walter, had been bringing informed and judicious comment on domestic and foreign affairs into the nation's breakfast-rooms. The pantry contained sinks, long tables for cleaning plate, cupboards for storing it, and, before the fire, an overstuffed chair, from the depths of which the butler controlled the footmen, the plate and the wine-cellar.

The portion of Blenheim's eastern court adjacent to the butler's pantry had been subdivided into a number of small rooms each designated for a special activity. There was a lamp-room, a brushing-room, a boot-room and a knife-room. The larder had been similarly partitioned into meat, game and miscellaneous, and a corridor off the kitchen into tiny rooms for vegetables, fruit and preserves. But perhaps the crowning complexity of Blenheim's body corporate was its six hundred towels and cloths, all clearly marked. There were towels for housekeeper, dairy-maid, laundry-maid, still-room maid and kitchen-maid. There were separate supplies of roller towels for use in kitchen, still-room, servants' hall, pantry and laundry, and by the groom, coachmen and cook. Work cloths were apportioned and parcelled out with a discrimination equally fastidious. There were china cloths for the footmen, glass-cloths for the butler and steward's room, lamp cloths for the lamp-room, dusters and china cloths for the housemaids. And woe betide any servant who accidentally used the wrong cloth.

By 8.30 a.m. Blenheim's complex mechanism of daily living was fully in motion. The butler ironed; the footmen cleaned and trimmed lamps; the scullery-maid washed up the breakfast dishes from the servants' hall; the still-room maid washed up those from the steward's room; the housekeeper unlocked the staples cupboard and passed out supplies to the cook; the nursery-maid scrubbed the nursery floor; everything hummed and turned with its usual well-lubricated precision.

Inside Blenheim Palace, the many hands of its workers performed, day after day, for very low pay, the same few mindless, repetitive tasks, all aimed at keeping Blenheim's overlords in a state of supreme comfort. Of the United Kingdom's twenty-two million inhabitants at this time, one million worked as domestic servants and their lives were not so very different from those of Britain's factory workers, whose hands only, not minds, were required to keep the country's factories turning out their products of wool and cotton, iron and pottery. In its Victorian years, Blenheim Palace itself was a dark, ugly factory with many cubicles and a tight corporate structure: a perfect microcosm of the industrial state beyond its gates.

The Great Exhibition, held at London's Crystal Palace eight years before, in 1851, had proudly demonstrated the power of machinery to lead Britain forward to unprecedented wealth and power. On 1 May, Queen Victoria had proclaimed Britain's real Golden Age – the eighteenth-century one of aesthetic achievement couldn't compare – seated on a throne in the Crystal Palace while 25,000 of her subjects cheered and cheered, and 'above them rose a glittering arch far more lofty and spacious than the vaults of even our noblest cathedrals', according to *The Times*. 'On either side the vista seemed almost boundless.' In the housekeeper's room at Blenheim, chosen by her after much deliberation from those rows and rows of wonderful, ingenious manufactured goods under the boundless arches, was a coal-scuttle of japanned metal, with a reproduction of Landseer's 'Dignity and Impudence' on its side.

If Blenheim was a proper hive of industry, John Winston, its resident Duke, the proudest, most self-satisfied Marlborough of them all, also directly reflected his countrymen's mood. The 1st Duke of Marlborough's victory at Blenheim in 1704 had sowed the initial seeds of national pride in the British breast; Wellington's victory at Waterloo in 1815 had added more, and the forty-four years of peace which followed, upset only by the distant war in the Crimea (1854–6), convinced all Britons that God was on their side, making them richer every day and well fitted to rule over such less blessed races of men as Indians and Africans. At home, Britain's manufacturing might, thanks to all those hands going through their boring motions, was truly awesome. Her total exports in 1850 were worth £71 m and by 1870 would rise to £200 m; imports had trebled, going from £100 m to £300 m. By 1870, Britain's foreign trade would be more than that of France, Germany and Italy together, and four times greater than that of the United States. Blenheim's crowded rooms bore mute testimony to the fact that Britain had become the 'workshop of the world', filled as they were with factory products, with many of the 4th Duke's beloved hand-crafted treasures stashed out of sight, and all those manufactured goods had to be dusted, washed or polished, scoured, ironed or starched, as the case might be, by Blenheim's many hands.

The servant activity at Blenheim, however, with its finely graded hierarchy of status and duties, was, so to speak, only its engineering plant, and before we move upstairs to where family and guests are now awake and being tended, we just have time to sketch the outline of the whole wondrous corporation of which the servants formed the lowest part. The Victorians had a genius for analysis, definition and logical division and in Britain's large country houses that genius found its fullest and most characteristic expression. At Blenheim Palace's head stood its pater-familias, John Winston Spencer-Churchill, 7th Duke of Marlborough, Knight of the Garter; Earl of Sunderland and of Marlborough, Wilts.; Baron Spencer of Wormleighton, Warwickshire; Baron Churchill of Sand-ridge, Herts. Under him was Frances Anne, Duchess of Marlborough, second-in-command over the household's three main divisions: guests, family and servants. The family was subdivided into grown-ups and children, and the children subdivided into nursery (Fanny, 6 and Anne, 5) and

The billiard room at Blenheim in Victorian times

schoolroom (Blandford, 15, had departed for further schooling at Eton; the three remaining were Cornelia, 12, Randolph, 10 and Rosamond, 8). The servants were divided into upper and lower, and subdivided into six main groups determined by their natural habitat: rooms; servants' hall; kitchen; nursery/schoolroom; stables; garden. Meals were routinely served in five places: dining-room, schoolroom, nursery, steward's room and servants' hall. The second principle of Blenheim's bureaucracy was that its three main departments converged only at recognized times and places, the first and underlying principle being that, apart from the convergences referred to above, the three main divisions of guests, family and servants didn't ever want to see, smell or hear each other. If lower servants were short-changed on privacy, upper servants, like guests and family, each had private apartments to which they could retreat when the world was too much with them, knowing that no one would cross the threshold uninvited. Lesser guests had bedrooms only; more important ones had bedroom and dressing-room; princes got a whole suite. The Duke and Duchess had a bedroom and dressing-room each on the upper floor, and a private sitting-room each in the main floor's eastern wing. If men from the guest and family divisions decided to congregate, but only with their own sex, they did so in billiard-room, gunroom and smoking-room. Prince Albert had started the fashion for smoking-rooms by installing one in 1845 at Osborne, the Isle of Wight house where he and Queen Victoria holidayed, and had ordered an A to be placed over the smoking-room door, rather than the V and A which were so closely intertwined above the other doors. By 1850, all the best country houses, including Blenheim, had smoking-rooms. If the ladies felt an urge to congregate with their own kind, they met in drawing-room or library. If both sexes were feeling convivial towards their opposites or, at specific times dictated by Blenheim's rigid schedule, whether its individual members felt convivial or not, they met in dining-room and drawing-room, and suffered the family occupants of nursery and schoolroom to join them in the drawing-room for tea.

The 7th Duke and Duchess were the first Marlboroughs who didn't sleep in the main floor's eastern wing, but with all the specialization and segregation which had taken place there, bedrooms had to go. The bedchamber of Fanny, Duchess of Marlborough, bore witness to another compulsion of the times. The Victorians suffered, it seems, from a mild form of agoraphobia and couldn't tolerate a large, unbroken space. Every inch of wall and furniture surface was covered with pattern, trim and a clutter of small objects. The wash-table was typical. It held three jugs, large, medium-sized and small, two porcelain basins, a dish for tooth-brushes, another one for soap, a water carafe and two tumblers. Doilies stood under every vessel. The bag of pleated magenta silk which hung from Fanny's rosewood work-table was adorned with two sizes of silk tassels; the cross-stitch flowers on the bell-pull had glass-bead trim; the dark velvet curtains had braid trim and bobble-fringe and a draped pelmet far too complicated in its geometry to describe. Fanny's bed was downy soft and very white and had four patterns of eyelet embroidery on its pillow-shams. Beside the bed stood a rosewood table; upon the rosewood table was a slab of marble; upon the slab of marble was a round linen mat; upon the round linen mat was a carved stand for holding a book; and upon the carved stand was the requisite book. All remaining surfaces in the room were covered with such useful objects as pincushions, ring-trees, paper spills in china vases, and little round covered dishes with holes in the top for hair-combings. There was, as well, a multitude of Marlborough relatives, mainly infants, unsmiling in their plush or silver frames. They bore witness to the fact that Blenheim Palace was a shrine sacred to the

A Blenheim bedroom furnished to Victorian tastes

Family, to 'Home, Sweet Home' and the notion that 'East or West, Home is Best', mottoes which, if one looked carefully enough, could be found thrice over in Fanny's bedroom: once in violet and yellow cross-stitch; once in multicoloured bugle beads; and once, in sepia arabesques, across the top of an advertisement for baking powder in *The Lady's Companion at Home and Abroad*. Soon after 8.30 the Duchess had finished her bath; the hip bath, with white crumpled towel beside it, still steamed on its linen mat before the fire. Blenheim still had only one bathroom; like the rest of their countrymen, the Marlboroughs had no use for 'luxury'. Excessive comfort was considered un-Christian. As the century progressed and more and more industrialists got rich enough to build themselves country houses and install the newest advances in plumbing, such technological comforts, among the peerage, came to be considered not only un-Christian, but also vulgar, *nouveau riche*, unhealthy and far too crassly North American.

Fanny had no private bathroom, but there was a water-closet near by and others placed here and there throughout the house. Joseph Bramah had patented his ingenious flush toilet in 1778, and by the beginning of the nineteenth century, country houses had a reasonable quota. No owner, however, could rival the water-closet obsession of the Duke of Wellington, who, in 1830, had large matching wardrobes erected in two opposite corners of all the bedrooms at Stratfield Saye: one to hold clothes and one to house the toilet.

The small French clock on the mantel in Fanny's bedroom said 8.42 as the Duchess and her maid stood in her adjacent dressing-room engaged in the complicated business of getting Her Grace dressed, something no Victorian woman, however humble, could manage on her own. (Against one wall of the dressing-room stood a cabinet, and within it, still in their red morocco cases, were the Marlborough Gems so beloved by the 4th Duke. Fanny never looked at them and had more or less forgotten that they were there. Pagan gods and dilettantism had long since fled from Blenheim, leaving God the Father and Duty in control.) Like the other upper servants, Fanny's maid didn't wear uniform, but her choice of clothes was none the less exactly prescribed. She was neatly dressed in one of Fanny's cast-off gowns – all personal maids got their mistresses' old clothes – but she had removed some of the ribbon trim, having read in *Friendly Hints on Dress* that the gown of a lady's maid 'should never be made in that Fashion which is suitable only for mistresses', nor was she wearing 'long drop earrings', since they were also forbidden. She could, however, on her day off, sport a veil and parasol, both of which were forbidden to housemaids. Fanny stood patiently in her long, white lace-edged pantaloons while the maid laced up her corset – but not too tightly because Fanny was in the middle stages of her tenth pregnancy. (In addition to the six children in the nursery and schoolroom, three sons had died in infancy.) Then, standing on a little stool while Her Grace held her arms straight up, the maid skilfully popped Fanny's crinoline over her head, and anchored it at her thickened waist.

It was only when she was safely inside her crinoline that Fanny felt completely and quintessentially herself; it was symbol and centre of her personality, her relationship to others and her philosophy of life. The crinoline had come into fashion roughly three years before to replace the many heavy petticoats previously worn under gowns. The crinoline had eight hoops of flexible steel wire sewn on to a circular petticoat reaching

OPPOSITE: Duchess Fanny, properly crinolined

to the ankles, and in 1859, according to fashion's dictates, it was still growing wider; in another year, it would be so immense that two ladies couldn't possibly pass through a doorway together, or sit on the same sofa. After 1864, fullness began to move towards the back, and by 1870, the crinoline would be replaced by a horsehair protuberance called a bustle. The 7th Duchess of Marlborough, however, was so enamoured of her crinoline that she would ignore the changing fashions and keep on wearing it until her death. Inside her crinoline, Fanny looked the picture of propriety, with her 'limbs' (the new euphemism for 'legs') hidden from the world, as they should be, yet within that carefully circumscribed womanly sphere, she could stride quickly and lightly and freely, without hindrance of any kind, towards her goals. The steel hoops were as strong as her will, and they kept the world at a respectful distance. No one could get too close to a crinolined lady, and the physical space somehow translated itself into emotional distance as well. In the hierarchical diocese of Blenheim, Fanny's crinoline marked the boundaries of the smallest and most sacrosanct parish.

At 8.47, Fanny's long-sleeved, high-necked gown, containing forty-eight yards of fabric and enough soutache-braid trimming to circle the Empire, was being buttoned up the back by her maid's deft fingers. Fanny stood before her mirror and adjusted the twin ringlets of chestnut hair which rested on each shoulder. At thirty-seven, Fanny's face, with its too-prominent grey eyes and aquiline nose, had settled into lines of stubborn self-possession. She had little personal vanity, being 'neither clever nor at all handsome', as one of her dinner guests once described her, but she was a Duchess, with what one relative called 'a God-and-my-right conception of life', based on the belief that 'an English Duchess was the highest position any woman not of royal birth could reach'. A future daughter-in-law would note her 'over-masterfulness' in ruling Blenheim and all those in it 'with a firm hand. At the rustle of her silk dress the household trembled.' To her children, Fanny was both domineering and fiercely devoted. Frances Anne Emily Vane-Tempest's sense of self-importance, which had ballooned at Blenheim, had begun with her birth, for she was the daughter of Lady Frances Vane-Tempest, an immensely wealthy heiress who had married a man twenty years her senior in 1819. In 1821, on the suicide of his half-brother, the Foreign Minister Castlereagh, Lady Frances's husband had become 3rd Marquis of Londonderry. The Marquis and his rich wife settled down at Wynyard, her palatial inherited estate in County Durham, and produced Frances Anne Emily in 1822. Little Fanny was raised there and in the stately Londonderry House in Park Lane, where her mother quickly became a great political hostess and close friend of Disraeli,

Britain's future Prime Minister. In 'Dizzy's' letters, he mentions Lady Londonderry's habit of sitting at her 'great assemblies' on a gilded throne-chair with a gold brocade canopy over her head. At one 1835 costume ball, Lady Londonderry came as Cleopatra 'in a dress literally embroidered with emeralds and diamonds from top to toe' which, according to Disraeli, 'looked like armour and she like a rhinoceros'. Her daughter Fanny inherited her mother's love of ostentatious finery but chose to express it, after her marriage, in her house rather than on her person. Lady Londonderry had enough clout in high circles and enough pounds in family coffers to secure for Fanny, in spite of her plainness and Pekinese eyes, the sober-whiskered, pious John Winston Spencer-Churchill, Marquis of Blandford and future heir of Blenheim. John Winston and Fanny were married on 12 July 1843, moved into Hensington House, just beyond Blenheim's boundary walls, and began at once to carry out what all Victorians considered to be their first duty, whether on the home or the manufacturing front: to increase and multiply. By the time John Winston succeeded to the dukedom in 1857, there were six little Marlboroughs to fill Blenheim's nursery/schoolroom area, and Fanny had bequeathed her suppressed rages and her protruding eyes to two of them: to George, Marquis of Blandford, born in 1844 and to Randolph, born in 1849.

While Fanny was being crimped and crinolined on that November morning in 1859, her husband, the 7th Duke, was being shaved and dressed by his valet. The valet, who earned £50 a year, had risen at 7 a.m., collected His Grace's polished shoes from the boot-room, his clothes from the brushing-room, his pot of tea and bread and butter from the still-room, his ironed *Times* from the butler's pantry and his letters from the Hall. He had entered His Grace's bedroom at 8 a.m., had drawn back its heavy window curtains while light snores still issued from the high, carved bed, had emptied the wash-basin into a slop pail, cleaned the basin thoroughly with one of Blenheim's six hundred cloths, put a can of hot water beside the basin and covered it with a much finer cloth. Then, since the Duke was to take his guest the Prince of Wales out shooting that morning with a party of gentlemen, the valet had laid out His Grace's tweed shooting-jacket and cord breeches on the seat of a chair, with socks and underclothes on top. He had moved about the dim bedroom silently, expertly, totally intent on his main purpose in life: to keep the 7th Duke of Marlborough immaculate and well-dressed at all times, so that His Grace could shine, in his large corner, with a pure, clean light, beaming forth a superb example of English gentleman to the nation beyond.

At 8.45, just as Fanny's crinoline was being lowered, the Duke was being shaved, but only on his upper lip and stubborn, protruding chin, leaving facial hair to flourish everywhere else it could. Victorian fashion, having agreed on the ideals of the Womanly Woman and the Manly Man, endorsed every artifice that could highlight the differences between them. The Duke's brown mutton-chop whiskers were consequently luxuriant from ear-lobe to jowl. Even sitting down, the Duke kept his back so straight that people always thought him taller than he was. Born in Garboldisham Hall, Norfolk, on 2 June 1822, son of George Spencer-Churchill, 6th Duke of Marlborough, John Winston had attended Eton and Oriel College, Oxford, and had emerged, not to put too fine a point upon it, as a full-blown Victorian prig. He began his exemplary public career as a lieutenant in the 1st Oxfordshire Yeomanry in 1843, took his seat as MP for Woodstock, the seat all Marlboroughs considered theirs by divine right, in 1844, and kept it until he became Duke and moved up into the Lords in 1857. 'His voice is very good,' Disraeli had remarked to Fanny's mother when Blandford made his maiden speech, 'and if he knew as much of other subjects, common in Parliament, as he does of theology, I think he might do very well indeed.' The Duke was as complete a Tory as anyone could be, totally opposed to any change whatsoever, including all political reform. He clung to the same hierarchical and aristocratic notion of society espoused by John Churchill, 1st Duke of Marlborough, of the rich man in his castle, the poor man at his gate. Because he had no time for secular books, John Winston could gaze smugly into his mirror, not knowing that in that very year John Stuart Mill's *On Liberty* had been published, a book which states that 'the despotism of custom is everywhere the standing hindrance to human advancement', which stresses the right of every individual, not just the rich, to a full hearing in the state, and which gives short shrift to ideals of obedience. Dukes, much poorer if not wiser, would be shunted eventually, thanks to John Stuart Mill and others, on to a permanent siding and left there to bemoan their fate. But not yet, not in 1859. The 7th Duke of Marlborough's mind chugged forward, straight and true, on a narrow-gauge railway rather like the one he would have built, a few years down the line, between Woodstock and Oxford, pulled by an engine called the Fair Rosamond. The Duke's mind never travelled very far in any direction; it never went off the rails, and religion was its mainline station. In 1856, he had indulged his passion for pigeon-holing, so evident at Blenheim, by instigating the passing in Parliament of the Blandford Act whereby large parishes were subdivided into smaller. In April 1858, from his place in the Lords, he saw to the formation of a Select Committee to inquire into the spiritual destitution of England and Wales. In February 1859, he urged a public thanksgiving for the fact that the Indian Mutiny had been so thoroughly put down that two thirds of India,

John Winston, 7th Duke of Marlborough

with all its trading wealth, was, thanks be to God, still part of the British Empire. John Winston became known as 'the good Duke'; he strongly supported sabbath-day observance, and found it shocking that 'from six to ten on Sundays the public houses were filled with persons carousing and reducing themselves to the level of beasts'. That the undernourished, underpaid labourers of England had good reason to drown their sorrows on the seventh day never occurred to the good Duke. He was armoured in smugness, in 5,000 acres of smugness, knowing himself to be the envy of every industrialist in the land, all of whom were toiling, as the 1st Duke of Marlborough had long ago toiled, 'to found a family, and to convert his wealth into land'. These 'twin thoughts', as Samuel Taylor Coleridge had written in the 1830s, were 'births of the same moment, in the mind of the opulent merchant'. As ruler of the kingdom of Blenheim, the reactionary, right-thinking Duke had set up a complex hierarchy of delegated authority so that he could be remote and sovereign at the same time. From Duke to governess to child, or from Duke to steward to head footman to lower footman, the chain of command was always rigidly in place. The Duke brooked no intimacy, and he ruled with a rod of iron. If Fanny had her crinoline to keep the world at bay, the Duke's carapace was the palace itself. Within that heavy stone circumference he walked in righteousness and thundered forth his imperial edicts. The system of command that worked throughout the Empire, from Queen Victoria down to lowest Calcutta clerk, worked, in microcosm, at Blenheim, from Duke down to scullery-maid.

In Sarah's day, the servants at Blenheim had mingled much more with their master and mistress, and some of them, such as Sarah's personal maid, Grace Ridley, had themselves been gentry. But as actual power in the land slipped from autocratic to middle-class hands, the rituals of subservience and the barriers of class were firmed up to offset the ongoing erosion. The yeoman farmer's son who was valet to the 7th Duke of Marlborough tried his best, as he went about the bedroom picking up wet towels and last evening's dress clothes, to be invisible. Every servant at Blenheim, when the Duke stalked past, had to flatten himself against a wall and look as much like a piece of wainscot as possible. Some of the 7th Duke's contemporaries demanded even more self-effacement from their servants. The first Duke of Abercorn couldn't bear the thought of common hands touching his bed-linen; his housemaids had to wear white gloves when they made his bed. At Welbeck, the Duke of Portland sacked any housemaid who had the misfortune to meet him in the corridors. One lord in Wiltshire never gave his valet any kind of greeting except on Christmas and New Year's Day. The Duke of Marlborough, with the Prince's visit preoccupying his narrow mind, may well have got completely dressed without a word to his valet. John Winston gave a final stroke to his whiskers, and regally descended the stairs, reaching the Hall's cold marble just as the groom of the chambers tolled the bell for chapel. It was precisely 9 a.m.

At the first solemn clang, the upper housemaids dropped their dusters, the under-housemaids their pails, the kitchen-maids their pans and all the other servants whatever they had in their hands. Blenheim's machinery came to a complete halt and every single inhabitant, with the exception of its four-footed ones, flew at once to the Chapel. It was Blenheim's central hub, the only place where family, guests and servants converged, and they did so every morning except Sunday. On Sundays, everyone attended morning worship in Woodstock church, and evensong at Blenheim with a good long, rousing, soul-cleansing round of hymn-singing. Blenheim had changed since the 4th Duke's time from house of pleasure to house of prayer. When it was first built, the palace had been declared 'extra-parochial' so that no tithe would be levied on it for the use of the poor, but on 1 January 1858, the 7th Duke of Marlborough had seen to it that 'Blenheim Park' became a parish in the Union of Woodstock, fully prepared to take up its charitable duties. As all the inmates of Blenheim hurried into Chapel, probably none of them knew that in addition to Samuel Smiles's *Self-Help* and John Stuart Mill's *On Liberty*, another incendiary book which would drastically alter England's social fabric had been published that year: Charles Darwin's *On the Origin of Species*. Its theories of evolution, which undermined the authority of the Scriptures, would eventually empty England's churches. Blenheim's little flock had, however, another forty years of sanctity ahead of it.

Family and guests entered the Chapel first, and took their places in the gallery reserved for them: a splendid affair draped in crimson velvet, with ample gold fringe. The upper servants filed in next and arranged themselves in the foremost pews; lower servants were strictly ranked behind them. The scullery-maid ran in last, trying not to slip on the marble stairs which were green as polar ice that had never seen the sun, and quite as cold and slippery. The present Duke had erected a fine alabaster pulpit in the chapel, but the spirit which reigned supreme there and always would, world without end, was that of John Churchill, 1st Duke. The massive Rysbrack monument above his tomb trumpeted forth, in intestinal shades of marble, his raw hunger for everlasting fame. The present Duke's chaplain, a mild-looking man in snow-white surplice, announced the hymn, read the lesson for the day, gave forth a long, extemporaneous prayer with several deft references to the Prince of Wales's continued well-being, and led his flock in the Lord's Prayer. And all the while that huge rearing marble mass behind him screamed its secular, power-crazed, discordant note.

The service ended at exactly 9.25; the Duchess and other ladies trooped back upstairs to remove their hats and pat their hair back into place and then joined the gentlemen in the dining-room which, as in the 4th Duke's day, was just east of the Saloon. The footmen had previously laid the table, folding all the table napkins into mitres, a most appropriate shape for saintly Blenheim, and placing bread, rolls, toast, butter dishes, bowls of jam, pots of marmalade and a whole honeycomb in the centre of the table, and at the top, a cream jug, sugar basin and the required number, ascertained by James from the butler, of cups and saucers. (The head footman at Blenheim, no matter what his Christian name, was always called James; it made things so much easier for family members with far more important matters on their overtaxed minds.) At 9.30, the butler and several footmen brought in the hot dishes: kidneys, bacon, eggs, cutlets and fish, as well as cold game pie and potted meat, and placed them on the sideboard so that guests could help themselves. All the boiled eggs had 'Wednesday, 30 November' pencilled on their uppermost curves.

While family and guests breakfasted, the housemaids were busy in the bedrooms above, coping with rumpled beds, dirty baths and trails of clothing. Tackling a Victorian bed was rather like trying to put clothes on a flip-flopping whale; one needed both strength and patience. There were three mattresses. The bottom one, stuffed with straw, was turned once a week; the middle mattress, made of wool or horsehair, was turned daily; the top one, made of feathers, was also turned daily and had to be shaken, punched and smacked until it was as light and puffed up and free from lumps as a giant soufflé. The Victorians took their beds seriously; it was in them, after all, that one entered and departed this life, and in between engaged in the fine Christian duty of begetting. Beds were the firm foundation of Home, Sweet Home, so the maids plumped and pummelled, pummelled and plumped, making all the Blenheim beds supremely smooth and supremely fat.

At 10 a.m. the butler and four footmen were in the pantry, wearing aprons and gloves, polishing the vast amount of plate which would be trotted out for the royal banquet. The housekeeper and still-room maid were in the still-room, the maid washing up the family breakfast china while the housekeeper replaced it in its cupboard and locked it in. The children were in the schoolroom settling to their lessons, with much sighing and biting of pencils; the ladies were sitting idly about in the morning-room reading the day's newspapers and their mail. The gentlemen were setting off, with two guns and a valet each, in the wake of the Prince of

Wales. He and five attendants had just arrived, all very informally, from Christ Church, Oxford, where His Highness was a student. After the briefest exchange of bows and curtsies with Fanny, who looked like a tiny bell-shaped doorstop on Blenheim's enormous portico steps, the men hurried off to the real pleasure of the day. The palace slipped into the usual low gear of its mid-morning rhythms.

At 12 noon, the lower servants clumped into the servants' hall for dinner, their one hot meal of the day. Goodness only knows how she'd managed it with all she had to do, but cook had prepared a roast with vegetables, and a rice pudding. It was a noisy, relaxed scene, with the footmen tossing crude *double entendres* across the table in the general direction of the housemaids, and the stable boys picking their teeth with a convenient straw.

In the steward's room, where the upper servants were dining, due punctilio and propriety were preserved. Everything, with the exception of the way knives were held and vowels pronounced, was as much like the proceedings in the family dining-room as the upper servants, after years of close study, could make it.

At 12.30, the housemaids hurried upstairs with cans of hot water so that the ladies could wash before luncheon. The upper footmen were laying the dining-room table under James's supervision. The Duchess and eleven lady guests sat down to luncheon with much rustling of skirts. The three eldest children, Lady Cornelia, Lord Randolph and Lady Rosamond, completed the party. The gentlemen out shooting would have a cold picnic in the woods. Luncheon had originated some forty years before to bridge the gap between breakfast and dinner, which had been gradually lengthening since the eighteenth century. Today there was salmon mayonnaise, a choice of hot beef, chicken or lamb, treacle tart and fresh fruit. As soon as the ladies had pushed back their chairs and swished from the room, the three children eagerly launched into one of their favourite daily routines. They took down from the sideboard the special tins and baskets piled there, and went carefully round the table and gathered up all the left-over food. It was piled higgledy-piggledy, treacle tart, salmon mayonnaise, everything, into the same tin. These unappetizing mixtures would be distributed to the poor and destitute of Woodstock when the children took their afternoon walk, and because in those mid-Victorian years everyone knew their place and what was expected of them, the little Marlboroughs would feel properly generous and the poor would feel properly grateful. Certainly the form which Blenheim's charity took was more civilized than that at Conisbrowth Hall in Yorkshire. There, each Christmas, the family celebrated by throwing mutton chops out of the dining-room windows while the poor scrabbled for them like dogs on the frozen ground outside.

The habitual tins on Blenheim's sideboard bore witness to the fact that Blenheim Castle, conceived in 1705 as show-place for wealth and power, then beribboned in the 1760s into Blenheim-house, exquisite cultural citadel, had now become Blenheim Palace, moral temple and training-ground for family and servants, and, by example, for the populace beyond its gates. Because the middle classes, through wealth and the franchise extensions of 1832 and 1858, were pushing their way towards the reins of power, aristocrats such as the 7th Duke of Marlborough realized that they must set their house in order and demonstrate their right to rule by dint of moral superiority, rather than by dint of wealth and rank alone. In his preface to the 1862 edition of *Alton Locke*, Charles Kingsley would rejoice that 'the attitude of the British upper classes has undergone a noble change. There is no aristocracy in the world, and there never has been which has so cheerfully asked what its duty was, that it might do it.' When the *Cornhill Magazine*, in the same year, took upon itself the task of defining a 'gentleman', it concluded its definition thus: 'There is a constantly increasing disposition to insist more upon the moral and less upon the social element of the word.' The Revd William Sewell, in a sermon preached to the boys in the chapel of Radley College, told them:

> Everything which is great, noble, high-minded, brave, generous, liberal, delicate, unselfish, God, who gives nobility, and men who honour nobility, expect from noblemen, and from all who have within them the blood of noblemen. Anything that is petty, mean, contemptible, selfish, disgraceful, or immoral, is in a nobleman infinitely worse than it is in a beggar. Noblemen, like Christians, are to be the salt of the earth.

The 7th Duke of Marlborough was surely the saltiest noble of them all, sprinkling spiritual and physical sustenance abroad every single day, via chapel and children, with a truly beneficent hand.

After luncheon, some of the ladies retired to their bedrooms to loosen their stays; others repaired to the drawing-room or library to net yet another reticule with long tasselled end, or to write yet another letter to a friend in which every fifth word was underlined for emphasis. Underlining their letters with a deeply scoring pen was, for most of them, their only outlet for intense emotion, supplemented by infrequent fits of hysterics. Ladies with intellectual aspirations picked up a book and made a fine show of reading. Fanny kept her drawing-room tables piled with the latest Miscellanies – collections of stories, verse and aphorisms – with covers wreathed in moss roses, under such titles as *Keepsakes*, *Amulets* and *Bijoux*. The fashion for Miscellanies had begun in 1828 with Rudolph

The Saloon in late Victorian times furnished as a drawing-room

Ackerman's *Forget-Me-Nots* and thereafter Victorian ladies couldn't get enough of them; they were sweetly sentimental, not too mentally taxing, and contained not a single reference to bodily functions or to sex.

At 3 p.m., cook, kitchen-maids and scullery-maid began their gigantic task of preparing a feast fit for a king-to-be. The long wooden table which ran down the centre of the kitchen was crowded with bowls in graduated sizes, flour-covered arms kneading and pummelling, and red, chapped hands chopping and grinding. The cooking equipment, ranged against one wall, was subdivided into roasting-range, stewing-stove, boiling-stove, turnspit, hotplate and hot closet. Above were ranged the gleaming copper pans which the scullery-maid spent roughly half her young life scouring and polishing. To the right hung the great sugar-nippers, used to cut the sugar which came from the grocer's in a giant cone wrapped in blue paper. Once cut, it had to be pounded, as one kitchen-maid was even then pounding it, with mortar and pestle, until the cook pronounced it fine enough for the moulded dessert she was concocting with twenty eggs, orange-flower water and enough hartshorn shavings to make it set.

While the kitchen staff slaved and sweated, the groom of the chambers was making one of his three daily tours of all the main-floor rooms. He was taller and handsomer than all the other male servants, and every footman, with a little help from Samuel Smiles, hoped some day to reach such eminence. The groom's physical labours could have been performed quite adequately by a small female child, but he looked so splendidly serious doing them that Fanny thought him well worth his £70 a year. He went from room to room patting cushions, adjusting blinds against the sun, placing footstools in exactly the right spot for ducal feet, replenishing Blenheim's crested notepaper, straightening the Miscellanies, and opening doors for guests to sail through.

At 3.30 p.m., the still-room maid and housekeeper began preparing afternoon tea in the still-room. The ritual of afternoon tea became common around 1840 among the upper classes, who now dined as late as 7 or 8 p.m. England's gentry, it seems, as eighteenth century gave way to nineteenth, needed sustenance as often as babies needed milk. The still-room maid cut the bread ever-so-fine, buttered it carefully edge to edge, made sandwiches and put out the cakes. The housekeeper supervised, and brewed the tea. At precisely 4 p.m. James carried the heavy silver tea-tray into the drawing-room, and put it down before the Duchess's chair, so that she could pour out the tea, and the parlour-maids, changed from morning prints into black dresses with white frilly aprons and caps, could pass it round to ladies and children.

At 5 p.m., a slightly plainer tea was served to upper servants in the steward's room, and a much plainer one to lower servants in their hall. At 5.20 p.m., Prince, Duke and gentlemen returned red-cheeked from their day's shooting and triumphantly reported the bag to the ladies: 146 pheasants, 81 hares, 10 rabbits and 2 deer. The Prince and his equerries then retired to his suite of rooms situated in the north-western curved arm of the palace, near the Long Library, and redecorated in His Highness's honour with enamelled white-and-gold furniture.

At 5.45, the house's sedate pulse began to quicken. A stream of housemaids rushed up the backstairs with hot-water cans covered with snowy cloths, and stoked the bedroom fires. At 6 p.m., the dressing gong sounded, and valets and ladies' maids began to help bathe and dress their masters and mistresses for the gala evening ahead. Outside, carpenters and stablemen were erecting a covered marquee up the front steps of the north portico. The temperature had dropped to 30°F and light snow had begun to fall. In the Saloon, the footmen had almost finished setting the oak dining-table, a massive Victorian design with rounded ends and skirted edge and no-nonsense legs. The table was laid for thirty-six, with napkins folded into water-lilies, hand-written menus in silver holders at each place, and a vastly crowded parade down the table's middle of silver candelabra, silver-gilt vases, marble statuettes and alabaster figures, all 'ranged artistically', if *The Times* social correspondent can be believed, and 'interspersed with fruits, flowers, confectionery, etc.' At each end of the table were vases piled high with pineapples and grapes 'remarkable for their size and beauty'. As soon as the footmen had finished, the butler came to check their handiwork, casting a critical eye on the grapes to make sure that not too much calcined magnesia had been applied to bring up their bloom. He also stared closely at the filberts in their silver dishes to be sure they had been sulphur-fumed to a uniform colour and glossiness.

Dominating the entire table, in the exact centre, loomed John Churchill, 1st Duke of Marlborough, in solid silver, writing his famous Blenheim dispatch to Sarah, intent on the crude contests of his age, oblivious to plump grapes and polished filberts, but noting, out of the corner of his solid silver eye, that all the magnificent gilt ewers and basins which he had saved and schemed for had disappeared from the large Saloon console table where they had always stood.

Where had they gone? Sold on the auction-block by George Spencer-Churchill, spendthrift son of George Spencer, reclusive 4th Duke and patron of the arts. Upon succeeding in 1817, the 5th Duke of Marlborough had spent £50,000 on Blenheim's grounds, 'transforming the rich draperies which Brown had thrown around Nature,' according to one disapproving visitor, 'into a harlequin jacket of little clumps and beds'. Perhaps it was from the 5th Duke, his grandfather, that John Winston, 7th Duke, inherited his need to divide and rule, for the 5th Duke subdivided the garden into a Chinese Garden, a Dahlia Garden, a Terrace Garden, a Rose Garden, a Botany Bay Garden and a Rock Garden. As his purse got ever thinner, he began to exploit the palace's money-making potential. When Mrs Arbuthnot came with her 'great friend' the Duke of Wellington to see Blenheim on 27 April 1824, she was most disapproving of the 5th Duke:

> The family of the great General is, however, gone sadly to decay, and are but a disgrace to the illustrious name of Churchill, which they have chosen this moment to resume. The present Duke is overloaded with debt, is very little better than a common swindler and lets everything about Blenheim. People may shoot and fish at so much per hour and it has required all the authority of a Court of Chancery to prevent his cutting down all the trees in the park.

Blenheim was suffering one of its greyest, blankest periods. When Prince Pückler-Muskau toured it on 7 January 1827, the 'horrid fog' was so thick that 'we saw Blenheim as if by twilight, for it was all shrouded in a veil.

As we entered', the Prince continues,

> there was such a smoke that we thought we had to encounter a second fog in the house. Some very dirty shabby servants ran past us to fetch the chatelaine, who, wrapped in a Scotch plaid, with a staff in her hand and the air of an enchantress, advanced with so majestic an air towards us, that one might have taken her for the Duchess herself. She required that we should inscribe our names in a large book; unhappily, however, there was no ink in the inkstand. We passed through many chill and faded rooms.

For the last few years of his life, the 5th Duke was as reclusive as his father, but for different reasons. 'He lived in utter retirement at one corner of his magnificent palace, a melancholy instance of the results of extravagance,' according to the *Annual Register*, subsisting on venison, fish and poultry from his grounds and on the fine wines stacked in the undercroft by former more frugal Marlboroughs. His sole income was £5,000 from the Post Office, one of the many perquisites which John Churchill had cannily obtained for himself and his descendants.

If the 5th Duke was a virtual bankrupt when he died in 1840, the 6th Duke, his son, was a suspected bigamist, having gone through a mock marriage to Susanna Law in 1817 with his brother disguised as clergyman. (The devout 7th Duke, John Winston, among his mind's many small compartments, had none ample enough to contain that shocking bit of his father's history.) While Susanna was still very much alive, the 6th Duke had gone ahead and married, properly and legally, no fewer than three times. His second wife, Charlotte Flower, had been plucked in her prime, one of Blenheim's victims. Disraeli has left us the details of Charlotte's demise, in the spring of 1850. 'I have heard all the particulars about the Duchess of Marlborough; they are striking,' Dizzy writes, quite enjoying himself. 'She would, not withstanding her [pregnant] state, show Blenheim in all its pomp and parts to the Grand Duchess; a premature confinement was the consequence, which left symptoms which according to the physicians, must end in death or madness. In her unhappy case, I believe both; she died, I hear at Mivarts [a London hotel] and her shrieks were terrible.' The 6th Duke mourned briefly, then married for the third time, showing the single-track mind passed on to his son, John Winston, for his third bride bore the same name as his first: Jane Stewart. When the American novelist Nathaniel Hawthorne came to see Blenheim several years before the 6th Duke died, he reported that there was 'much public outcry against the meanness of the present Duke in the arrangements for the admission of visitors'. The Duke 'sells tickets admitting six persons at ten shillings. If only one person enters the gate, he must pay for six; if there are seven in company,' fumed Nathaniel, turning scarlet, 'two tickets are required to admit them. The attendants, who meet you everywhere in the park and palace, expect fees on their own private account – their noble master pocketing the ten shillings.' While touring the garden, Hawthorne caught sight of 'the besotted Duke (ah! I have let out a secret which I meant to keep to myself, but the ten shillings must pay for all) and, if in a condition for arithmetic, was thinking of nothing nobler than how many ten-shilling tickets had that day been sold.' The 6th Duke cannily covered up all his other sins from posterity by giving the order, just before he expired, that all his private papers be burnt.

AT 6.25, ON THAT NOVEMBER EVENING TWO YEARS LATER, THE first guests in their carriage passed through the entrance gate, noted the large sign which said: 'The Duke of Marlborough begs the persons who may walk through the park to keep to the high road, and not to walk on the grass' and proceeded over Vanbrugh's bridge. The carriage contained two Oxford dignitaries, Francis Jeune, Vice-Chancellor of Oxford, and Henry George Liddell, Dean of Christ Church, and their wives. Forty-one-year-old Margaret Jeune, like so many Victorian ladies, was an avid diarist and has left us a full account of the evening. Along with the High Sheriff of Oxford and his wife, who were following in a second carriage, these six would, in addition to Blenheim's house guests, form the select company of thirty-six around the banquet table. As the Jeunes and Liddells pulled their wraps closer against the snow, they expressed the fervent hope that the temperature inside Blenheim would be higher than it had been at dinner there the previous November, when it was so 'bitterly cold' that only 'furs and hot-water bottles' had kept pneumonia at bay. Dean Liddell, a curly-haired, long-faced man of forty-eight, was smiling to himself at the prospect of dining in stately Blenheim, never mind the cold. He well knew the value of a showy house in broadcasting one's elevated social position to the world. Born in a 'good square stone house' at Binchester where his father was rector, Henry George Liddell had sat next to the novelist William Makepeace Thackeray at Charterhouse School, drawing houses as fast as Thackeray drew faces, both of them ignoring the lesson. As soon as he moved into Christ Church deanery in 1855, Liddell had panelled the drawing-room, designed an impressive staircase and built a 44-foot-long gallery for musicians. (And Liddell's second daughter, Alice, was the little girl for whom Lewis Carroll wrote *Alice's Adventures in Wonderland*.)

The four guests left their cloaks in the Hall which 'looked *very* grand, well lighted and with a dozen footmen in the showy Marlborough livery drawn up at the entrance'. Then, on their way to the Grand Cabinet, just as they were passing Carlo Maratti's 'The Triumph of Christ over Sin' in the small green drawing-room, a painting wherein the Virgin stamps on a serpent and infant Jesus nails it with a long staff, the servant conducting them, 'being evidently on the watch', turned and announced 'the Prince is coming'. HRH advanced at once to the Jeunes and Liddells and in his 'gracious pleasing manner' shook hands. Then all four followed him and his five equerries into the Grand Cabinet where the house guests had already assembled. The Prince's attendants were: Earl Vane, Earl Denbigh, Lord Chelsea, Col. the Hon. R. Bruce and Col. Keppel.

The Prince himself was a slim youth of eighteen, and had been first honoured at Blenheim on the day of his birth in 1841, when John Winston's father, the 6th Duke, had stopped counting his shillings long enough to order a royal salvo to be fired from one of the 1st Duke's cannons. The Prince had grown into a fine-looking, fair-haired young man with a nose which Margaret Jeune thought 'remarkably well-shaped'. He had enrolled at Christ Church six weeks before, on 18 October, when Dean Liddell, meeting him for the first time, pronounced him 'the nicest little fellow possible, so simple, naïve, ingenuous and modest, and moreover with extremely good wits, possessing also the royal faculty of never forgetting a face'. Prince Edward Albert wasn't reading for a degree, but attended history lectures, played cricket, 'not at all minding being bowled out', and immediately became 'wonderfully popular and most justly so'. Margaret Jeune had first met him on 24 October at Oxford Town Hall where the Prince had 'seemed amused' as Charles Dickens read from *Pickwick Papers*. The Prince still had a marked German accent learned at the paternal knee of Prince Albert, but his Oxford experience would gradually erase it.

The company eyeing the Prince surreptitiously in the Grand Cabinet stood about looking stiff and self-conscious. 'I saw one lady make a deep curtsey to the Prince, but there did not seem to be many recognitions or much conversation,' writes Margaret. Perhaps it was the room itself, so oppressively furnished with dark colours and a confusion of objects, that flattened the guests into silence. The pier-glasses in one colour of gold so skilfully carved with a shell motif by Mr Ansell for the 4th Duke reflected what those two Men of Taste would have pronounced an excessively ugly décor. Candlelight had given way to gilt gasoliers on the walls (only Buckingham Palace, which always seemed to drag behind, still used candles) and the gas lighting gave off a blue-white glare. The pale eggshell colours which had helped light Blenheim's dim rooms in the eighteenth century had been replaced by garish aniline dyes of puce and plum and a dark green never found in Nature. Overstuffed chairs and sofas with dachshund feet had their plumpness held in check by hundreds of buttons which were the despair of Blenheim's housemaids, who could never get all the dust, no matter how hard they brushed, out of those dimpled crevices. Fanny, always conscious of Blenheim's bleakly bellicose façade, had done her best to make the Grand Cabinet 'homey', a 'homey' effect being the current ideal in home decorating, and to say that the room's clutter and padding gave it a 'lived-in look' is the only kind comment we can make.

'There was evidently some difficulty about the pairing' for the procession into dinner, with 'considerable rustling of a sheet of paper,' writes Margaret, 'which was being appealed to by a man or gentleman who was arranging the matter'. At 7 p.m., the difficulty somehow resolved, eighteen pairs of ladies and gentlemen trooped into the Saloon, with Fanny and the Prince leading. As the Prince reached the Saloon doorway, an orchestra struck up 'God Save the Queen'. The band was seated in the gallery above the Saloon which John Churchill had ordered from Vanbrugh for just such a royal occasion as this one, but had never seen in use. The orchestra continued to play 'pretty airs' throughout the meal. The ladies, as soon as they were seated, drew off their tight, above-elbow kid gloves. The banquet was served *à la russe*, according to the new fashion whereby, once the soup had come and gone, the entrées were no longer placed on the table as in the 4th Duke's time. Instead, the footmen, wearing white gloves, carried each dish round, offering it from the left side first to ladies, then to gentlemen. If the food was rich – lobster soufflé, stuffed quail, truffles poached in champagne – the conversation was anything but. Convention decreed, in those mid-Victorian years, that it be ground down to the lowest common denominator of mediocrity. 'The great spell of high life in this country seems to be *repose*,' commented one typically energetic American visitor who dined at various noble tables about this time.

> All violent sensations are avoided, as out of taste. In conversation nothing is so 'odd' as emphasis or startling epithet, or gesture, and in common intercourse nothing so vulgar as any approach to a 'scene'. For all extraordinary admiration the word 'capital' suffices; for all ordinary praise, the word 'nice'; for all condemnation in morals, manners or religion, the word 'odd'. To express yourself out of this simple vocabulary is to raise the eyebrows of the whole company at once, and stamp yourself under-bred or a foreigner.

The French historian Hippolyte Taine, who was in England in 1859, found that at many dinners 'there is no conversation at all. Several inconveniences arise from this, and tedium is one of them.' 'The general aspect of Society,' remarked Charles Francis Adams, the American Minister in London, 'is profound gravity. People look serious at a ball or dinner' and seemed totally preoccupied with their social position. 'I suppose state dinners

cannot well avoid being formal and rather dull,' sighed Margaret Jeune with thirty-five sobersides around her. If anyone thought the banquet 'capital' it was probably the Prince, for compared to Windsor dinners with Mama and Papa, Queen Victoria and Prince Albert, it was positively bacchanalian. There conversation was carried on entirely in whispers, and when the Queen spoke, even whispers ceased, while the whole company listened attentively.

And so the Blenheim banquet dragged ponderously forward; platitudes thudded like spent tennis balls on to the table. In its centre, the lean and hungry 1st Duke concentrated on the silver successes of his Blenheim dispatch; the false marble, painted so long ago by Laguerre, circled the room in red-veined right-angled rectitude, and high above the subdued company, the Saloon ceiling blared forth its trumpet note of lustier times. In cerulean blues and pinks and scarlets, still as bright as the day one hundred and forty years before when Laguerre had brushed them in, steeds reared and lunged, warriors aimed clubs and spears, and John Churchill, helmet-plumes and crimson cape flying in the wind of his ambition, forced his chariot ruthlessly forward. Nothing dull or puce-coloured up there.

At 8.15 precisely, as soon as all fingertips had been delicately dipped into crystal bowls, the Duchess gave the nod to Countess Vane, the second highest ranking lady, and all the ladies stood up, drew on their gloves, and flung their napkins on their chairs. The gentlemen stood too, and the groom held the door while the ladies swished through, one crinoline at a time, in strict order of rank. Then the gentlemen drew closer together, circulated the silver wagon which held decanters of claret, port and madeira, and began their desultory talk. There was none of the lewd, drunken ribaldry of the 4th Duke's time, and there were most certainly no chamber-pots hidden in the sideboard. At 8.45, only a little less sober, the gentlemen joined the ladies in the red drawing-room.

As soon as the Saloon was cleared of gentry, the footmen removed all signs of the sober feasting, shoved the heavy table against one wall, quickly carried in more tables, and began to set out evening refreshments for the large company about to descend on Blenheim. The butler began bringing up from the wine-cellar champagne which John Winston had ordered the house steward to buy from an Oxford wine merchant for 25s. per dozen bottles. Meanwhile, in the scullery, the scullery-maid was beginning the long evening's task of washing up: thirty-six of everything and more to come. She got a short break at 9.15, when the lower servants sat down to

OPPOSITE: The silver tablepiece of John, 1st Duke of Marlborough, writing his Blenheim dispatch

supper in the servants' hall, and the orchestra members helped themselves to cold meat, cheese and beer, eating quickly before they had to begin playing for the evening's dancing.

In the drawing-room, the hour between 9 and 10 p.m. was 'a little dull' according to Margaret Jeune, while the flagging thirty-six slumped against the buttons of the ladies' and gentlemen's chairs and awaited the fresh stimulation which the evening guests would surely supply. The long hour 'gave time and opportunity however,' Margaret writes, 'for admiring the toilettes of which the most elegant was Lady Portarlington's [Fanny's sister], the most distinguished-looking woman there – and the jewels (diamonds) of Lady Macclesfield, the Austrian ambassadress, Countess Vane and others. The ambassadress had superb shoulder knots of rubies and diamonds and the tiara of Lady Macclesfield and the necklace of the Duchess were well worth notice.' Fanny's necklace was most certainly worth notice, for its three largest diamonds had been filched from the sword presented to John Churchill by Emperor Leopold I of Austria and subsequently carried in the 1719 Bow-window Room production of *All for Love*.

Margaret was pleased that her two daughters arrived with the first influx of those invited for the evening 'while Her Grace was still near the door "receiving" so they were specially introduced and graciously received and shaken hands with, a compliment not shared by those who arrived after Her Grace had gone into the ballroom, and who have since expressed dissatisfaction thereat'. The Misses Jeune's engraved invitations had requested the honour of their presence at an 'evening party', which had led their mother to comment that 'the real thing intended is a Ball, but from the Duke's reputation in the religious world, I fancy the Duchess thinks it would not be quite consistent to own this, and accordingly scrupulous people can accept the invitation.' From 10 to 11 p.m., three hundred scrupulous people poured through the marquee, up the portico steps and into the first and second staterooms west of the Saloon, where *the ball* (we shan't sink to euphemisms) was taking place.

There was champagne, cold lobster, light-hearted music and 336 beautifully dressed people; moreover, a whole army of servants had been labouring for sixteen hours to make the ball a success, but the plain truth was: with one exception, no one was enjoying themselves and the fault lay partly with Blenheim's haughty Duchess. Margaret Jeune describes it all:

> Of course there were a great many who could not dance, wanting both room and partners, but a great many did, and if the Duchess had requested those who knew more of her company than she knew herself to make more introductions nothing would have been wanting, but she has not very agreeable manners

herself and is very deaf, which gives her an appearance of awkwardness unfortunate in her position. A very large party of Officers of the University Rifle Corps came, and plain and quiet as their uniform is, it was very ornamental and effective in the *coup d'oeil* of the party, as they grouped about the room. Some of the Oxford people certainly roamed about looking somewhat disconsolate.

The only person inside Blenheim having a good time was the Prince, who 'did appear to enjoy himself thoroughly – he danced every dance of every kind'. There were waltzes and polkas and quadrilles, the last an old dance form rather out of fashion, but much favoured by the conservative Duke. Without respite, the Prince whirled and smiled and skipped and the select three hundred sulked self-consciously from room to room, consoled only by the fact that just being inside Blenheim was, even as they yawned and glanced for the hundredth time at their pocket watches, greatly enhancing their social position, always their prime concern.

Outside Blenheim, however, was a very different scene. Looking in through the brightly lighted windows along the south front, standing where Henry Wise's parterre had given way to Capability Brown's sheep-dotted green carpet, were several hundred of Woodstock's underprivileged, gazing enchanted at their Prince and their social superiors. If the company inside was cold and inhibited, the company outside was just the opposite. These were the descendants of those earthy Blenheim workmen who had downed their ale 150 years before at Jockey Green's tavern, and they were just as full of jokes and ribaldry. They didn't miss a thing; they saw every snub and every missed step in the quadrille. They placed bets on whose tiara had the greatest number of diamonds and how many glasses of champagne the gentleman with the frayed cuffs could knock back. They dug each other in the ribs and filled the frosty air with much laughter and hooting and many a 'Lor' love us!' and 'Did you ever!' 'The great houses in the land are the centres to which at stated times the country comes up as to shrines of refinement,' the Revd William Sewell had pontificated from his pulpit that very year, 'and then in due time the country goes back again home, enriched with a portion of the social accomplishments, which those very visits serve to call out.' The Revd Mr Sewell had never stood on the south lawn of Blenheim while what one newspaper called 'the most brilliant spectacle in the county for a century' took place on the far side of the glass. The common folk certainly went home enriched but not quite in the manner the Revd Mr Sewell suggested.

While the scrupulous simpered within and the unscrupulous guffawed without, the housemaids were very busy on the floor above. They were turning down the beds, closing the windows, setting everything out for the morning bath, removing dirty shoes and used towels. They would be up very late, for they would have to return, just before the guests retired, whenever that happened to be, with cans of hot water and warming-pans for the beds.

So the night wore on. At 4 a.m. the crowd on the lawn, all of whom had to rise with the lark, had disappeared as silently as mist and the Prince was dancing the cotillion with as much energy as ever, and everyone else was asleep on their feet, and the ladies' maids were still awake, but only just, in their carpeted rooms, waiting to release their mistresses from their corsets and to put away their jewels, and the butler was dozing over a racing sheet in his pantry waiting to extinguish all the gasoliers and lock all the doors. At 5 a.m. Prince, Duke, Duchess and the hardiest house guests were falling gratefully into their nicely plumped, nicely warmed beds, and the footmen were bent all in a row over basins washing powder from their itchy scalps, which they hadn't dared to scratch with so many stony stares upon them. Finally, at 5.21 a.m. the last candle in Housemaids Heights was blown out, and everyone in the palace, from Prince to scullery-maid, having so satisfactorily performed the duties to which God had called them, took their well-earned rest.

THUS THE MILLS OF BLENHEIM GROUND SLOWLY FORWARD DAY after day, efficiently manufacturing for the Marlboroughs the plush upholstery of living which muffled the real world's nasty poking pro-tuberances – and, quite as efficiently, their hearts' passion and their souls' growth.

The children supplied Blenheim's only spontaneity and spark. Around the time of the Prince's visit, ten-year-old Lord Randolph persuaded his father to buy him a pony called The Mouse, owned by the telegraph boy who brought cables to Blenheim. What Randolph wanted, using fair means or foul, Randolph always got. The Mouse became his, and he proudly joined the Heythrop Hunt for the first time, relished the fox's death in King's Wood, was presented with the brush and properly initiated. He burst into Blenheim with his cheeks well smeared with fox's blood. It had been a century and a half since the palace had caught that familiar stench of bloody violence.

In the following year, another little Marlborough, Georgiana, was added to the plentiful nursery harvest, and due thanks for the Duchess's safe delivery sent heavenwards from the Chapel.

On 4 February 1861, the Duke went up to London, leaving Fanny at Blenheim with the usual large party of house guests. Sometime after midnight, the porter at the main gate was awakened by a strong smell of

smoke and a sudden glare. 'He immediately rang the alarm bell,' as
the *Annual Register* reported, and 'on the household assembling it was
ascertained that the north-eastern wing of the outer quadrangle was in
flames.' There, in a long room above the steward's office, bake-house and
store-room, the 7th Duke had hidden away the nine Titian paintings, 'The
Loves of the Gods', presented to John Churchill by Victor Amadeus, Duke
of Savoy, and hung originally in Blenheim's Hall. When William Hazlitt
came to Blenheim in the 1820s, the Titians were still in plain view. Hazlitt
waxed ecstatic on their 'purple light of love, crimsoned blushes, looks
bathed in rapture, kisses with immortal sweetness' and on a Cupid in the
'Venus and Mars' painting 'who might well turn the world upside down'.
After John Winston, the good 7th Duke, succeeded, however, the Titians
had been banished to a locked room to languish unseen and unappreciated.
Now – how had it happened? – they were all on fire, their incendiary
nature dramatically confirmed. 'The intelligence that Blenheim was on fire
spread a most lively excitement through the city of Oxford,' noted the
Annual Register; all available fire-engines and thousands of curious people,
on foot or horseback, came rushing to the scene. Blenheim's most dutiful
servants tried to cut the canvases from their frames, but were driven back
by the extreme heat. All the Titians burnt to a black crisp, as well as
Rubens's 'Rape of Proserpine', a magnificent painting of which no copy
existed. It too had been locked away so as not to offend scrupulous
Victorian eyes. Blenheim's resident females, particularly its crinolined
Duchess, heaved a sanctimonious sigh that the palace had been purged of
its obscenities, and next morning the hymn 'God moves in a mysterious
way/His wonders to perform' was sung most fervently in chapel. Thus it
was that on a dark February night in 1861, Blenheim Palace lost most of
its remaining Eros, and sank even further into the cold ashes of hypocrisy
and prudery.

Blenheim grew even more sedate when Lord Randolph left for Eton in
1863, taking with him smells of fresh air, dogs and horses, and his raucous
jay-like laugh, leaving the field to his sedentary sisters with their embroidery
hoops. At Eton, Randolph became known at once as a 'scug', a 'scug'
being someone bumptious, ill-mannered and irresponsible. His one
accomplishment was to recruit the largest group ever of personal 'fags',
no less than fifteen smaller, younger boys to cater to his every whim. He
was only slightly less rebellious at Eton than his elder brother Blandford,
who had gone so far he had been expelled. Both boys reacted to the
heady release from Blenheim's constraints, and what Blandford called 'the
overbearing manner and assumptions of superiority' which their father
always 'displayed to us'.

The Duke and Duchess produced another daughter, Sarah, in 1865. Fanny was forty-three, and eleven pregnancies had rather sapped her maternal zeal. In 1866, the dutiful Duke became a Privy Councillor; he was made Lord President of the Council on 8 March 1867. In that year, sporting a walrus moustache and a dandified dark-blue frock coat, Randolph transferred his rebellious ways to Merton College, Oxford, where he was duly fined for smoking while in academic dress, breaking the windows of the aptly named Randolph Hotel and being drunk and disorderly. His colleagues nicknamed him 'Gooseberry' in deference to his eyes, and Randolph stalked about with all the arrogance and assertiveness which Blenheim's hard stones had given him.

On 8 November 1869, Westminster Abbey's bells pealed for Blandford's marriage to Albertha 'Goosie' Hamilton, daughter of the fastidious 1st Duke of Abercorn, whose housemaids wore white gloves to make his bed. 'Goosie' had black hair, a thin, plain face and small blue eyes which, after her marriage, took on a hurt, disillusioned look, for she discovered soon enough that Blandford nursed a lukewarm passion for science, an inflamed one for pretty women and none at all for her. 'Goosie' vented her spleen mildly in the form of practical jokes: an ink-pot poised over a doorway ready to descend on her husband's head, pieces of soap among the cheeses at dinner, that kind of thing.

Four years later, in 1873, it was Randolph's turn to think of matrimony. That August he went, with the rest of the fashionable world, to Cowes on the Isle of Wight, for regatta week, and strolled about with his pugdog, whose eyes were remarkably like his master's. On Tuesday afternoon, 12 August, Randolph attended a ball given on board HMS *Ariadne*, guardship of the regatta. There he met Miss Jennie Jerome, a nineteen-year-old American. She was incredibly beautiful, with deep-set grey eyes, thickly fringed black lashes, an extremely high colour, very red lips, and a radiant vitality. One admirer felt that Jennie 'had more of the panther than of the woman in her look'. Her appearance was as flashy and flamboyant as the country of her birth. Randolph fell violently in love and three days later asked Jennie to be his wife; she said an enthusiastic 'Yes!' Next day, Saturday, Randolph ended an impassioned note with the words: 'I shall hope to see you after church tomorrow. You see I keep turning up like a bad shilling.' Not a penny, mind; no son of Blenheim would value himself so lowly. By Tuesday, 19 August, Randolph was back at Blenheim,

---

OPPOSITE: John Winston, 7th Duke, and Duchess Fanny, *c.* 1865, with five of their daughters (and an unidentified female). Photographed outside Blenheim's east front

wondering how best to drop his bombshell. He was relieved to find that his father had gone to shoot in Scotland, so Randolph sent off a letter announcing his engagement, and then held his breath, awaiting the explosion sure to follow. 'Such a melancholy journey away from you,' sighed the besotted Randolph to Jennie,

> and then to have to listen to the twaddle and gossip of my mother and sisters when my heart and thoughts are elsewhere. It is so curious that my rooms and my things and my occupations here which I used to take interest in are quite hateful to me now. My whole life and energies should be devoted to making you happy and protecting you from harm or wrong. Life should be to you like one long summer day.

The Titian Cupid who 'might well turn the world upside down' had gone up in smoke, but his vengeful spirit had returned to stir things up at Blenheim. 'It is not likely,' the Duke thundered through the post to Randolph on 31 August, 'that at present you can look at anything except from your own point of view; but persons from the outside cannot but be struck with the unwisdom of your proceedings, and the uncontrolled state of your feeling which completely paralyses your judgement.' The paterfamilias absolutely refused to give his consent to the match. He had made preliminary inquiries concerning Leonard Jerome, Jennie's father, who sounded 'a sporting, and I should think vulgar kind of man'. He was 'of the class of speculators' and had already been bankrupt once. It would be a connection 'which no man in his senses could think respectable'. Leonard Jerome was bad enough, but his wife Clara – horror of horrors! – was the great-granddaughter of an Iroquois squaw. 'Under any circumstances,' declared the Duke to his son, himself the great-great-great-great-grandson of a speculator far more ruthless and ambitious than Leonard Jerome, 'an American connection is not one that we would like. You must allow it is a slightly coming down in pride for us to contemplate the connection.'

When the Duke returned to Blenheim from his shooting, a stiff interview took place between His Grace and his headstrong son. The Duke forbade the marriage; Randolph played his trump card and threatened blackmail. (It was the first, but not the last time that he would use blackmail to get what he wanted.) There was an election pending, and the Duke wanted Randolph to stand for the Woodstock seat. Since the Duke had ousted his brother, Lord Alfred, from it, because the latter had taken too liberal a view on a bill dealing with church rates, the seat was being kept warm for

---

OPPOSITE: Lord Randolph Churchill

a Marlborough by the Duke's nominee, a middle-class banker called Mr Barnett, who had set himself up as squire of nearby Glympton Park. In spite of Randolph's threats that if he couldn't marry Jennie he wouldn't stand for Parliament, the Duke stood his ground, with Blenheim's weight around him. He forbade Randolph to see Jennie again, and since Randolph had no income beyond what his father doled out, he was forced to obey. 'It is very wretched for me here,' Randolph wrote to Jennie from the fortress-prison of Blenheim, 'time drags itself along like lead and I am getting quite to hate this place.' Eventually, however, hard-hitting Randolph was victorious. The Duke, after weeks of continual bombardment from his son, consented to a provisional engagement with the wedding date set far in the future.

Randolph was planning to join Jennie in Paris, where she was then living, for her birthday, on 9 January 1874, but the Duchess's sister, handsome Lady Portarlington, fell mortally, and most conveniently, ill in Ireland. The crinolined Duchess, from within her steel circumference, insisted that Randolph stay rooted with the rest of the family round the deathbed and sent off her first letter to Jennie: 'He [Randolph] was on the point of starting when my poor sister had a relapse to the state of fearful gasping for breath. It was almost impossible for him to go while she was in such a state for if the worst had happened he would have blamed himself.' The rigid forms of Duty and Decorum wouldn't bend, and Jennie blew out her birthday candles alone.

In February, Randolph was busy campaigning for the Woodstock seat. 'The number of houses I have been into – many of them dirty cottages – the number of unwashed hands I have cordially shaken, you would not believe,' he wrote to Jennie from Blenheim's superior vantage point. Randolph won handily, which is not surprising, in view of the fact that his father had commandeered Woodstock's three leading hotels for his son's cause, leaving only a 'wretched, low, miserable pothouse', thus described by Randolph with a sneer, for the Liberal candidate Brodrick. On election night, Randolph was carried in triumph from Woodstock to Blenheim by a canny crowd of townsfolk who knew which side their bread was buttered on.

The Duchess of Marlborough's birthday, 15 April 1874, was chosen for Randolph's and Jennie's wedding-day – an ineffectual ploy, as it turned out, for when the wedding took place in the chapel of the British Embassy in Paris neither Duke nor Duchess deigned to attend. Randolph brought

OPPOSITE: Lady Randolph Churchill

his American bride to Blenheim for the initial encounter in May. The newly-weds were met at the station by the same canny crowd of townsfolk, who unhitched the horses from the Marlborough carriage and themselves pulled it along the main street of Woodstock, under the Triumphal Arch erected by Sarah, past the Blenheim porter holding a long wand topped by a red-tasselled, silver knob – Jennie's eyes grew bigger as she took it all in – and into Blenheim Park, where Capability Brown's blue lake swirled out from the golden knot of Vanbrugh's bridge. 'This is the finest view in England,' Randolph announced to Jennie in his habitually loud voice which silenced all opposition. The Duke and Duchess and family awaited them on the portico steps, and Jennie felt the pop-eyed hostility of eight female eyes as Fanny and her three youngest daughters – the three eldest had married, all most suitably – looked Jennie over, inch by inch.

With Jennie's arrival, the life of Blenheim Palace turned a fresh corner. She resolutely refused to feel intimidated by its stultifying bulk, and fought back with typical North American gusto and brashness. She did what no upper-class English person would ever do, she showed off. She sat down at the piano and gave clear evidence with every cadenza that she had been taught by a master, and had practised five hours every day for years. She peppered her racy conversation with French and German phrases, for she was fluent in both languages. She talked intelligently of books, meaty books which no female at Blenheim, existing on the watery gruel of *Keepsakes* and *Bijoux*, had ever read. She swept through Blenheim's cluttered, dark-plush rooms looking ravishingly beautiful in her chic Parisian gowns in pale lilac and white, and incredibly *alive*. Instead of admiring Blenheim, she raved about the Château de Compiègne. Pasty-faced Rosamond in her drab, drooping frocks, began to hate her new sister-in-law, and fourteen-year-old Georgiana and nine-year-old Sarah stared entranced at this being from another planet. Jennie was already pregnant, and couldn't ride. Inside Blenheim, she paced like a tigress caught within the bars of regimented days. In the mornings, she read the carefully smoothed-out news in *The Times*; in the afternoons, she practised the piano or walked slowly about the grounds; in the evenings she played a subdued game of whist. 'Many a glance would be cast at the clock, which sometimes would be surreptitiously advanced a quarter of an hour by some sleepy member of the family,' reported Jennie. 'No one dared suggest bed until the sacred hour of eleven had struck. Then we would all troop out into a small anteroom, and lighting our candles, each in turn would kiss the Duke and Duchess and depart to our rooms.' Jennie paced and chafed, and found one small avenue of release for her pent-up feelings. She wrote, on Blenheim's crested paper, long naughty letters to her mother, making fun of the Marlboroughs' frumpy clothes and of such lapses from elegance as thick, ordinary tumblers on the dinner table, 'the kind we use in bedrooms'.

She and Randolph had rented a house in London's Curzon Street, but throughout 1874, they were frequently at Blenheim so that he could attend to constituency business. 'On our return to Blenheim,' Jennie fumed to her mother, '[we] found the drawing-room full of lots of people having tea [a new batch of house guests]. I escaped as soon as I could. You cannot imagine how stiff and uncomfortable the first hour of their arrivals is. No one knows each other and so content themselves with staring.' Jennie found a second safety-valve: she began to flirt with susceptible Blandford, who was appearing at Blenheim more and more frequently. One day he gave Jennie a ring which she promptly showed to Fanny, and which the Duchess promptly declared the property of dearest Goosie. A terrible family row ensued, conducted in the usual Blenheim manner, which was very different from the way Jennie and her two sisters conducted theirs. They screamed at each other, threw hairbrushes across the room, got rid of all their resentments within minutes, and then embraced warmly, feeling wonderfully relieved. The Marlboroughs, however, kept their resentments growling for days, years even, under the plush and politeness of their palace life. Candour and passion bumped against the invisible walls of cant and hypocrisy in their minds, and against the real ones of privacy and division in their house, and couldn't find a way out. The Marlboroughs gave vent to their emotions only on paper. Face-to-face they were forever courteous, but their letters to each other were etched in acid. The affair of Goosie's ring ran to many deeply scored and underlined sheets. Blandford wrote scathingly to his mother; the Duke added his sonorous note, and sent the swelling package on to Randolph; eventually the whole family took up their pens and marched into the thick of it. Through it all the insouciant Jennie, more or less oblivious to the consternation and commotion her disturbing presence was causing in well-oiled, orderly Blenheim, sailed through its rooms, in full glamour and drama, leaving a provocative trail of expensive scent, Alençon-lace parasols, and pretty little objects in amber and tortoiseshell with her name flashed across them in gold. Jennie had been raised in a country very large, very expansive, very energized and just then entering on what Mark Twain called its Gilded Age, twenty-five years of phenomenal economic prosperity and optimism, marked by 'invitation in the air and success in all the wide horizon'. America, and particularly New York, had made Jennie what she was, for she was exactly like her native land: in her vitality, her spontaneity, her inventiveness, her distrust of tradition and formality, her childish love of superlatives and anything larger-than-life.

At Blenheim, Jennie was the enemy within because she brought into its sanctuary the crass New World, with all of its threat, and all of its promise. Inside the neat closets of their minds, the Marlboroughs felt, and rightly feared, that rushing wind. By 1874, the smug fortress that was Britain, centre of a vast thriving Empire, was, like Blenheim, already being besieged. In 1867, the franchise had been widened for the third time and household suffrage given in the towns, thereby strengthening the power of the populace to rule through their representatives, much to the delight of Mr Barnett at Glympton Park, and other middle-class barons. Britain's birth-rate began to decline after 1870; her industrial and commercial strength, and even her naval supremacy, began to be challenged by the United States. England's imperial sun had already begun to set, just as it was rising in Jennie's native land. The winds of change blew strongly eastwards across the Atlantic, and once Blenheim had opened its doors to Jennie, the palace felt that keen blast in every crevice, and trembled. Three of Blenheim's future chatelaines would be American; all of them would radically alter Blenheim's traditional fabric, introducing innovations which were un-English, inappropriate, wildly eccentric or even materially destructive.

On Saturday, 28 November 1874, there was a shoot at Blenheim. Jennie, seven months pregnant, followed the shooters in a pony-trap, and a rattling drive over rough ground brought on labour pains. She was hustled back to Blenheim, and into the drab little main-floor bedroom which had belonged to Dean Jones, the rotund Marlborough chaplain whose likeness Laguerre had painted on the Saloon wall. The Dean's ghost, the only one ever seen at Blenheim, often toddled along the corridors, finding it difficult, among all that ball-fringe and bric-à-brac, to recognize the stark, gilt-ridden castle of his day. Jennie had intermittent labour pains through Sunday, and at 1.30 a.m. on Monday, 30 November, she gave birth to Winston Leonard Spencer-Churchill. Perhaps it was Dean Jones, hovering curiously just above his bed to see what Jennie would bring forth, who endowed Winston Leonard's spirit with all the martial valour of the Dean's hero-employer, John Churchill. Winston Leonard himself would later strengthen the link to his bold ancestor by dropping the 'Spencer' from his surname, leaving 'Churchill' to resound anew through the halls of British history. Early Monday morning, 'a merry peal was rung' from Woodstock church, and Fanny scribbled a note to the baby's other grandmother in Paris: 'We had neither cradle nor baby linen nor anything ready, but fortunately everything went well and all difficulties were overcome.' Randolph was thrilled to have a son, and told Mrs Jerome that Jennie 'suffered a good deal, poor darling, but was very plucky and had no chloroform. The boy is wonderfully pretty so everybody says, and very healthy considering its prematureness.' He added a frantic postscript: 'We hope the baby things will come with all speed. We have to borrow some from the Woodstock solicitor's wife.' A nanny and wet-nurse came down at once from London. The nanny, who would for many years to come be Winston's greatest comfort and confidante, was Mrs Elizabeth Ann Everest, a plump, forty-one-year-old widow in dark silks and bonnet, ready to give unbounded love and loyalty to her new charge.

It was on that cold, dark morning of 30 November 1874, one hundred and sixty-nine years after its corner-stone was laid, that mighty Blenheim, first gaunt and beleaguered, then beguiling and cosseted, then pigeon-holed and proper, embraced its second British Hero, and its renaissance of fresh renown. Like America itself, Jennie was a puzzle and a paradox, filling the palace with crossed signals concerning its future. Sometimes the events which she sparked were disturbing and disruptive; sometimes, as on that November day, they were bracing and beneficent, but always they were rampant with life.

'I can't tell you how jealous Randolph says the Duchess is of Jennie,' her sister Clara wrote to their mother while visiting Blenheim in 1875. Rosamond had come out that year and was desperately seeking a husband. She was suffering from a liver complaint, and the sight of her yellow skin beside Jennie's rosy radiance did nothing to improve Fanny's temper, nor did the discovery that Randolph and Blandford were forever 'abusing and ridiculing' their parents behind their backs. The paper war hotted up again. 'Fanny,' Jennie complained to Randolph, referring to his sister, 'is the most "bottled up" creature I have *ever* met.' 'Blandford's eternal lectures and harangues always about himself are awfully wearying,' Randolph countered to Jennie. '*Dieu! comme il m'ennuie.*'

The Duke's response to this epistolary snake-pit inside Blenheim was to grease the machinery of polite living, and pile on more padding, all of which, to his chagrin, was taking a great deal more than £40,000 per annum to maintain. The good Duke, pious, proper John Winston, consequently did what none of the earlier Dukes, however spendthrift or lecherous, silly or sottish, had dared to do: he began the systematic spoliation of Blenheim's treasures. The Marlborough Gems were auctioned off at Christie's in June 1875 – were there, one wonders, mute stirrings in the 4th Duke's vault? – and knocked down for 35,000 guineas to a Mr Bromilow of whom nothing is known. One suspects, however, that Mr Bromilow was a wealthy industrialist who relied on the wondrous classical gems to take the sting of '*nouveau*' out of '*nouveau riche*'.

In the autumn of 1875, Blenheim's stones shook with fresh crisis and scandal. The Prince of Wales, no longer as slim nor as naïve as in his cotillion days, went to India in search of fresh *frissons* in the form of tiger hunts and sumptuous banquets where Indian nautch-girls slid their brown flesh slowly past his appreciative eyes. Prince Edward took with him 'Sporting Joe' Aylesford, a pig-sticking, polo-playing crony. As soon as Sporting Joe had left the field in England, the Marquess of Blandford promptly moved his horses and household, but not his wife Goosie, down to an inn handy to the Aylesford seat, Paddington Hall, near Coventry, and seduced Sporting Joe's wife, Edith. Blandford informed his stunned parents that he planned to divorce Goosie, and then he ran off to Paris with Edith. There they set up housekeeping as Mr and Mrs Spencer and eventually produced a son.

Oh, the consternation at Blenheim! The tight-lipped, white-knuckled, poison-pen consternation! Divorce was unthinkable, for divorce meant the Divorce Court and the Divorce Court meant Public Scandal and Public Scandal was the ultimate sin, far, far worse than a little discreet adultery! The Duke tugged at his side-whiskers, and Fanny's crinoline swayed and dipped like a foundering ship at sea, and Randolph, for the second time in his life, resorted to blackmail. He went round to Marlborough House in London where the Prince of Wales resided, for after the 4th Duke's death in 1817, the house that Sarah built had reverted to the Crown. Randolph showed Princess Alexandra, Prince Edward's beautiful wife, love letters which her royal spouse had written to Edith Aylesford. Randolph threatened to make them public unless the Prince persuaded Sporting Joe not to divorce Edith, naming Blandford as co-respondent. The Prince refused to cooperate and gave the order that he never wished to see the Randolph Churchills again.

The newspapers at Blenheim arrived every morning on the breakfast table as nicely ironed as ever, but screaming, in bold, black type, nasty gossip and slander about the Marlborough family. The Duke and Duchess conferred behind closed doors in their dressing-rooms, and decided that they would have to leave Blenheim's inadequate carapace and flee the country. The Duke appealed to his Tory friend Disraeli, the Prime Minister, who often stayed at Blenheim and, unbeknownst to his host, sent off letters to his friends complaining of the palace's excessive chill and dullness. The Duke asked Disraeli to send him to Ireland as Lord Lieutenant, a post he had refused two years before. Disraeli agreed. 'There is no one else to appoint,' he wrote to a friend, 'for the wealthy avoid the office and paupers won't fit.'

The summer of 1876 was not a pleasant one at Blenheim. Little Winston crowed and cavorted in the nursery and the servants tiptoed about as attentively and silently as ever, flicking the dust from the silver phalanxes of smiling family photos and from the cross-stitched Home, Sweet Homes, but the Duchess and Jennie sniped at each other from behind the velvet *portières*, and Randolph began a fresh feud with sister Cornelia, over some trifle. 'There is no doubt, however, that Cornelia behaved very piggily,' Randolph wrote to Jennie; 'she cannot have the least feeling or affection for me' and consequently he would henceforth 'forget that she is my sister'. The Duchess grimly began her list-making and packing, not at all relishing the thought of a four-year exile in Dublin's bleak Viceregal Lodge, among peasants and papists. 'It's all most unpleasant and humiliating,' she wrote, wishing she could bury her head in her crinoline; 'when will all this annoyance be at an end?'

In November, Queen Victoria invited the Duke and Duchess down to Windsor Castle, on condition that the dinner whispers were to include no reference to the 'domestic circumstances' (the royal euphemism for the Aylesford affair) which had caused Her Majesty 'anxiety and deep regret'. The Queen was grieved to find both the Marlboroughs looking 'so *distressed*, and *wretched*'.

It really was too aggravating. The Duke had spent his life setting a moral example to the nation, and now Blandford had spoiled it all with one foul swoop. The Aylesford affair not only besmirched the Marlborough name in public, but also gave fresh fuel to the growing number of social critics who felt that heredity alone, unallied to intellect and honour and ability, was an insufficient claim to one fifth of the kingdom's land. They pointed out that England's 600 peers owned 14 million acres and pocketed a total of £66 m annually in rents. Thackeray had led the pack of critics by publishing *The Book of Snobs* in *Punch* in 1846–7, deploring the 'peerage-worship' still rampant in the country:

> A man becomes enormously rich, or he wins a great battle and the country rewards him for ever with a gold coronet and a title and a rank as legislator. 'Your merits are so great,' says the nation, 'that your children shall be allowed to reign over us, in a manner. It does not in the least matter that your eldest son be a fool; we think your services so remarkable that he shall have the reversion of your honours when death vacates your noble shoes.'

Now the eldest son of the Duke of Marlborough was amply demonstrating his right to the title of fool, but to no other.

On 12 December 1876, the Marlboroughs took up their cross in Dublin, and Blenheim was left to the care of a small skeleton staff. While the Marlboroughs were in Ireland, not-so-fair Rosamond, at the age of twenty-five, finally received a proposal, and got herself engaged, in 1877, to Captain William Fellowes. 'I am afraid your mother,' wrote Jennie to Randolph, 'worries herself about what people will say. She seems to think it is a great comedown.' The Randolph Churchills, lured by the fine hunting, often went to Dublin's Viceregal Lodge on visits. It was there, in 1878, that Winston, a sturdy four-year-old with red sausage curls, experienced his 'first coherent memory', and it seems fitting that it was a martial one. 'The old Duke, the formidable grandpapa', as Winston would recall years later, was unveiling a statue to Lord Gough, while 'scarlet soldiers on horseback' formed a phalanx and grandfather thundered forth the unforgettable phrase: 'and with a withering volley he shattered the enemy's line'. 'I quite understood,' writes the adult Winston, 'that he was speaking about war and fighting.'

The Marlboroughs returned to Blenheim in the summer of 1880, the Duke with a much depleted purse. He had been forced, against all personal inclination, to go to Ireland to keep his fine moral façade from cracking beyond repair. Since he was not a philosopher nor even a thinker, it may not have occurred to the good Duke that what he had relinquished in the process was not only his bank-roll but also his independence and power of choice. As with the 7th Duke of Marlborough, so with the Empire as a whole. 'When the white man turns tyrant,' George Orwell would write many years later in his essay 'Shooting an Elephant', thinking of all those Englishmen who ruled in colonial outposts such as India, 'it is his own freedom that he destroys. He becomes a sort of hollow, posing dummy, for it is the condition of his rule that he shall spend his life in trying to impress the "natives", and so in every crisis he has got to do what the "natives" expect of him.' The 7th Duke of Marlborough had spent his life trying to impress the English lower orders, and in the Aylesford crisis he had done what they expected of him: he had publicly demonstrated, from the Dublin outpost of his self-imposed exile, how splendidly he could still do his duty.

Back home at Blenheim Palace, the Duke knelt on his crimson velvet chapel cushion, dined in his starched shirt, and strutted about, as he always had, with the weight of Blenheim on his squared shoulders. He was quite as unaware as the 4th Duke had been, though for different reasons, that Blenheim had taken him prisoner, and henceforth would call the tune, allowing its Duke to rule only as hollow, posing dummy, never in real autonomy and liberty. The Duke was being crushed and emasculated by the pressing demands, as he saw them, of his mighty palace. The mills of Blenheim ground slowly, day after righteous day, but they ground exceeding small.

Jennie was at Blenheim with Winston for the summer and autumn of 1880 while Randolph pursued his political ambitions in London. Unlike the Marlboroughs, Jennie was never one to hide from the truth. She gazed at her reflection in the pewter waters of the lake and faced the hard fact that Randolph valued her as a beautiful possession, but that he did not love her because he was incapable of loving. He knew only how to take, not how to give. One November evening when mist wrapped round the palace like a cold grey shroud, Jennie revealed her unhappiness in a letter to her mother:

> The fact is I *loathe* living here. It is not on account of the dullness, *that* I don't mind, but it is gall and wormwood to me to accept anything or to be living on anyone I hate. It is no use disguising it, the Duchess hates me simply for what I am – perhaps a little prettier and more attractive than her daughters. Everything I do or say or wear is found fault with. We are always studiously polite to each other, but it is rather like a volcano, ready to burst out at any moment.

Jennie sometimes escaped into a false persona. She disguised herself in an old cloak, hat and reticule, and joined the tourists still flocking to see where the good Duke lived with his happy family. 'My, what poppy eyes these Churchills have!' she heard one sightseer exclaim as he gazed at the massed bull-frogs in their silver frames.

The Duke was very busy pushing through Parliament, with the help of his friend Earl Cairns, the Lord Chancellor, the Blenheim Settled Estates Act whereby all the heirlooms which Sarah had cannily entailed lost their protected status. Once the Act was passed, the 7th Duke rubbed his hands with glee and eagerly sold off the Sunderland Library, in two ten-day auction sessions held in December 1881 and July 1882. He raised £56,581 6s. od. and felt not a single pang at parting with exquisitely bound editions of the classics, Bibles from very early presses, Renaissance vellum folios, rare English county histories and illuminated medieval chronicles. The empty Long Library shelves, with their splendid Georgian woodwork and latticed doors, were torn out and some third-rate portraits of Marlborough ancestors were hauled from attics, dusted off and hung on the protesting, pillaged walls.

Unlike the 4th Duke and his fellow peers, the 7th Duke of Marlborough and his noble friends were definitely *not* Men of Taste. 'The Barbarians' is what Matthew Arnold, that stern critic of his society's values, calls England's aristocrats in *Culture and Anarchy* (1869). Their culture was confined totally to such 'exterior graces' as courteous manners. Speaking of 'the good looks and politeness of our aristocratic class', Arnold cannot resist making 'the one qualifying remark, that in these charming gifts there should be, for ideal perfection, a shade more *soul*'. He might well have been thinking of the 7th Duke of Marlborough, the crassest Barbarian of them all.

In June 1883, the Duke made a slow-chugging, slow-puffing speech in the Lords, detailing all the sacred objections to marriage with a deceased wife's sister. It was his latest and, as it turned out, his last religious crusade.

On Wednesday morning, 4 July 1883, the Duke felt slightly unwell at his London house in Berkeley Square. In the afternoon, he and Fanny drove, as usual, in Hyde Park, returning, as usual, an hour before dinner. The Duke went to bed that night protesting that he felt quite alright, thank you. Next morning, however, when his valet came to draw back the curtains at 8.01 a.m., he found His Grace lying dead on the floor of his bedroom. All the Duke's children and their spouses rushed round at once to Berkeley Square. Queen Victoria expressed her sympathy by telegraph; the far too liberal Prime Minister, Mr Gladstone, left his card. The ladies of the Marlborough family ordered their heavy mourning veils and black gowns, and the gentlemen their black silk hat-bands, scarves and black kid gloves. The servants were immediately provided with mourning clothes, and secretly looked forward to the funeral feast.

On Saturday, 7 July, *The Times* ran a small notice on page 11: 'The funeral of the late Duke of Marlborough will take place at Blenheim on Tuesday next at 1 o'clock. The ceremony will be private, but any friends desirous of attending will be conveyed from Paddington Station to Wood-stock-road (where carriages will be in waiting) by the 10 o'clock train on Tuesday morning. They return from Woodstock station at 3.30 p.m. or 5 p.m., arriving in town at 5.25 p.m. or 7.15 p.m.' One Duke and eighteen Lords, together with assorted Sirs and even one or two mere Esquires, sent their valets out for black arm-bands and prepared to catch the Tuesday train to Blenheim.

On Monday morning, 9 July, when all England picked up its morning *Times*, ironed or unironed, as the case might be, they read the next instalment of the Duke of Marlborough's demise:

The sad event of the sudden death of the Duke of Marlborough, for many years the president of the institution, came specially under notice of the large and influential meeting of the committee of the Shipwrecked Fishermen and Mariners' Royal Benevolent Society, held at the society's central office, Hibernia-chambers, London-bridge, on Friday. His Grace was to have presided at the 44th annual meeting of the society, announced to take place in Fishmongers' Hall, on Wednesday next, 11 July, for arrangement of the final details of which the committee had been brought together. A resolution of condolence, tendering to the late Duke's family the unanimous expression of the committee's heartfelt sympathy, was specially passed, as well as a further resolution postponing, under all the melancholy circumstances, the holding of the proposed annual meeting, *sine die*.

The Marlborough family, on that same Monday morning, accompanied the body of the Duke, with all due pomp, down to Blenheim. There Dr Acland, the family physician, did a *post mortem* and determined the cause of death as angina pectoris. The body of John Winston, 7th Duke of Marlborough, aged sixty-one, was then laid in state in an oak coffin in the Hall. During the day, a steady stream of solemn dignitaries, respectful tenants, and curious villagers, three thousand persons in all, filed past the bier. 'The private chapel of the Palace and the opening to the crypt were also visited' and everyone went away feeling amply rewarded for their long wait in line, and pleased with themselves for having done their duty by the Duke.

The funeral service took place as meticulously planned on Tuesday, 10 July, and when everyone – no, not everyone, there was one exception – picked up *The Times* on Wednesday morning, 11 July, they were properly gratified to see a full account:

> The weather yesterday was rather fine, and long before the hour appointed for the ceremony there was a large assemblage in the park. Among the earliest to arrive were the Duke's tenantry numbering nearly 100. The Mayor and the Corporation of Woodstock assembled in the Town-hall and walked in procession therefrom in their robes to the Palace. The midday train brought down Lord Carrington, who represented the Queen, the Duke of Leinster, [and assorted Lords, etc.] . . . Punctually at 1 o'clock the coffin, covered with superb wreaths, was borne down the steps of the entrance to the north front of the palace, the tenantry lining each side of the way. The body was met at the entrance to the chapel by the Revd A. Majendie, the Rector of Woodstock, who read the funeral service throughout. After the mourners came the magistrates and many gentlemen of the county, the tenantry and Corporation of Woodstock, and others. While the company were being seated in the chapel, the choir of Woodstock parish church sang the hymn 'I heard the voice of Jesus say'. The coffin was placed over the opening to the vault in front of the monument to the 1st Duke, which stands on the north side of the chapel, a few feet from the altar steps. At the close of the ceremony the hymn 'Thy will be done' was sung by the choir and those assembled. The members of the family . . .

The members of the family, all dressed in deepest black down to the last jet button, sat around the breakfast table at Blenheim quite as usual on that Wednesday morning, 11 July. Voices were perhaps a little more subdued, but there were no impulsive hugs, no hand-clasps, no tears, not even a sniffle. Fanny decapitated her pencilled egg with one neat stroke, and picked up *The Times*:

> The members of the family, headed by the Marquess of Blandford, deposited

several beautiful wreaths and crosses upon the coffin, among them being a large cross composed of stephanotis, white lilies, roses and maidenhair fern from the Marchioness of Blandford.

From the Marchioness of Blandford! 'Goosie' had long since severed all connection with her erring husband and in a few more months they would be divorced. She was no longer a member of the Marlborough family, let alone purveyor of the funeral's most exquisite and expensive wreath. Fanny turned bright red down to the ruffled collar of her black silk gown, laid down *The Times*, finished her egg through grim lips, and said nothing.

On the morning of Friday, 13 July, the polite world picked up its *Times* and was presented with one final snippet concerning the Duke of Marlborough's last rites, and it was quite the juiciest one of all, not only in content, but because it was such an unexpected, bonus morsel:

> We are requested by the family of the late Duke of Marlborough to state that the floral cross which was placed on the Duke's coffin after the funeral service by the present Duke was sent by his mother, the Duchess of Marlborough, and placed there by him at her express wish, and not on behalf of the Marchioness of Blandford.

Thus, in the midsummer of 1883, Blenheim gathered in another Duke to its grim harvest under the Chapel floor. In due time, the Chapel, at Fanny's command, was adorned with a large white marble standing figure, sculpted by Sir Joseph Boehm, of John Winston, 7th Duke of Marlborough, in his Garter robes. He stands very straight-backed and plain, to the right of the 1st Duke's baroque form, sculpted by Rysbrack in wild, curvacious excess. Beneath the 7th Duke's well-shod feet is a dark grey rectangular marble plaque bearing words carefully chosen by Fanny and inscribed thereon in gold:

> He filled the high office of State of Lord Steward of the Royal Household in 1866, Lord President of the Council in 1867, Lord Lieutenant of Ireland 1876–80. Eminent for his public and private virtues, he won in every department of life respect and esteem. The constitutional and loyal servant of the crown, he was a true son of the Church of England ever anxious to broaden and deepen her foundations in the hearts of the people. The responsibilities which his wide estates devolved upon him did but illustrate a devotion to local duties, a wisdom, courtesy and liberality, which secured him the abiding regard of his neighbours and tenants. An appalling sudden death, for which few can have been better prepared, inflicted an irreparable loss on his sons and daughters and bequeathed a sorrow, to end only with life itself, to his mourning, loving, and devoted wife, Frances Anne, Duchess of Marlborough, by whom this monument has been erected, in fond remembrance of forty years of happy wedlock.

No one but Fanny mourned the Duke's passing, because no one but Fanny had loved him. His daughters had merely feared him, and always obeyed. His son Blandford had feared, then rebelled in his own rakish, self-indulgent way. His son Randolph had feared, then backed away. Raised by a father who never gave a physical sign of affection, Randolph treated his son in exactly the same way. Winston would long remember the moment when once, but only once, his father had patted his knee.

If, during his twenty-six-year reign at Blenheim, the Duke's children didn't love him, what about the palace? What imprint did the 7th Duke of Marlborough leave upon Blenheim's soul? Who knows? Under all that starch and plush and tufting it is impossible to detect any firm outline – or even to know if, in fact, Blenheim Palace still *had* a soul.

Its 7th Duke had come and gone, but the complicated paraphernalia of doilies and divisions and distinctions which he had accentuated and accelerated at Blenheim, not so much to make life comfortable as to make it pretentious and punctilious, would continue without him, heading into the future with a mind and momentum of its own, like a runaway engine on a downward slope.

On the morning of Saturday, 14 July 1883, at exactly 6 a.m., the first head lifted from its pillow in Blenheim's Housemaid Heights. The housemaids rose and dressed, pinned up their hair and flew down the stairs. The scullery-maid lit the huge kitchen range; the still-room maid lit the fire in the still-room and set out the morning tea-trays. The under-housemaid cleaned the grates; the upper-housemaid dusted the bell-jars of plump, waxed fruit and the rose-wreathed *Keepsakes*. The horizontal belt of powdering-footmen-at-their-basins and the vertical belt of mounting-and-descending-housemaids-on-the-backstairs began to move. The mid-summer sun rose with slow dignity above the eastern wing and kitchen court, casting down its golden shafts upon the 1st Duke's trumpeting eastern gate, the 4th Duke's orangery theatre and the 7th Duke's blackened, empty Titian gallery. Inside Blenheim Palace, transmogrified over the years from showy castle to house of art to philistine workplace, its complex machinery of living started up for almost the sixty-thousandth time, and no one, least of all its long line of future Dukes, would be able to bring it to a full stop.

4
DISSIPATION

But when the master's buried, mice can play,
And maybe the great-grandson of that house,
For all its bronze and marble, 's but a mouse.

W.B. Yeats, 'Ancestral Houses'

DUSK HAD CLOSED IN EARLY ON MONDAY, 22 NOVEMBER 1896, for all day heavy clouds had hovered over Minerva and her two chained captives atop Blenheim's north portico. Below these dark shapes, the palace's many windows blazed with light – not the golden nimbus of candles or the blue-white hiss of gas, but the merciless glare of electric light which exposed every imperfection. Strong shafts were hitting the bases of the giant pillars, revealing the scabrous condition of their stone.

Inside the Great Hall, an elaborate banquet in honour of Edward, Prince of Wales, was in progress. Bacchus, God of Wine, his white marble thighs gleaming, leered lasciviously at the revellers from one corner of the Hall; near by loomed a Louis XIV battle drum and a cluster of battle standards brought triumphantly to Blenheim by John, 1st Duke of Marlborough. The gaudy standards which had once reeked of blood and gunpowder were faded, and smelled faintly of pot-pourri. They had been most artistically arranged in Chinese porcelain vases by Blenheim's two resident 'decorators' who, early each morning, filled all the ground-floor rooms with flowers. The battles which had engendered Blenheim and plagued its growth were almost two hundred years behind it. Now a different kind of battle was being waged by every one of the thirty aristocrats arranged around the banquet table: an unremitting life-long struggle against the dragon called Boredom. They fought valiantly, frantically, to keep that cold, slimy weight at bay, using two main weapons: Play and Parade.

Their dedicated leader, Prince Edward, seated half-way down the table was, as always, giving his main attention to the food, but from time to time he raised his pale-blue codfish eyes to stare glumly at the solid-silver 1st Duke of Marlborough who, directly in front of him, was still writing his interminable Blenheim dispatch to Sarah. How slim and young and hopeful the Prince had been on that November day thirty-seven years before when he'd dined at Blenheim as an Oxford undergraduate and seen himself reflected in the Duke's shining expanse! Who could have imagined that Mama would go on reigning year after year – next year would mark her sixtieth on the throne – while her eldest son waited and waited to become King, and Queen Victoria had fiercely, jealously, denied him even the tiniest participation in the mighty task of ruling an Empire comprising four hundred million souls and one-quarter of the world's land surface?

He'd done his best, with eating and buttoning and unbuttoning, hunting and horse-racing and shooting, to keep himself busy and amused. At his Norfolk country seat, Sandringham, a red-brick mansion, more neo than Tudor, which resembled a large railway-station (a most fitting shape for one who waits) the Prince and his friends held tricycle races in the ballroom, played bowls in the library and tobogganed down the stairs on large silver trays. The Prince loved practical jokes: brandy poured over a guest's head, a dead bird slipped into his bed – His Royal Highness was wonderfully ingenious. When the Duke and Duchess of Marlborough had come to Sandringham at the beginning of November, the Prince had angled for an invitation to shoot at Blenheim. Now here he was for the next six days with twenty-seven dear friends and relations, including his wife of thirty-three years, Princess Alexandra, and his daughters Victoria and Maud, the latter with her new husband, Prince George of Denmark.

All twenty-eight guests had come down to Blenheim that very afternoon by special train, its long baggage-car piled high with trunks. In each lady's trunk, carefully folded by her maid between layers of tissue, with more tissue stuffed into every sleeve, were six velvet breakfast outfits, six tweed or serge luncheon suits, six silk tea-gowns (the ladies called them 'teagies'), six satin dinner gowns and six everything elses to match. The ladies had to bring twenty-four costumes because it was considered very bad form – and boring – to appear in the same one twice.

It was the Prince's trunk, however, which was by far the largest, for he loved dressing up and often changed his clothes twelve times a day. He always travelled with two valets while another two stayed behind at London's Marlborough House, where the Prince had lived since his marriage, to brush and care for his fifty military uniforms and hundreds of suits. To Sarah's original no-nonsense design for Marlborough House, the Prince had added wall-to-wall pitch-pine cupboards in his enormous dressing-room, and then done up the private rooms facing the garden in nut brown and rose with plenty of plump pouffes and potted palms. There he entertained 'the Marlborough House Set', a motley group of actresses, opera singers, playboy peers and Jewish millionaires, including Sir Ernest Cassel, son of a Cologne money-lender, who had lined his Park Lane mansion with 800 tons of white Carrara marble and whose friends always called the hall, ignoring its lapis lazuli pillars, 'the Giant's Lavatory'. The 9th Duke of Marlborough had seen to it that none of the Prince's Jewish cronies came to Blenheim; only old money and very blue blood now sat round the table and sipped its soup from the correct side of the bowl.

There were two soups to choose from: one hot, one cold. Prince Edward ate both, with frequent napkin-dabs at his drooping moustache and the neatly trimmed pepper-and-salt beard which hid his receding chin. As he ate, the tunic of his splendid military uniform grew tighter across his forty-eight-inch chest and waist, its fine scarlet cloth and gold braid concealing layers of fat and a diseased liver. The fifty-five-year-old Prince, only five feet six inches tall, was beginning to resemble a battle drum in shape, in spite of annual dieting cures at Homburg, a German Spa where English duchesses were upended, with shrieks and flying underwear, for wheel-barrow races. 'Tum-Tum' the English press called their Prince, or 'Spuds', for his head, with outsize nose and ears, did look rather like a potato ready for the pot. His prestige with press and public had never stood higher, for earlier in the year he'd won the Derby with a horse appropriately named after a mouth-watering fruit: Persimmon. The Prince had celebrated with a huge meal at the Jockey Club and after the sweet had taken Georgiana, Countess of Dudley, to bed. It was only two years after his 1859 Blenheim banquet that the Prince had first helped himself to a pretty woman: actress Nellie Clifden had been smuggled into his tent at Curragh military camp. Queen Victoria always claimed that what really killed dear Albert was not typhoid inexpertly treated but 'that dreadful business at Curragh'. The Prince moved on to Lily Langtry and Sarah Bernhardt, and when a straight diet of actresses began to pall, switched to well-born ladies whom he seduced on their sofas between luncheon and afternoon tea, while their husbands turned a blind eye and his own very beautiful wife, one of her two deaf ears. The Prince, at the moment, was cooling towards 'darling Daisy' Brooke, afterwards Countess of Warwick, and in another two years Alice Keppel would gently guide him into a quiet corner where a rubber of bridge was enough to satisfy him. Prince Edward had finished his soups, and turned his attention to the fish courses, one hot, one cold, while a royal footman stood behind his chair and Herr Gottlieb's Viennese Band began another popular tune from the gallery behind him, and the Duchess of Marlborough, as pretty as a Japanese doll, with her slightly slanted, sad brown eyes, masses of dark hair and funny little turned-up nose, poured a thin trickle of gossip into his large, fleshy ear.

Consuelo, Duchess of Marlborough, was finding it heavy-going keeping the Prince amused, for she knew he liked only scandal and sport whereas her own interests were more intellectual. Her slender hands twisted in her lap; she was only nineteen and had been Duchess for a year. The prospect of all the hard work ahead of her being hostess to the Prince for six interminable days and mistress of Blenheim for goodness knows how many interminable years made her small head on its very long white neck droop like a lily. This was Consuelo's first big house-party and she felt extremely nervous, and exhausted before it had barely begun. She'd been rushing about the palace for days, ordering ginger biscuits from Biarritz and bath salts from Penhaligon's and so many other things which the Prince had to have, and getting the Duke's approval of her twenty-four costumes and trying to sort out who should sleep in easy proximity to whom and ... Consuelo was feeling slightly dizzy, and the diamond clasp on the nineteen-row pearl dog-collar which Sunny, 9th Duke of Marlborough, had bought her on their honeymoon – fit symbol for a young wife to be brought instantly to heel – was, as always, rasping her neck. And she could feel her page-boy's hot breath on her bare back, just below the dog-collar.

Mike, as the servants had named him, was the black Mohammedan boy whom Sunny had insisted they bring back with them from Egypt, one of their honeymoon treasures. From ten in the morning till seven at night, Mike sat in a hooded leather chair in the Hall, ready to open doors and run messages; then he stood behind the Duchess's chair at dinner, doing nothing, but looking splendid in yellow satin turban, tunic, tasselled sash and skirt. The Duke of Marlborough saw only the yellow satin and approved; the Duchess saw the violence beneath and feared it. Mike's only English was a volley of swear-words fired off frequently in the servants' hall; he'd smashed a jug of beer over the head of Gerald Horne, the fourteen-year-old who ran Blenheim's thirty-seven-line switchboard, and pulled a knife on an old lady in Woodstock who sold toys. And Mike was growing taller and stronger every day.

The six Blenheim footmen who were now removing the fish-bones looked as magnificent as Mike in maroon coats, silver-braided waistcoats, maroon plush breeches, flesh-coloured stockings and silver-buckled patent shoes. ('They were devils, those footmen,' according to young Gerald Horne. One night they broke down the locked door of the bedroom he shared with Mike, dragged the two boys roughly from their beds, blackened Gerald's face, and whitened Mike's.) Consuelo watched them bringing in the meat course, their white gloves spotless, their powdered heads held high. She had spent hours with the French chef who presided over a staff of four in the kitchen, deciding on the banquet's eight courses. The Prince was helping himself so very liberally to beef; should she perhaps tell him that after the sorbet, the game course would be his favourite dish: pheasant stuffed with woodcock, the woodcock stuffed with truffles, and the whole smothered in a rich sauce? Since September, Blenheim's gamekeepers had

---

OPPOSITE: Consuelo, Duchess of Marlborough

kept the Duke's table supplied with grouse, partridge, pheasant, duck, woodcock and snipe; during the summer, the Duke had upheld the honour of the game course by importing, at great expense, quails hatched in Egypt and ortolans from France.

Consuelo toyed with her *boeuf médaillon*. She was seated in the middle of the table with her husband across from her, for they had adopted the English Royals' custom of sitting thus rather than at the table's ends. Prince Edward's bulk loomed on her right, Prince George's on her left and the silver 1st Duke's directly in front. Consuelo thought the statue of the latter looked grotesque on the table, far too big she'd told Sunny, quite out of scale with the delicate arrangements of orchids, but Sunny had replied petulantly that the Great Hero *always* stood as centrepiece for important Blenheim dinners. The 1st Duke, Consuelo now realized, had one redeeming virtue: he completely hid Sunny from her view.

The Duchess of Marlborough was not and never had been in love with her husband, nor he with her (as he took pains to tell her less than a month after their marriage, confessing that he loved another). Consuelo had married a ducal house; the Duke had married the fortune needed to prop up that house in the days of its decrepitude. Dollars for dukedoms: the pattern of the times had been set by Consuelo's godmother and namesake, a wealthy American who had snared the Duke of Manchester. The younger Consuelo's fortune had been founded by great-grandfather Cornelius Vanderbilt, whose ancestors had come from Holland to New York in 1650, and by the time her father, William Kissam Vanderbilt, inherited, the family coffers held $65m. Consuelo's mother, Alva, dipped into them freely to furnish the mansions which it became her consuming passion to build. Born in March, 1877, Consuelo grew up in a huge white-stone Fifth Avenue one whose dining-room boasted a stained-glass window depicting England's kings and attendant knights, and at Marble House, Newport, Rhode Island, whose symmetrical pillared façade resembled a smaller Blenheim. There Consuelo came out at a sumptuous ball where fake humming-birds hovered above the real flowers. She was deeply in love with a young attorney called Winthrop Rutherford, but her mother, frantic to recover Society's approval, which she had lost by divorcing 'Willie K.' for adultery, was angling for bigger fish than Winthrop – bigger, that is, in all the senses that counted. Alva Vanderbilt had set her heart on hooking for Consuelo the undersized but over-pedigreed 9th Duke of Marlborough, master of the grandest mansion in Britain. Consuelo had first been pushed into the Duke's proximity at a London dinner-party where she had noted his unhappy little face and well-shaped hands, of which he seemed 'inordinately proud'. He, in turn, noted her well-heeled state, for the Vanderbilt fortune had grown to $200m, and invited her and her mother down to Blenheim for a spring weekend in 1895. On a Sunday tour of the estate, Consuelo saw how village women curtsied and men touched their caps to the little Duke sitting so erect beside her in the shabby carriage. In September, the Duke came to Newport, where Consuelo had been kept a prisoner by her mother all summer, not allowed to see or communicate with Winthrop. One sultry evening, in the Gothic Room, the Duke proposed, while visions of beloved Blenheim's three acres of decaying roofs danced in his head. Consuelo said an inaudible 'yes' and burst into tears. Next morning, only Alva Vanderbilt was wreathed in smiles; the Duke merely sent off a telegram to his estate agent, Mr Angus: 'Have the lake dredged.' On the grey morning of 6 November 1895, Consuelo 'like an automaton', as she described it, climbed into her wedding-dress of Brussels lace over white satin with long court train. A bouquet of orchids from Blenheim's hothouse was slated to arrive, but didn't – the first of many disappointments Blenheim would hand her. Consuelo was half an hour late at the altar of St Thomas's Fifth Avenue church because it had taken that long to sponge her eyes, swollen from hours of crying. Walter Damrosch led a sixty-piece orchestra in 'O Perfect Love' while Consuelo sniffled and Sunny gazed stonily ahead with his pale-blue protruding eyes, and Alva Vanderbilt raised hers thankfully heavenwards and floated up to a Higher Social Sphere than anything America could offer. Consuelo's father settled $2,500,000 worth of railway stock on Sunny, which would bring him in an assured annual income of $100,000, and then Willie K. added another $100,000 per annum for good measure.

Since Blenheim was in a chaotic condition, already undergoing extensive repairs and refurbishing, the newly-weds took an extended honeymoon in France, Spain, Italy and Egypt, where Sunny spent his days in antique shops and galleries buying furniture and paintings and tapestries for Blenheim, and his nights impressing on his bride that she was 'only a link in the unbroken chain of succeeding generations of Marlboroughs'. On their return to England, Sunny ordered a crimson state coach whose coachman would wear a two-tiered scarlet cape, and a smart phaeton with a platform behind for the groom to stand on. Sunny planned to drive the phaeton himself dressed in grey swallow-tailed coat, grey top hat and white gardenia buttonhole. Several days after their return, in March, 1896, Sunny took Consuelo to 50 Grosvenor Square to meet his formidable grandmother, Dowager Duchess Fanny, widow of the 7th Duke. Crinolined in black, with a lace cap on her head and an ear-trumpet in her hand, Fanny 'bestowed a welcoming kiss' on Consuelo, as she recorded, 'in the manner of a deposed sovereign greeting her successor'. She hoped to see

Consuelo, Duchess of Marlborough arriving at Blenheim after her marriage

dear Blenheim, she informed Consuelo, fixing her popping grey eyes on her, restored to its former glory. 'Your first duty,' she continued, 'is to have a child and it must be a son, because it would be intolerable to have that little upstart Winston become Duke. Are you in the family way?'

It was shortly after this crisp interview that the 9th Duke finally took his bride home to Blenheim, insisting that she wear her splendid sable coat. They went by train to Oxford, and by the 'Fair Rosamond' to Woodstock, where the Mayor in scarlet robes assured the young Duchess that 'Woodstock had a Mayor before America was discovered', after which the Marlboroughs were drawn up to the palace with loyal tenants between the shafts of the carriage, just as Randolph and Jennie had been twenty-two years before. Like Jennie, Consuelo stared in awe at the porter at the eastern gate, with his long staff, silver-buttoned black coat, buff breeches and cockaded top hat. Blenheim's eighty servants (forty inside ones and forty outside) were ranged on the portico steps, along with a vast crowd of curious villagers. Too many speeches and presentations of bouquets followed. Consuelo's sable coat grew heavier on her narrow shoulders, her big hat was buffeted by strong winds, and at her back she could feel the oppressive presence of the huge, scaly house which was claiming her as victim as surely as if she had been stretched out in sacrifice on its highest cold marble step.

She had been caught, since that day eight months ago, in the relentless grip of Blenheim's conventions, and now here she was with five Royals to worry about. She had put the Prince in the scarlet stateroom just west of the Saloon, which Sunny had refurnished for the occasion with Boulle cabinets and gilded French chairs, and the rest of the Royals in the eastern wing where she and Sunny usually slept. Consuelo picked at her twice-stuffed pheasant, while the Prince muttered 'Capital! Capital!' between large mouthfuls. He would be beside her for another thirteen meals and already she was scraping the bottom of her tin of conversational gambits. Across from her, Princess Alexandra was chattering volubly to the hidden figure of Sunny. There was something so natural and spontaneous and *girlish* – yes, girlish was the right word – about Alexandra, who was looking particularly young and lovely this evening with pearls and diamonds cascading to her slim waist, brown hair piled high behind her diamond tiara, her oval face slightly flushed as she talked to the Duke.

She was telling him how she'd kept tripping over the white bearskin rugs strewn on the floor of Consuelo's bedroom when she was dressing for dinner. And when it came time for bed, she would have to ask a Blenheim carpenter – the Princess was laughing merrily – to quickly knock together a ladder. Could he manage that while her maid brushed her hair? Because without a ladder she would never be able to get into the Duchess's bed on its high dais – *far* too elevated!

The 9th Duke of Marlborough frowned and looked uncomfortable. Dais and bearskins had been his idea; he castigated himself severely; he who prided himself on being the perfect host, ever thoughtful for his guests' comfort, had forgotten Alexandra's damaged knee, the legacy from a bout of rheumatic fever. Outdoors she always walked with a steel umbrella in lieu of a cane. His face puckering, Sunny began a long apology, quite unnecessary, for Alexandra clearly regarded the bedroom incident as 'such fun!', nothing more. It was the catchword of the time. *It Was Such Fun* the society matron Mrs Hwfa Williams would call her memoirs. Only the 9th Duke of Marlborough, living in the gay nineties, found no fun anywhere, not a glimmer. Sunny: was ever a nickname so unsuited? It derived not from his disposition but from his title of Earl of Sunderland, and indeed it was his noble position that formed the main plinth of the

9th Duke's personality. He was, before all else, Charles Richard John Spencer-Churchill, 9th Duke of Marlborough and Master of Blenheim. He didn't regard his palace as grandfather John Winston, 7th Duke had, as a carapace of authority, nor as George, 4th Duke had viewed it, as a mistress to be decked in splendid raiment. For Charles, 9th Duke, Blenheim was icon and cross, inner shrine and holiest crusade. Every breath and act was drawn and done for Blenheim. He wore the palace like a religious medal next his heart.

Born on 13 November 1871, Sunny hugged to himself, like a hair-shirt, a large fund of hard-luck stories, most of them concerning his boyhood. Sunny had been permanently bruised when the 8th Duke, his father, fittingly known as the Wicked Duke, had divorced his wife, fittingly known as 'Goosie', and run off with Joe Aylesford's wife, Edith. Sunny was put in his father's 'care', if one could call it that, and 'entirely crushed', as Sunny put it, for his father 'never spoke a kind word to me'. Sunny retreated into his shell and crept through Blenheim's empty spaces trying his best to keep out of his father's way.

His frail shoulders drooped as Sunny listened to Alexandra and ate, with no relish at all, the gay nineties' favourite dessert: peach melba, its peaches artificially brought to ripeness in a hothouse, enfolded in rich cream and richer sauce, all of it pale and insipid in colour on the plate. It was Sunny's father who had indirectly supplied the peaches, and all the other hothouse fruits piled in profusion in silver-gilt epergnes.

The 8th Duke had converted the former Titian gallery – where thirty-five years before the 'Loves of the Gods' had flamed so high and crumbled into black ash – into an elaborate hothouse for fruit and his special passion, orchids. The 8th Duke, to be sure, had turned all of Blenheim into a sensually gratifying hothouse. John Winston's and Fanny's eldest son had had quite enough of grim-lipped rectitude; once Blenheim was his, in 1883, and his father's all-pervading presence reduced to one mute marble form on the chapel wall, the 8th Duke of Marlborough felt free to indulge himself. He turned Blenheim's top floor into a laboratory for experiments in chemistry, electricity and metallurgy. Strange acrid smells and muffled explosions filled Blenheim with a new unease. He installed in the ancient palace the first private telephone system in the country, which he had invented quite independently of Alexander Graham Bell. Wires lay along all the corridors, entangling the housemaids' feet. 'He's a sorcerer, that one,' they agreed as they let down their hair in Housemaids Heights; '*and a seducer!*' the prettiest one would add. By 1886, the Duke was running out of funds and sold at auction 227 of Blenheim's best paintings, including the Rubens, Rembrandt and Van Dyck masterpieces which the 1st Duke

'Sunny', 9th Duke of Marlborough

had hung so proudly on the walls of his hard-earned home. They brought the 8th Duke £350,000; he bought rarer orchids, more laboratory equipment and installed his mistress, Lady Colin Campbell, in a Venetian palazzo. By 1888, the Duke's purse was empty again, so he headed for America to find a rich wife. 'Where the great Marlborough conquered campaigns,' remarked one New York newspaper, 'the little Marlborough conquers courtesans,' and another, noting his thirty-five pieces of luggage, commented: 'Everything His Grace brought with him was clean, except his reputation.' Jennie's father, Leonard Jerome, introduced him to a widow whose name rhymed with million: Lilian Hammersley. She weighed 160 lb and sported a definite moustache but she was so rich – with a fortune of $5m – that she fed her spaniels on chicken fricassée and macaroons. The Duke ignored the beard on this rare Lily and promptly made her Duchess of Marlborough. Back at Blenheim, Lily in turn ignored the nude portrait of Lady Colin Campbell which hung in her husband's bedroom, and opened her purse: £40,000 was spent on Blenheim's lead roof, and electricity and central heating were installed throughout the palace, even in stables and dairy. When brother Randolph came to visit he acknowledged these 'great improvements' but thought the drawing-rooms done up in very vulgar taste, and ended a letter to his mother, the formidable Fanny: 'I don't think the Duchess Lily looking at all well in health, and the moustache and beard are becoming serious.' It was Lily's idea to remove Rysbrack's Queen Anne from the north end of the Long Library where Sarah had placed her, and install a Grand Willis pipe organ instead. Queen Anne stared disapprovingly from her new spot against the south wall while such popular singers of the day as Fanny Ronalds and Plunket Greene sang 'The Lost Chord' to the organ's mighty swell.

On 9 November 1892, the forty-eight-year-old Duke dropped dead from a heart attack in his top-floor laboratory 'with a terrible expression on his face', according to the housekeeper. His hirsute widow immediately ripped Lady Colin Campbell off his boudoir wall, and tore up all photos of her, posting the fragments to Her Ladyship in Venice. In his will, the Duke left Lady Campbell £20,000 'as proof of my friendship and esteem', and asked to be buried anywhere except at Blenheim: 'I dislike particularly the exclusiveness of family pride and I wish not to be buried in the family vault in Blenheim Chapel.' He was the first Churchill, but not the last, to be buried in nearby Bladon churchyard.

So it was that four days before his twenty-first birthday, Sunny took up his true calling: Master of Blenheim. The little Duke stopped creeping about the palace; he rapped out orders to the servants and wore the house like a pair of elevated shoes or tall top-hat, to enhance his self-image. He took a solemn vow: he would repair the 5th, 6th, 7th and 8th Dukes' plunder, for all of them had ripped precious paintings and books from Blenheim's walls and left her ugly and ravaged. He would do more: he would gild not only house and setting, but the very myth itself; he would vindicate the ways of Blenheim to man. Dukes and their land-owning way of life were becoming, more and more, an anachronism. Late-nineteenth-century Britain espoused an industrial and urban, rather than agricultural and rural way of life. Its population – which had doubled during Queen Victoria's reign – had deserted the countryside and flocked into the cities to earn its living manufacturing raw materials and exporting the finished products round the Empire (external trade had increased by 600 per cent since 1837). The great landowners were hit hard, not only by loss of real power and staffing problems, but by steadily rising rates of income tax and by death duties, which would be imposed in 1894 and increased in 1909 and 1919.

Sunny dug in his heels and became a reactionary with a hatred of any innovation whatsoever, and a fanatic belief in all the feudal traditions associated with the Marlboroughs and their palace. The 9th Duke worshipped its material objects, not as the 1st Duke, because they were costly, nor as the 4th Duke, because they were beautiful, nor as the 7th Duke, because they were imposing, but simply because they had been around for a long time. Sunny didn't make political or aesthetic or moral choices that suited his personal needs; he made those that suited Blenheim, because he *was* Blenheim, as no earlier Duke had been. 'Do you know,' the 9th Duke once complained to a fellow peer, 'that I have been criticized for insisting on my guests wearing white ties at Blenheim, and also for signing myself "Marlborough" even to my dearest friends, who in conversation would call me "Sunny"? I am afraid they do not understand that people in certain positions have to maintain a certain dignity.' The 9th Duke of Marlborough's ancestral pride was the only really large thing about him but it was quite as gargantuan as the house that engendered it. The Earl of Carnarvon called him 'a pompous little man' and recalls in his memoirs sitting at breakfast on Boxing Day before a Blenheim shoot. The butler informed the Duke that the head keeper sent his respects but was too ill to supervise the shoot. 'Sunny listened in chilly silence. "My compliments to my head keeper; will you please inform him that the lower orders are *never* ill,"' replied Blenheim's master as he decapitated his two brown eggs. (A little girl from one of his farms at Folly Bridge, two miles away, carried the new-laid eggs to Blenheim each morning in a basket.)

Tomorrow, decided Sunny, as he listened to Princess Alexandra and pushed his peach melba round his plate, he would invite her and the Prince into his holy of holies, the Grand Cabinet, and show them the diamond-hilted sword given to the 1st Duke by Emperor Leopold (and used so cavalierly in the 1719 theatricals) and the scrap of paper on which John Churchill had written his Blenheim dispatch, for which Sunny had designed a special glass case. (George, 4th Duke, living at a time when Blenheim was more house than hallowed institution, had unaccountably lost the Blenheim dispatch; miraculously it turned up some years later on the stall of an Oxford second-hand book dealer.)

The footmen were bringing in the hot savoury now, and the butler followed with the port. Since Consuelo's infusion of dollars, Sunny had engaged two wine specialists from London to come to Blenheim for a week at a time and refill one cellar with the finest French wines and the other with champagne (which one could buy for 48s. a dozen bottles.) The dinner was proceeding smoothly and Prince Edward looked pink and pleased. Sunny came very close to a tiny secret smile as he looked down the length of the orchid-strewn table, where ladies in sweet-pea colours alternated with gentlemen in white ties, tails and all their decorations, their short hair side-parted, as Sunny's was, and gleaming with macassar oil. The ladies' hair was puffed up to resemble large bowls, but underneath these gleaming basins were hideous pads called 'rats'. As the savoury gave place to fruit, the ladies were ever fearful that a bit of pad might somehow show itself among the diamonds and the gloss. Soft white hands were frequently raised to make sure no rat peeked through, and the conversation was never so mentally taxing that soft white hands forgot to feel. There was much talk of money and amorous affairs. 'Did you hear about Celia's gaffe? She invited Violet *and* Verena to her house-party. Well, you can imagine ... Are you going to Chips's costume ball next week? It's sure to be deevie [divine]...' Eyes met, most of them in a glassy, unseeing, fish-like way, but a few with the first sparks of sexual interest already, on this first night, beginning to smoulder.

Jennie Churchill's brown eyes were sparkling as they always did when she told a *risqué* story. Jennie was still beautiful but she had put on weight, and the past decade had been a troubled time in her life. It was in 1886 that Randolph suddenly grew cold and left her bed. Jennie had appealed to her mother-in-law, Fanny, for advice on how to win Randolph back. 'If you wish to regain your influence over him and make him fonder of you,' wrote Fanny, 'you must sacrifice yourself and lead a different life. You *must* feel now that life cannot be all pleasure and oh, dearest Jennie, before it is too late I do pray you to lay my advice to heart and give up that fast lot you live with, racing, flirting and gossiping.' In December of that year, Randolph rashly, in a moment of rage and pique, threw his promising political career to the winds by resigning as Chancellor of the Exchequer and Leader of the House. Underneath this son of Blenheim's suave façade – violet waistcoat, tan shoes, diamond-studded amber cigarette-holder – there had always been a smouldering violence; now it erupted more and more frequently. 'So mad and odd,' sighed Queen Victoria. By 1890, Lord Randolph's political cronies and his wife knew why his behaviour grew ever more erratic: he had syphilis which he had contracted – according to the most credible story – from a Blenheim housemaid soon after his son Winston's birth. Randolph was so ill by the time he and Jennie started on a trip round the world in June 1894, that they took along a doctor and a lead-lined coffin. A month after their return, on 24 January 1895, Randolph Spencer-Churchill, aged forty-five, died of *paralytica dementia*, the final stage of syphilis, in his mother's dignified home, with Jennie and Winston distraught beside his bed. 'The illness which has killed him,' wrote Duchess Fanny to Lord Salisbury two days later, 'is due to overwork and acute mental strain,' thereby drawing a plush curtain across the hard facts of Randolph's death which would stay pulled, when it came to public pronouncements, for all the Churchills. Randolph was buried near his brother, the wicked 8th Duke of Marlborough, in Bladon churchyard.

Jennie had mourned briefly, then her zest for life had bubbled up again stronger than ever. Now, at the Blenheim dinner table, as she leaned forward to help herself to a ripe peach, her breasts rounded voluptuously below the black silk of her décolleté. She had that freshly seductive glow which comes of taking a new lover; in this case, Charles Kinsky, a Hungarian count and sportsman. Jennie knew that every man round the table, with the exception of her wan little nephew Sunny, would like, if they hadn't already, to take her to bed. The novelist George Moore claimed that Jennie had enjoyed more than two hundred lovers, and some said Prince Edward was among them. For the past ten years, ever since the Prince had got over his anger at the Aylesford affair and consented to dine with the Churchills, he and Jennie had been close friends. He often lunched with her tête-à-tête at 35A Cumberland Place, her London house, which Jennie had decorated with her usual flair and flamboyance, and their frequent notes to each other were full of private jokes and saucy *double entendres* fringed with exclamation marks.

On Jennie's right sat George Nathaniel Curzon, whose pomposity came not from age – he was only thirty-seven – but from his ancestral seat, Kedleston Hall, a magnificent eighteenth-century mansion in Derbyshire designed by Robert Adam. Lord Curzon loved old houses – 'a house has to my mind a history as enthralling as that of an individual,' he would later write – and his favourite, after Kedleston, was Blenheim, to whose august stones some Oxford wag had for ever linked him with the verse:

> My name is George Nathaniel Curzon,
> I am a most superior person.
> My cheek is pink, my hair is sleek,
> I dine at Blenheim once a week.

He and Jennie were merrily recalling the time George had dined at Blenheim and, when asked to stay the night, had borrowed a nightgown of Jennie's. Like Sunny, George had been thinking of decaying, ancestral roofs when he'd married, and had chosen Mary Leiter, an American heiress whose father had made his millions from a Chicago department store. In another two years, Lord Curzon would become Viceroy of India. But beneath George Nathaniel's pink cheek and sleek hair lay a granite stubbornness and overweening pride which would, at the end of his viceroyalty, trip him up and send him crashing from his most superior heights. No one in England would take much note of his fall. The Empire, more and more, was becoming a bore and a burden.

On Jennie's left was Fanny's nephew, the Marquis of Londonderry, who owned Wynyard, a fine Durham estate blessed with coal under its greensward, and Mountstewart, a beautiful eighteenth-century house in Ireland. The Marquis's bland smile and starched shirt-front hid a bitter vindictiveness. Some years before, his wife 'Nellie', Lady Theresa Chetwynd-Talbot, daughter of the 19th Earl of Shrewsbury, having duly presented her husband with the requisite heir and one to spare, fell victim to the charms of the Honourable Harry Cust, the lady-killer of the century. A jealous rival for the Honourable Harry's attentions got hold of his and Nellie's love-letters and sent them round to the unsuspecting Londonderry. He read and rewrapped them, scribbled a note and rang for a servant. The curt note – 'henceforth we do not speak'– and the bundle of letters were deposited by the servant on Nellie's dressing-table. After that he spoke to his wife only when necessary in public and never in private. (When he lay dying thirty years later, Nellie sent a servant with a note begging to see him and the answer came back 'No'.) Further down the table, Nellie sat, pensive, popping grapes into her mouth, her haughty beautiful face balustraded by the heavy diamond tiara which she always called 'the family fender', and her rather squat figure hidden by the resplendent table. 'She had the proudest face I have ever seen,' one friend commented. Nellie had consoled herself for a dumb husband by becoming London's foremost society hostess, and her happiest moments came when she stood like a proud pillar at the head of her impressive staircase in Londonderry House, receiving her guests as they ascended slowly from below. As Lady Londonderry munched her grapes without much relish and looked across the table at her daughter, Lady Helen, frown-cracks appeared on her porcelain brow. Helen had gone through two London seasons thinking only of dogs and not at all of possible husbands. Nellie could hear her at this very moment heatedly discussing hounds with the Right Honourable Henry Chaplin, seated on her left.

Henry's Savile Row dress suit, so faultlessly cut, gave his girth a certain dignity, but the red, mottled skin above his collar belonged to one who has drunk and dined too well for far too long. Thirty-seven years before, as an undergraduate at Oxford, Henry 'the magnifico' had brought his own chef and introduced untutored Prince Edward to the pleasures of the table. Henry had inherited great wealth and a country house aptly named Blankney where he and his house guests filled their vacant days with gourmandizing. Beside him, Lady Helen abandoned hounds long enough to gaze upwards at the trumpeting stone angels sculpted so long ago by Grinling Gibbons on the arch below the musicians' gallery. 'What beautiful carving,' she remarked. Henry, still thinking of the delicious *boeuf médaillon*, replied, 'Yes, the service is always very good in this house.' He ignored Blenheim's splendours partly because he had recently had to sell Blankney to pay some of his enormous debts. The grapes on his plate tasted rather sour.

On Lady Helen's other side was Lord Chesterfield, whose father had died of typhoid twenty-five years before while attending an autumn shooting party in honour of Prince Edward at Londesborough Lodge near Scarborough. Poor Lady Londesborough had been so very sorry; Londesborough House was palatial in every respect except plumbing, and its drains had seeped – how *had* it happened? – into the drinking water. Lord Chesterfield's water goblet in the array of glasses before his plate was still full; who knew to what lengths ancient Blenheim's drains might go?

On Lord Chesterfield's other side, vivacious Ettie Grenfell was speaking in a low voice to Arthur Balfour. Ettie was married to Willie Grenfell, the future Lord Desborough, and at their country seat, Taplow Court, Maidenhead, where they had frequent house-parties, the athletic Willie punted their guests down the Thames while he told them how he had twice swum the pool at the foot of Canada's Niagara Falls and cleverly avoided the undertow. Dear Arthur, thought Ettie, as she rambled on, he was *such* a good listener. Unknown to Willie, his wife and Arthur had been lovers. 'Tell me,' Arthur was murmuring, stretching out his long legs beneath the table and leaning back in his chair, his pale blue eyes gazing upwards to where the 1st Duke of Marlborough, in blue mantle, knelt at Britannia's feet. Forty-eight-year-old Arthur was First Lord of the Treasury and his ambition would eventually raise him to Prime Minister. There was something 'mellow in outlook' and 'infinitely serene' about Arthur, according to a friend, a mellowness emanating from the ivied stones and meandering sprawl of his mother's home, Hatfield House, built in 1607, which gave him, as he himself said, 'a special quality of continuity'. Bachelor Arthur was no longer Ettie's lover; he had moved on to Hugo Charteris's wife, Mary, Lady Elcho, who had been raised in a house called 'Clouds' and who had recently written gloomily to Arthur of a self-induced abortion. Arthur was the closest thing to an intellectual at the Blenheim banquet, and he who had thought – but not too deeply – about the essence of his age perceived that 'games which may seem to the careless observer but trifles' had 'profoundly affected the social life of the period'.

Arthur kept his eye on Consuelo – surely it was time to leave the table? The emotionally frigid Louisa, Lady Gosford, who lived in Gosford Castle, a huge, forbidding Victorian mansion in Northern Ireland, sat on Arthur's right. When he had leaned towards her during the savoury, pince-nez trembling, and murmured 'tell me', she had stonily refused to fling wide the door of her secret chamber.

At long last, Consuelo rose from her chair and taking Prince Edward's arm, led her guests, closely followed by the limping Princess and the little Duke, into the Long Library. From his new vantage point beside the organ, Rysbrack's white-marble 1st Duke, commissioned long ago by Sarah, with shoulder-length ringlets and armour-clad torso, looked at the elaborate bookshelves and leather-bound books which the present Duke had recently installed.

The frivolous company sank into soft, deep armchairs as Charles William Perkins from Birmingham, regularly summoned to Blenheim to perform, began to play the Prince's favourite composer on the organ. The orgasmic crescendoes of Wagner rose slowly, slowly, towards the ceiling's two false domes, stuccoed and painted in the 1720s to look roundly tumescent, though actually flat. At midnight, the footmen brought in a cold buffet of ptarmigan and salmon with every sort of liqueur, and the guests helped themselves with renewed appetites. After that, they would have to manage with no food at all until breakfast, except, of course, for the sandwiches and mineral water placed on their bedside tables.

Breakfast was served in the dining-room at 9.30 next morning, with the ladies trailing over-trimmed velvet gowns across the Aubusson and the

---

OPPOSITE: The Long Library, 1909

men dressed for shooting in tweed Norfolk jackets and breeches. At 10.30, the ladies settled round the fire in the green drawing-room east of the Saloon. Its furniture was all white-carved wood, with a large autographed photo of Princess Alexandra prominently displayed among the alabaster and ormolu. While the ladies gossiped and read the papers, George, 4th Duke, and his wife Caroline looked down from the golden-age refinement of Reynolds's portrait on this over-dressed group clinging feverishly to a social order they no longer quite believed in, and disguising their insecurity with flash and glitter that were more than a little vulgar, and tinged with the phosphorescence of decay.

The gentlemen, meanwhile, rushed eagerly outdoors, as they would each following morning, for the real business of the day. They had all trekked to Scotland in mid-August to shoot grouse and had hurried south on 1 September to shoot partridge and had been regularly felling pheasants since October. Awaiting the men beyond Blenheim's north front were the Duke's twenty keepers in brown leggings and breeches, green velvet coats with brass buttons and black billy-cock hats. There was no sound in the misty morning air except the cawing of a few rooks in Capability Brown's elms; on the far side of his lake, the beech woods hung like a soft, russet curtain. The smart-looking game cart, drawn by one of the Duke's twenty bay horses, began its creaking way across Vanbrugh's bridge and into the beech woods. The small army of gentlemen and keepers followed with their double-barrelled guns. The beaters, dressed in white smocks and red tam-o'-shanters so that even after an imbibing lunch no gentleman would mistake them for pheasants, fanned out in the woods, each with a long stick in his hand. Until Prince Edward came on the scene, English gentlemen had gone in for 'rough shooting' or 'walk-ups' in which they walked slowly forward with dogs ahead of them flushing birds into the air. Since Prince Edward had neither the shape nor temperament for the hard work of a 'walk-up', a new style of shooting had come into fashion, in which the gentlemen merely stood in one spot, and the beaters drove the birds towards them, beating their sticks against tree trunks and shouting at the same time. The rotund Prince stood waiting now as the beaters walked slowly towards him and the pheasants, first singly, and then thickly, began to rise. The Prince liked a cloud of pheasants to come over about the height of a tree, and then very deliberately he would select his bird – he never fired at a difficult one – and drop it dead. The pheasants flew up, up towards the blue, feathers iridescent in the sun, stopped in mid-air, jerked unnaturally, and plummeted, lifeless, into damp earth.

At exactly 1.30, the shooting stopped and all the gentlemen, feeling vastly proud of themselves and as noisily keyed-up as children at a birthday

The royal shooting party, 1896, photographed in front of High Lodge.
Consuelo, Duchess of Marlborough is seated third from left; the Duke of Marlborough
is sitting on the grass in right foreground

party, assembled at High Lodge for luncheon. The food, including the Prince's favourite, ptarmigan pie, arrived in padded baskets from Blenheim's kitchen and was re-heated on a stove. The ladies, who had climbed out of their velvets and into their tweeds, joined the gentlemen for lunch. Then everyone trailed out to the front of High Lodge where a few, but only a few, crimson threads still flamed in the brown, dying Virginia creeper, and arranged themselves self-consciously on the grass for the ritual photograph.

Promptly at 2.30 the shooting began again, with the ladies accompanying 'the guns' for a drive or two. Consuelo stood beside Sunny as a pheasant landed right at her feet, writhed and twisted like a colourful Chinese dragon, and then lay still, a thin trickle of blood running from its mouth. Consuelo felt sick and cornered. The pheasants were prisoners of Blenheim; thousands of pheasants' eggs were hatched each spring under hundreds of hens and the chicks were reared in captivity until they were large enough to be turned loose in the coverts. They were also, by that time, so heavy that they couldn't fly beyond Blenheim and their own inevitable destruction.

The Duke prided himself on being a good shot – not perhaps as good as the legendary Lord Walsingham, who, on one memorable August day in 1882, had bagged 100 grouse all by himself. Blenheim's record was set on the sunny day when the Duke and four others killed 7,500 rabbits, using three guns and two loaders each. It was quantity, not quality, which counted now in shooting; the goal was simple slaughter, and the far-reaching sound of the guns was as deafening and terrifying as warfare. The violence which had always lurked in Blenheim's battlements and spiralled smokily up from her Brussels battle tapestries was taking a new, macabre twist.

As the men trooped triumphantly towards the palace's golden windows, the sunset blazing at their backs, more than one maimed rabbit, which earlier in the day, had screamed like a tortured child as a stray bullet pierced its haunch, crept into a grassy hollow, trailing blood behind it like a very small red carpet, and lay down modestly to die, its soft, dark eyes turned, unseeing, on Blenheim's evil towers.

Within the house, Arthur Balfour, the only gentleman who had absented himself from the carnage, was scribbling a letter to his lady-love, Mary Elcho, in his own cool style:

> There is here a big party in a big house in a big park beside a big lake ... We all came down by special train – rather cross most of us – were received with illuminations, guards of honour, cheering and other follies, went through agonies about our luggage, but finally settled down placidly enough.
>
> Today the men shot and the women dawdled. As I detest both occupations equally I stayed in my room till one o'clock, and then went exploring on my bike, joining everybody at luncheon. Then, after the inevitable photograph, I again betook myself to my faithful machine, and here I am writing to you. So far you perceive the duties of society are weighing lightly upon me!
>
> Now I must go down to tea and leave this scrawl.

Five o'clock tea was served in the Saloon, furnished with plump settees covered in hand-embroidered cloth, plus palms and ferns and flowers and decorative screens, none of which effectively softened the Saloon's stark marble symmetry. The gentlemen recounted, shot by shot, what fun they'd had. They bluffed and boasted and stuffed themselves with ginger-snaps filled to overflowing with double cream from Blenheim's all-electric dairy, while the marble wainscot, its colour the exact shade of dried blood, squared off around them. Above the real marble was the fake, festooned with gilded laurel sprays and gilded fruit garlands, all of it most skilfully painted by Laguerre 177 years before, but not so skilfully that one could fail to see – if only one cared to look – that none of it was real.

And so the week's festivities ground forward. On Thursday evening, as the *Illustrated London News* reported,

> several thousands of people from Oxford and the neighbouring countryside assembled in the park to witness a great display of fireworks and a procession and cycle parade by torchlight. After dinner, the royal and other distinguished members of the house-party emerged to the grand entrance of the Palace to watch the firework display, and received a very hearty greeting from the assembled crowd. Some 800 more subsequently took part in a torchlight procession, which was rendered strikingly *bizarre* in its effects by the lights of different hue which at intervals lit up the scene.

Bizarre: it was perhaps the best word to describe that week of frolic. By Thursday evening, the very-late-night entertainment was also flaming high. A country house was the locale of choice for the best game of all. It had begun on Monday afternoon as soon as all the guests had ascertained their bedroom locations. Before their arrival, the Blenheim housekeeper had inserted their names into little slotted brass plaques on every bedroom door. Consuelo had given her the clever master plan for, like the other guests, the Duchess knew the rules, formulated by their racy leader, the Prince, who – with that small part of his brain which still worried about what Mama would say – saw to their strict propriety. No married couple were given a single bedroom to share, nor were any lady and gentleman already known to be lovers given connecting bedrooms. On the other hand, Consuelo had to see that lovers weren't *too* far apart – country-house corridors, even centrally heated Blenheim's, could introduce an unwelcome chill. Preliminaries had been laid downstairs in daylight, and rule number one was that no gentleman stalked a lady until she'd been married for at least ten years; she needed a running start in order to fill her nursery with legitimate offspring, but no one cared who sired the tail end of a family. Having made his choice, the gentleman had fired off some incendiary glances over Monday tea and dinner (but with no touching, for touching in public was taboo). Walks in the shrubbery and whispered exchanges in the Long Library as Wagner swelled on the organ took up much of Tuesday and Wednesday. On Thursday evening came the last clinching whisper as the gentleman bid his chosen lady good-night; then they both mounted, with covert smiles, to their separate beds.

So it was that on the night of Thursday, 25 November 1896, ladies lay in their Blenheim beds in their most fetching nightgowns, watching fireplace flames leap on their bedroom ceilings, and listening for a creak in ancient floorboards, as slippered male feet made their way purposefully along them. Was there, the ladies asked themselves, curling their toes and fanning out their long hair on embroidered pillows, was there any sound in the whole deevie world as exciting as that first oh-so-close creak?

All night long, as Blenheim stood foursquare and forbidding in its blackness, there were soft slidings and shufflings, tip-toeings and tappings, and quick flarings of matches held in trembling male hands long enough to illuminate a name slotted into a brass plaque. Then came bed-spring squeakings and restrained gruntings and little bird-like cries, and in more than one bedroom John Winston in sober side-whiskers and Fanny in sacrosanct crinoline exuded moral wrath from silver frames. Finally, a solemn warning bell from downstairs announced that it was half-an-hour till breakfast, at which time everyone scurried back to their original places on the Blenheim-board before housemaids came to draw the curtains on a brighter day.

Blenheim below stairs also spent its nights in frolic, but with less punctilio. Servants now, their masters all agreed, were a most inferior breed; the brightest and best of their class had joined the mass exodus from the country of artisans and agricultural workers and gone to work in city factories for higher pay. The Blenheim menservants played cards for high stakes and tormented the boy servants with rough practical jokes. They drank more than earlier generations of servants, and danced more and fornicated more in the housemaid's broom cupboard. The musk of self-indulgence which had first entered Blenheim in the 1790s, in the 4th Duke's time, was all-pervasive now, for by the 1890s, Blenheim's function had changed yet again.

John, 1st Duke, had viewed Blenheim Castle as propaganda piece, proclaiming power and privilege to the world; George, 4th Duke, had seen Blenheim-house as arbiter of aesthetic taste. John Winston, 7th Duke, had turned the palace into a moral temple preaching to the nation. But since then, the seats of social and economic power had permanently shifted from country to city. Sunny, 9th Duke, ran Blenheim as the last amusement park in a world more and more exclusively geared to commerce. Blenheim was a luxurious private club far removed from the hectic bustle of ordinary living.

It was on 1 November 1896, less than a month before Blenheim's shooting party convened, that laws were passed permitting motor cars to be driven along public highways; their legal speed limit was raised from four to fourteen miles per hour, and a man was no longer required to walk ahead, warning pedestrians and cyclists of the monster's approach. England's aristocrats began to dash about the country as they never had been able to before; their country houses, more and more as time passed, became recreational retreats where they rested and refuelled. Blenheim's 1896 frolic also coincided with the creation of *Country Life* magazine by a romantic called Edward Hudson. Its glossy pages ushered in the first wave of nostalgia for country living, to be reinforced soon by such novelists as John Galsworthy and H. G. Wells. Edward Hudson perceived, as they did, that the English country house was doomed and dying, that it was already more historical product than pivot, more husk than hub. In 1899 and in 1909, four issues of *Country Life*, a total of thirty-two pages, waxed sentimental on the glories of Blenheim. 'If the question were asked, "Which is the greatest of English country seats?",' wrote the anonymous author of the 1899 article, 'the answer "Blenheim" would leap to the lips. Chatsworth, Welbeck and Belvoir among ducal houses might arise in the mind, but Blenheim would claim precedence, alike by its famous origin, its stately character, and the greatness of its vast domain.' Its 9th Duke and Master also began to enhance Blenheim's myths in print. In 1900, 'Blenheim and its Memories' appeared in A. H. Malan's *Famous Homes of Great Britain and Their Stories*, in which the 9th Duke of Marlborough retells, and retouches, the story of Blenheim's building by his revered ancestor, John Churchill.

If, during the 1896 shooting party, it was the 9th Duke who polished Blenheim's prestige with plenty of parade, it was the Duchess who had to stage-manage it all. 'On Friday I awoke with a sense of exultation that the last day of what had seemed an interminable week had finally dawned,' she would later write of her ordeal. That night, six hundred guests thronged the three staterooms, listened in the Long Library to Herr Gottlieb's Viennese Band and the fine singing of Clara Eissler and Oxford baritone Henry Sunman, and took their sumptuous supper in the Great Hall. On Saturday morning, twenty-seven guests departed – in style, for they were escorted to Yarnton by the Woodstock division of the Oxfordshire Yeomanry Cavalry under Sunny's splendidly garbed command, and from Yarnton to Oxford by the Oxford division of the same regiment. The University Volunteer Battalion formed a guard of honour at the railway station, and, at long last, as Consuelo's tired arm waved goodbye, a special train carried twenty-seven well-spoiled and well-padded passengers back to London.

Meanwhile, the one guest who had remained at Blenheim, Jennie Churchill, sat at her bedroom desk writing to her beloved son Winston on Blenheim's proudly crested notepaper. Winston was far away in India, but his mother knew that Blenheim was the citadel, and always had been, ever since his precipitate birth within its walls, of her son's imagination. Winston himself was fond of saying that he had chosen to be born prematurely so that he could begin his life at Blenheim and take his cue from its embattled stones. At the age of eight he had penned his very first letter, which set the cornerstone of his strenuous life firmly in place, from Blenheim, where he had celebrated Christmas: 'I thank you very much for the beautiful presents,' wrote little Winston to his mother, 'those soldiers and flags and Castle. They are so nice.'

For the first nine years of his life, until Grandfather John, 7th Duke, died in 1883, Winston was often at Blenheim. A cousin who played soldiers with born-to-win Winston on Blenheim's schoolroom floor never forgot the two rules, both strictly enforced, of those war games. 'Firstly, Winston was always General and secondly there was no promotion.' After the 8th Duke succeeded, Winston was deprived of Blenheim's life-blood for the next ten years, for his father Randolph and the 8th Duke kept their distance, particularly after the latter sold off Blenheim's best paintings, an action his brother Randolph angrily denounced. Winston was thrilled when Blenheim's new master, cousin Sunny, invited him down for Christmas 1893, and it was then that he and Sunny cemented their lifelong friendship. 'I am enjoying myself here very much,' Winston wrote to Jennie. Sunny 'is very good company and we have sat talking till 1.30 every night since I have been here. Altogether I am quite content at the prospect of staying a week.'

Two years later came the shock of his father's ignominious end. Winston recalls how he ran across the snow of Grosvenor Square in the darkness, to keep vigil as Randolph expired, leaving his eldest son nothing but large debts. 'I was now in the main,' wrote Winston, 'master of my fortunes.' At twenty, he was a red-haired, freckle-faced, watery-eyed, accident-prone youth who had done poorly at Harrow and been bullied by his class-mates. He stood pale but erect – being only five foot six tall he could never look imposing – beside the grave in Bladon churchyard as his father's coffin was lowered. 'Over the landscape,' he recalls,

> snow had spread a glittering pall. He lies close by the tower of the village church, and the plain granite cross which marks the spot can almost be discerned, across a mile of lawn and meadow, from the great house which was his childhood's home and whose sinister motto ['faithful but unfortunate'] his varied fortunes had not ill sustained. A statue is erected to his memory in Blenheim Chapel.

(The statue, in burgundy and black and ochre marble, contrasts sharply with father John Winston's pristine white on the opposite wall.)

After Randolph's death, Winston turned instinctively to Blenheim, feeling keenly the loss of a father and political mentor, and needing

Blenheim's girth and age and firmness. It was among the palace's triumphant towers and golden cannon-balls that Winston's ambitions
unfurled and stiffened: he would take the world by storm; he would be
spectacular soldier and statesman, in that order. At Blenheim, Winston
found his conquering hero and his context: not only a father-substitute and
role-model in John Churchill, the self-made man whose image dominated
almost every room, but also roots going deep into Britain's past which
would help Winston's historical sense grow strong. With Blenheim behind
him, Winston felt fully confident that he could seize fame and fortune just
as John Churchill had, by his own sweat and driving will. Only his mother
believed in him. Society laughed at his bumptious ways and called him 'a
bounder'; mothers kept their daughters out of his way and Prince Edward
often snubbed him. Winston was too self-absorbed to notice and too self-
possessed to care. He passed out of the Royal Military College at Sandhurst
twentieth in a class of 130, and in February 1895, a month after his father's
death, was commissioned in the 4th Hussars, a dashing cavalry regiment.
He was so eager for battle-smoke that during an autumn leave, Winston
dashed off to Cuba to join a column scouting the interior jungle for
guerrilla rebels. To his great delight, he came under fire for the first time
on 30 November 1895, the day of his majority, twenty-one years after his
first red-faced bellow under Blenheim's crowning muskets. In the autumn
of 1896, before the Blenheim shooting party began its frivolities, Winston
sailed off to India to the 4th Hussars' station at Bangalore. Living in 'a
palatial bungalow, all pink and white', Winston chafed at the inactivity,
for he wanted to climb the highest heights at once, and unlike his peers at
Blenheim that November, he had no time for silly sports and idle drifting.
When, some years later, he found himself at a shooting party at Warter
Priory in Yorkshire, he wrote to his wife: 'Tomorrow pheasants in thousands. On the whole survey, how much more power and great business
are to me, than this kind of thing.' Winston alone, in that generation of
aristocrats, was reaching for the stars, like a thrusting cathedral spire in
the midst of a haphazard heap of little hovels.

On 21 October, Winston had written to Jennie from Bangalore: 'The
regiment is completely isolated. I find no one worth speaking to. If I can
only get hold of the right people my stay here might be of value.' He
begged his mother to get him out of India, which he considered a hopeless
backwater. Sitting in her bedroom on Saturday, 27 November, as the
shooting-party guests rattled away with all due pomp, Jennie told her son
that she would write to Lord Kitchener and see if she could get Winston
transferred to Egypt. Meanwhile, Winston lounged under the punkahs
reading Gibbon and Macaulay and honing his sense of history. He was

'grieved to read [Macaulay's] harsh judgements upon the Great Duke of Marlborough'. It was in the sandy wastes of Bangalore that Winston vowed that some day he would redress John Churchill's bad press. He sharpened what would be for him, in any fight, his most powerful weapon, words, by writing *Savrola*, an adventure novel based on his Cuban skirmishes and filled, by his own admission, with 'plenty of fighting and politics'.

Jennie did what she could, among her many friends and lovers, to help Winston win his spurs. She spent Christmas 1896 at Blenheim, along with Dowager Duchess Fanny, who was, according to Consuelo, proving to be a great trial, expecting the youthful Duchess to 'conform to a dignified decorum even then considered old-fashioned'. Blenheim's whale-boned matriarch would die three years later, aged seventy-seven.

In April 1897 'that little upstart' Winston raced off to India's North-West Frontier where Sir Bindon Blood, so aptly named, was organizing what he called a 'pheasant shoot' to punish the unruly Pathans, an Afghan mountain people who were struggling for independence. Winston wrote dispatches for London's *Daily Telegraph* for £5 each, and published them in book form in *The Story of the Malakand Field Force* (1898). His cousin Sunny, on the other hand, spent the spring of 1897 designing his costume for the Duchess of Devonshire's spectacular ball: a Louis XV creation of straw-coloured velvet with pearls and diamonds sewn on by hand. It took several seamstresses a month to make and cost £300.

On 18 September, Sunny and Consuelo's first son was born in London, and christened John after the 1st Duke, Albert Edward after the Prince of Wales and William after Consuelo's father. The Blenheim servants celebrated the arrival of their future master with a rowdy palace dance where refreshments were tossed from hand to hand by a row of waiters reaching from kitchen to dining-room, and beer flowed freely from the beer cellar, which held two dozen barrels. It was while Consuelo was still convalescing in London that Sunny fell under the spell of Gladys Deacon, a sixteen-year-old who would have a profound influence on Blenheim.

Gladys (pronounced Glay-dus) was born at the Hotel Brighton in Paris on 7 February 1881, to wealthy American parents who had made France their home. When Gladys was eleven, her father, Edward Deacon, crept into his wife's hotel room in Cannes, and fired three shots at her lover Abeille, crouching behind a sofa, one of which killed him. Edward went off to prison and ended his days completely mad in an asylum, while his wife, a silly woman with nothing but dress and sex on her mind, was ostracized henceforth by polite society. Gladys, for her part, studied Latin, Greek and five other languages and turned herself into an intellectual with an informed taste in art. When she day-dreamed, Blenheim's far-off faerie turrets beckoned her. 'I suppose you have read about the engagement of the Duke of Marlborough,' she wrote to her mother in 1895, seeing the newspaper headlines announcing Sunny's betrothal to Consuelo. 'Oh dear me,' sighed fourteen-year-old Gladys, 'if I was only a little older I might "catch" him yet! But alas! I am too young though mature in the arts of woman's witchcraft.' When Gladys finally met the 9th Duke of Marlborough face-to-face in the autumn of 1897, she turned on him the full force of her gamine charm, her mercurial moods and her enchanting conversation. Her eyes flashed blue fire; she had already learned how to roll them provocatively; with her boyish figure and arresting profile, she was like a 'lascivious young god', according to one friend. The small, pallid Duke warmed himself at that bright flame, and even Consuelo, when she met Gladys, fell victim to her charms.

Consuelo was desperately unhappy in 'the gloom that overhung our palatial home'. The year's hit song 'Only a Bird in a Gilded Cage' ran through her head over and over as she paced restlessly round Blenheim's dark confines. 'It is strange that in so great a house there should not be one really liveable room,' she mused. 'We slept in small rooms with high ceilings; we dined in dark rooms with high ceilings; we dressed in closets without ventilation.' She woke every morning to the irony of golden cupids cavorting round her bedroom ceiling and to the grim reality of the inscription which the 8th Duke had incised in the marble mantelpiece in black letters: 'Dust. Ashes. Nothing.' She came to dread dining *à deux* with her husband. As soon as the butler and footmen had served a course 'with all the accustomed ceremony', they left the dining-room, and a malevolent silence slithered on to the shining table and stayed there. Sunny 'had a way of piling food on his plate; the next move was to push the plate away, toy with knives, forks, spoons and glasses – all this in considered gestures which took a long time; then he backed his chair away from the table, crossed one leg over the other and endlessly twirled the ring on his little finger'. Eventually he would begin to eat, complaining that the food was cold. Then silence coiled up again sluggishly while Consuelo took to knitting in desperation and the butler read detective stories in the hall.

Consuelo fled the palace whenever possible to take long, lonely walks in the park or drives in the electric car which her mother had given her. The palace became more than a mere prison, it became venomous and vengeful. One morning, a horrid smell of putrefaction hit her in the face when she opened the door of the Chapel, where Blenheim's masters lay buried, and pursued her down the corridor. 'On investigation,' reports Consuelo, 'it was found that some of the coffins were such light shells that they had burst open.' Then too, Dean Jones's ghost seemed to be growing more vicious, so that anyone who slept in his room was 'terrified' by his appearance. A young woman miniature painter who was doing Consuelo's portrait pleaded for another bedroom, 'hysterically declaring that she had been awakened in the night by a blaze of light and had seen the Dean bending over her'. A male guest had a similar experience and impressed Consuelo with 'his evident terror'. The Duchess gave orders that henceforth no one was to be domiciled in the bedroom where the newly aggressive Dean had slept (and Winston had been born).

Meanwhile, Sunny was busy enhancing his shrine with Consuelo's money. He had the two-mile avenue north of Vanbrugh's bridge planted from Ditchley Gate to the Column of Victory with elms, for the original trees, after two centuries, were dying off. Sunny liked to look at his new elms and think of them providing shade and greenness for his great-grandchildren. (The trees would all die some seventy years later, destroyed in their prime by Dutch elm disease.)

While Winston took part, in 1898, in the last cavalry charge in history at Omdurman in Egypt under Lord Kitchener, Sunny turned his attention to the three staterooms west of the Saloon, and had their walls and ceilings decorated in the French manner with gilded wood, or *boiserie*, all of its precious prettiness far too refined for Blenheim's gaunt, uncompromising spaces. Twenty decorators from Paris worked for six months carving and gilding. The effect, at first glance, was of lavish superabundance – but the gilding was only nine-carat gold.

On 14 October of that year the Marlboroughs' second son, Ivor Charles, was born and, in the following year, Winston rushed off to South Africa to fight the Boers. They captured him briefly but he escaped on 12 December 1899, and after a series of daredevil stunts reached Durban on 23 December to find himself a popular hero. He returned to England in July 1900, in time to see his coquette of a mother, in frilly pale blue chiffon with osprey-feather hat, marry George Cornwallis-West, who was blond and handsome and penniless and exactly Winston's age, twenty-five. The Duke of Marlborough gave Jennie away and at the end of the ceremony, everyone sang 'Now Thank We All Our God'. In the autumn, Winston sprinted into the second lap of his career by becoming Conservative Unionist Member of Parliament for Oldham. 'How long can he keep up his present pace?' asked *Harper's Magazine*. 'Is his star to shine clearer and clearer or is it to burn itself out by its very vehemence?' While Winston was mastering his stutter and perfecting his oratory in the House, Sunny, in *his* house, was restoring the three-acre Great Court on Blenheim's north side. In John and Sarah's day, according to Vanbrugh's decree, it had been paved. Then along had come the 4th Duke and Capability Brown to rip out the paving-stones and plant grass. Sunny came down squarely on tradition's side and ordered Achille Duchêne, a French architect, to re-pave. The 9th Duke also had a parapet, sunken wall and tall, elaborate iron gates put up beyond the Great Court to keep the masses at bay. This project would occupy Sunny for the next ten years.

On 22 January 1901, Queen Victoria drew her last breath beneath the flowered cretonne draperies of her simple bed at Osborne, the family's Isle of Wight retreat, and Prince Edward, sitting by her side, realized that at last he had inherited the keys to the kingdom and could open all its windows and let in some fresh air. 'Get this tomb cleaned up!' the new King thundered, referring to Buckingham Palace, which he had always called 'the Sepulchre'. The fantasy furniture ordered by George IV for Brighton Pavilion, with its golden dragons and serpents and overwrought bamboo, was brought out of storage, staircases and galleries were carpeted in bright blue, enormous mirrors were installed, and the sooty gas chandeliers were, at long last, electrified.

In August of that year, Gladys Deacon – a very wealthy Gladys, for her insane father had died in July and left her a fortune – came to Blenheim for a six-month stay. Winston made frequent pilgrimages from London, and the 1901 appointments diary of that busy MP shows that he had already formed the habit of spending several days each month, unless he was out of the country, at grandiose Blenheim. He and Consuelo became friends, although she had no illusions about him. 'Winston was even then,' she noted, 'tremendously self-centred.' Winston and Gladys skirted each other warily, competing for centre stage, a battle which Winston easily won. 'Winston is still on the talk – never stops and really it becomes tiring,' sighed Consuelo. 'Sunny is still devoutly attentive to Winston's every remark,' she added, and Winston, for his part, would recall that 'Sunny and I were like brothers.'

The two men were very different: Winston aggressive and abrasive, Sunny anaemic and over-polite; Winston foraging for fame in the wider world beyond Blenheim's fortress, Sunny locking himself within its gates to play fastidious curator; Winston comparatively poor, strenuously earning his own wealth, Sunny immensely rich, thanks to his wife, smugly resting on his ducal escutcheon; Winston waging external battles either military or political, Sunny waging internal ones against the threatening void. What made the cousins close, in spite of these differences, was their common creed. They were both, before all else, Churchills of Blenheim, tied to the palace by their heart-strings, both intent on raising its attendant myths to greater heights and popularity. Sunny and Winston understood and respected each other, for Sunny saw in Winston the fierce energy of the 1st Duke; Winston saw in Sunny the supreme head of a famous family and a famous house.

Winston settled into Blenheim's Muniments Room in the summer of 1902 to sort through its massive papers and write his father's biography. 'There emerges from these dusty records a great and vivid drama,' he told Jennie excitedly, preparing to apply the first coat of varnish to the Churchill saga. Gladys came down that summer, and the next, for long visits, her profile now as ideal and finely chiselled as the young god's on William Chambers's eighteenth-century mantelpiece where Cupid was still marrying Psyche. Gladys had improved on nature by the artful injection of paraffin wax to fill out the hollow between forehead and nose. She was still in love with the palace, seeing it through a rosy, romantic haze.

In the spring of 1904, Winston impatiently took an impulsive leap forward – across the floor of the House, deserting the Conservatives to join the Liberals, and earning for himself the epithet 'Blenheim rat'. For some time Winston had 'drifted steadily to the left', as he put it, drawn to the Liberals' espousal of free trade, financial retrenchment and social reform – and fully aware that he could reach the seats of power sooner with the Liberals. (He was proved right when they had a landslide victory early in 1906 and Winston, at the age of thirty-one, became Under-Secretary of State for the Colonies.)

In September 1904 Winston was working long hours at Blenheim in a 'most comfortable' arcade room beneath the Long Library on his life of Lord Randolph. John Singer Sargent, a big man, impeccably tailored, with neat brown beard and searching green eyes, came to Blenheim at the Duke's request to paint a family portrait to match the 4th Duke's family, depicted by Sir Joshua Reynolds 127 years before. The 9th Duke of Marlborough gave explicit orders: he would wear his Garter robes; all available dogs and children would be included, and a statue of the 1st Duke would loom behind. (Sargent cunningly placed Consuelo on a high step so that it would not be obvious to the viewer that she was taller than her husband.) When completed, the huge painting, which measured eleven feet by eight, was hung in the same drawing-room as the Reynolds, and the diminutive Duke was pleased to have added one more link to the ancestral chain.

The first of November 1905 found Winston proudly writing 'Blenheim Palace, Woodstock' at the end of his Preface to *Lord Randolph Churchill*, which he had just completed. Where but from Blenheim should that

OPPOSITE: The 9th Duke and Duchess of Marlborough with their two sons. Portrait by Sargent

Charles Spencer Churchill, Duke of Marlborough, Consuelo, Duchess of Marlborough, John, Marquess of Blandford, Lord Ivor Spencer-Churchill.

Winston Churchill and Consuelo at Blenheim, 1907

monumental and romantic work go forth into the world? Three quarters of the book's 840 pages focus on Lord Randolph's six years as a successful politician (1880–86). The Aylesford affair, which, by causing a ten-year rift with Prince Edward, certainly affected Randolph's career, is dismissed in one sentence: 'Engaging in his brother's quarrels with fierce and reckless partisanship, Lord Randolph incurred the deep displeasure of a great personage.' There is no hint of Lord Randolph's blackmailing tactics, and he dies 'of a very rare and ghastly disease' which Winston nowhere specifies as syphilis. He portrays his father as a tragic hero destroyed by the Conservative party, so that the book is a clever propaganda piece (the 1st Duke wasn't the only Churchill adept at propaganda) justifying Winston's own desertion of the Tories. Blenheim is equally haloed along with Randolph, particularly for its hoary associations. 'The whole region is as rich in history as in charm,' enthuses Winston, 'for the antiquity of Woodstock is not measured in a thousand years, and Blenheim is heir to all the memories of Woodstock.' When the book appeared, in January 1906, the *Daily Telegraph* reviewer referred to Lord Randolph's treatment of his friends as 'often atrocious, even not honourable'. Sunny dashed off an incensed letter to the *Telegraph* and told Winston that he was 'the proper person to administer a good and sound trouncing to that dirty little Hebrew' (referring to the newspaper's manager Harry Levy-Lawson, son of its owner, 1st Baron Burnham).

Sunny cooled his ire at Blenheim by pushing the button recently installed in the wainscot of Sarah's Bow-window Room. It activated a fine fountain-spray in the centre of his new formal garden, so that a cascade of water fell prettily from the coronet of Venus, sculpted by the American Waldo Story, into a lily pool at her feet. While Winston had been whitewashing his father, Sunny had been busy with Achille Duchêne planning a formal garden to duplicate the one Sarah had seen when she looked out of her favourite bow-window. When completed, it had stiff, predictable arabesques in dwarf box on a ground of hand-crushed brick, with orange trees stuffed into tubs and flowers constricted into earthenware wine-jars.

Sunny discovered that autumn that Consuelo had taken a lover: the Honourable Reginald Fellowes, whose mother was not-so-fair Rosamond, daughter of John Winston, 7th Duke. The tensions between Sunny and Consuelo which had been smouldering for years exploded, and they decided on a legal separation. With great glee, Consuelo turned her back on the evil palace where she had known nothing but misery and moved into Sunderland House in London, which Sunny had built in 1902 with her father's money. 'In a spirit of bravado not untinged with humour,' as she put it, she had bas-reliefs sculpted at both ends of its Long Gallery: one of the Great Duke of Marlborough and one of Commodore Vanderbilt, her great-grandfather, two hard-nosed buccaneers who, thought Consuelo, lifting her glass to toast them both, weren't so very different after all. Winston, for his part, hurried down to Blenheim to console his cousin Sunny, deprived of more than a wife. 'We are very miserable here,' Winston told his mother, 'it is an awful business.' Jennie noted in December 1907 that Sunny appeared 'thin and seedy', while Consuelo looked 'very well and quite fat'.

In the following year, beloved Blenheim was the chosen stage for the next crucial event in Winston's life. Four years before, he had met briefly at a London ball a tall young lady with lustrous ash-blond hair and green eyes flecked with brown, who seemed quite unaware of her beauty. She was Clementine Hozier, granddaughter of the 10th Earl of Airlie, then living with her mother and twin sisters at 51 Abingdon Villas, a modest house tucked in behind London's Kensington High Street. When she and Winston met again four years later, she had broken off two engagements, and Winston had been rejected thrice: by enchanting Pamela Plowden who preferred to wed the Earl of Lytton, by wealthy heiress Muriel Wilson whose family were Hull shipowners, and by actress Ethel Barrymore who felt that she 'would not be able to cope with the great world of politics'. 'Let us all go to Blenheim for Monday and Tuesday,' Winston wrote to Clemmie on 7 August 1908. 'I want so much to show you that beautiful place, and in its gardens we shall find lots of places to talk in, and lots of things to talk about.' Clemmie hung back; Blenheim would be far too grand and she was then visiting at Cowes and down to her last clean cotton frock. Winston wrote again next day: 'I think you will be amused at Blenheim. It has many glories in the fullness of summer. Pools of water, gardens of roses, a noble lake shrouded by giant trees; tapestries, pictures and monuments within.' Winston wooed her through Blenheim, and of course Winston won her round. Monday, 10 August, found Clemmie on a train Blenheim-bound, dashing off a note to her mother: 'I shall get to Oxford at 5.20 where I shall be met by motor. I feel dreadfully shy and rather tired.'

Next afternoon, Winston and Clemmie went for a walk. It began to rain and they took shelter in the Temple of Diana which William Chambers had built for the 4th Duke. Clemmie and Winston sat side by side on its stone bench, looking out at the serene, dimpled lake caught between thrusting, solid pillars. 'If that beetle reaches that crack,' Clemmie said to herself, 'and Winston hasn't proposed, then he isn't going to.' But the miracle happened; Winston proposed and she accepted. When they emerged to clearing skies and diamanté grass, Clemmie swore Winston to secrecy until they could tell her mother, but Winston, seeing a little knot of people on the lawn, including Sunny and his mother, raced ahead, arms waving wildly, and blurted out his glorious news.

Next morning, notes flew along Blenheim's corridors and landed like little white doves on morning tea-trays. 'My dearest,' wrote Winston, 'I hope you have slept like a stone. I did not get to bed till 1 o'clock for Sunny kept me long in discussion about his affairs which go less prosperously than ours.' Clemmie replied: 'I never slept so well and I had the most heavenly dream. Je t'aime passionnément, I feel less shy in French.' Sunny viewed the ecstatic couple sourly and sank further into self-pity. Only a week after the betrothal, he was already writing to Winston: 'I fear alas! that I shall be unable to be present at your wedding. I have had a long and trying year; I have had to tick curs that would snarl, and stamp on my heel vipers that would bite. I hope you will allow me to spare myself the mingled pleasure – and pain – of such a ceremony.' The wedding took place at St Margaret's, Westminster, on 12 September 1908. Clemmie looked ravishing in Jennie's *point de Venise* lace and Winston talked politics with Lloyd George in the vestry. Jennie sighed with relief at Winston's luck and confided to a friend: 'My Winston is not *easy*; he is very difficult indeed and she is just right.'

Winston predictably had decided to honeymoon at Blenheim. The wedding presents included twenty-one inkstands for his future word torrents and he spent much of the time revising his next book, *My African Journey*. Back in London, the newly-weds rented 33 Eccleston Square, a modest house which felt minuscule after Blenheim. Theirs proved a successful marriage because Clemmie was quite willing to focus all her energies on Winston. She became his shield and fine reflecting mirror. 'Sometimes I feel as if I could lift the whole world on my shoulders,' Winston exulted to a friend. With Blenheim at his back and Clemmie by his side, Winston felt impregnable.

King Edward died on 6 May 1910, from too much rich food and too many cigars, and stately Queen Mary and simple-sailor George V, whom Sunny and Gladys in their letters soon christened 'King Log', ushered in a much more sober age. Gladys had taken a London apartment in Savile Row, and had to be content, since Sunny and Consuelo were separated but not divorced, with being mistress of Sunny but not mistress of Blenheim. Her face looked puffy and her mouth had a 'curious twist', as a friend put it, for the wax injected above her nose had begun its downward slide, and would eventually settle, hideously and disfiguringly, round her jaw. But Gladys still clutched her illusions. 'Am I not the last of the Marlborough gems,' she asked Sunny pertly in a letter of 1911, 'Greek in temper with a more modern dash of Roman about certain parts?'

As antidote to his loneliness and lumber-room past, Sunny began to lavish hospitality on his acquaintances like a Renaissance prince. He formed the habit of filling the palace for Christmas and New Year with twenty or thirty guests. They arrived with children, nannies, maids, valets, grooms, horses and children's ponies; sometimes a hundred people slept in the palace. The regulars included Winston and Clemmie and F.E. Smith, Lord Birkenhead, a big, athletic man who lived like a Regency buck at the top of his bent, gambling, drinking, squandering vast sums of money, and delighting Parliament with the wittiest oratory of the time. At his country house, Charlton, he had built fine stables for his ten hunters, a swimming-pool and three tennis-courts. He would burst into Blenheim bubbling with plans for wild escapades, his wife and three children – Freddie, Eleanor and Pam – trailing behind.

Eleanor writes graphically of these Blenheim Christmases where the housekeeper, Mrs Ryman, greeted their arrival in the Great Hall, her huge bunch of keys dangling at her waist. Another child guest recalls that Blenheim had a distinctive smell 'rather like the weighty smell of locked-in history, with hints of decaying velvet' and that he hated 'the clatter of eating from gold plates' and feared that 'some of the gold would chip off and get mixed with the vegetables'. The children often lay along the huge radiators in the Hall, gazing upwards at the 1st Duke in his cerulean splendour, or played hide-and-seek in the pitch-dark staterooms. Sunny grew livid and forbade this game after one child knocked over a precious screen. The little ones gaped in awe, one Christmas, as Lord Blandford and Ivor pelted their governess with scones and cakes in the schoolroom. The adults amused themselves with billiards, bridge and other larks, but Blenheim's mood had changed since the house-parties of the gay nineties. It was no longer frivolous yet formal. Under the mistletoe was a tamped-down ferocity, its sparking fuse winding through rooms packed with jarring memories as densely as black gunpowder in a cannon's mouth. 'F.E.' and Winston and some of the other men would join the children in the Great Hall after tea to play a war game called 'French and English', but it grew so vicious that the children fled in terror from those crashing, bruising arms. Then came the awful day when a housemaid went mad. She ran through the staterooms shrieking, 'stalked by grim, powder-headed footmen'. Her screams were so terrible, according to Lady Eleanor Smith, that 'I will never forget them. They reminded me of a hare's.' The footmen cornered the wild housemaid in the darkness of the Long Library. Perhaps she crouched beneath the Herschel telescope which poor mad George III had given to the 4th Duke and which Sunny had placed in a window embrasure. Four footmen carried the maid, who was beating her fists on their heads, raising clouds of powder, back through the three staterooms, across the Great Hall and through the green baize door into the servants' quarters. That night she was removed to a lunatic asylum, but her shrieks still hung, in shreds and membranes, in all the gilded staterooms.

The 9th Duke of Marlborough burrowed deeper into Blenheim's past, and on 18 April 1914, just before the First World War destroyed his ducal world for ever, he wrote a twenty-nine-page introduction to Stuart Reid's *John and Sarah, Duke and Duchess of Marlborough*. It was a paean with all stops out to Sunny's noble home and its founder. 'What I would ask,' he wrote, referring to the 1st Duke, 'is whether he was really the selfish miser that his enemies represented him. As I read him, he worked for his house, not for himself.' 'Had he lived in an age which glorified its heroes,' Sunny continued, 'Marlborough, like Alexander, would have been viewed as a god.' It was up to his 'descendants to support worthily their heritage of his fame', the 9th Duke concluded, flourishing his *raison d'être* like a proud flag.

During the Great War, while Britain felt tremors in the foundations of her mighty house which would crack her social hierarchy beyond repair, Sunny was confined to Blenheim's east wing, for the Long Library had been turned into a fifty-bed ward for wounded soldiers. They lay still, the human spoils of war, row on row, while the organ's peals spread balm but did not heal, and above them on the roof, Grinling Gibbons's stone spoils thrust out their jagged edges at the sky.

Sunny served his country in 1915 by substituting sheep for mowers in the gardens and planting cabbages in the flower-beds. 'The national food problem,' commented *The Times* dryly, 'may not have been greatly lessened by these practices, but it was a patriotic gesture.' In November of that year, Major Winston Churchill of the Oxfordshire Yeomanry joined the whizzing bullets in France, Europe being the fourth continent where he had inhaled the exhilarating stench of gunsmoke. 'Filth and rubbish everywhere,' he told Clemmie, 'water and muck on all sides. Troops of enormous rats creep and glide to the unceasing accompaniment of rifle and machine-guns.' But this son of Blenheim exulted: 'I have found happiness and content such as I have not known for many months,' he confided. He always began his letters to Clemmie from the front with 'My dearest soul', the salutation John had always used to Sarah when writing of another bloody war.

In 1916, Winston, still in France, was promoted to Colonel of the 6th Battalion Royal Scots Fusiliers and Sunny fell off his horse at Blenheim and fractured his foot. He wrote to Gladys on 9 August, 'I expect to have a limp for all time. It is as well to tell you this for if you hate that – you will have an excuse for leaving me.' Gladys's jowls were growing heavier by the day and she was now a parody of her pretty, younger self with hair too yellow, lips too red, but she had no intention of abandoning Sunny before her dream of being Blenheim's chatelaine had materialized.

Whenever he was home on leave, Winston came down to Blenheim, bringing his painting gear, for he had recently taken up oil painting. 'Painting a picture,' he would later write, 'is like fighting a battle,' for both require 'a good plan' and 'a strong reserve'. He would eventually do a painting of the Great Hall, making it look more like a rosy bower than a grey-marble mausoleum by placing a huge, pink bouquet of flowers in the foreground, and filling in the background in faulty perspective. Winston also did a painting of the Brussels tapestry in the second stateroom, in which John Churchill outmanoeuvres the Sun King at Bouchain in 1711.

The heir to Blenheim, 'Bert', Lord Blandford, survived his service in the Great War, much to his father's relief, and married Mary Cadogan, daughter of Viscount Chelsea, on 17 February 1920, just as his father was getting divorced. Eleven days after his son's wedding, the 9th Duke of Marlborough booked into Claridges under the name 'Spencer' and spent the night with a hired co-respondent establishing the necessary 'grounds'. In the following spring, just ten months after Consuelo's father had died, leaving $54m, Sunny's decree became absolute. Consuelo promptly married a charming Frenchman, Jacques Balsan, and quitted England for ever. At long last, Sunny was free to marry Gladys, which he did on 24 June at the British Consulate in Paris where Randolph had wed Jennie.

When Gladys and the Duke returned to Blenheim on 28 July 1921, she formally signed 'G. Marlborough' with a proud flourish in the Visitors' Book where 213 years before John Churchill had written the first signature. Then she took *Burke's Peerage* from its shelf in the Long Library and ascertained, with a slight shudder of foreboding, that she was the thirteenth person to bear the title Duchess of Marlborough and mistress of Blenheim. In the beginning, Gladys gloated and glided through its echoing halls; she imprinted her own taste by hanging French Impressionist paintings from her fine collection in the empty spaces where Rubens and Rembrandt had reigned until Sunny's father had traded them for pounds sterling.

From now on, Blenheim would be bereft of one of its brightest spirits, for Jennie Churchill, aged sixty-seven, had been buried beside Randolph in Bladon churchyard while Sunny and Gladys were honeymooning abroad. Jennie had been staying at Mells Manor, an Elizabethan house whose oak floors had been wax-polished for three hundred years. Rushing to dinner one evening in very pretty but very high-heeled Italian shoes, Jennie had slipped and broken her ankle. Gangrene had set in; the leg had been amputated; an artery had burst and killed her. Much of Blenheim's glamour and verve seemed to die with her.

Sunny, meanwhile, was feeding into Blenheim's insatiable maw the dollar fortune of its third American Duchess within thirty-three years. He launched his last great improvement, his final bid to inscribe his name in Marlborough annals. It would be written in water, for he was closeted with the faithful Achille Duchêne designing the water-terrace gardens for the west side of the palace. The challenge, Sunny told Duchêne, was 'to make a liaison between the façade of Vanbrugh and the water line of the lake made by Brown'. Somehow, it had to be done: a connection must be made between the rigidity and stasis of the house and the fluidity and caprice of the lake. The Duke took to standing on the terrace site, as still as an urn, for hours at a time. Once, when a guest sauntered by, he asked

Aerial view from the south-west showing the water terraces designed by Duchêne

her opinion of his great work. 'I think it's a topping idea,' she replied. 'A topping idea,' Sunny muttered over and over, his thin shoulders suddenly straightening. 'That's what it is, a topping idea.' 'Try and inspire in them,' the Duke told Duchêne, referring to his designs, 'a feeling of joyousness, for joy means the birth of everything.' It was the one quality, before all others, which Blenheim, and its current Duke, had never, ever had, and Sunny was poignantly aware of that lack. 'You have never made a drawing for the pots on the first terrace. These decorative objects are very important and if skilfully handled may just give the life to the whole Scheme which it now lacks,' Sunny told Duchêne. It was a lot to ask of clay pots: to animate and redeem the best-laid schemes of a mousy man. The Duke devoted, in his own words, 'six years of labour and study' to this great project of creating, in water, 'a worthy frame to the Palace'. Finally, the mighty task was done, and two terraces of water basins and clipped box, linked by a wall of caryatids and *vasques*, led from palace to lake. Gladys's ideal Grecian head, as it had appeared before the wax began to slip, surveyed the limpid scene enigmatically not once but twice, sculpted by H. Ward Willis on to the bodies of two lead sphinxes. On the lower terrace were two large reflecting pools; in the centre of one was the baroque energy and dash of Bernini's model of the River Gods fountain in Rome's Piazza Navona, given to the 1st Duke by the Papal Nuncio; in the middle of the other pool was a vastly inferior modern approximation.

Gladys's feelings for the palace, like her ravaged face, were deteriorating rapidly. The vast Blenheim machine hummed silently day after tedious day; by eight o'clock every morning the lawns were rolled, the dead leaves were raked, the servants were creeping in their accustomed places and the clocks were chiming thinly ... and meaninglessly. The past, but only the past, filled every room with must and memory. As in the 4th Duke's last days, life was leaving the palace, slowly but surely. It was all, thought Gladys, escaping one dead room only to be caught in the clammy grasp of another, far too much like a waxwork show. At first she fought valiantly against the spreading torpor. A French friend who came to visit remarked that 'a battle has been joined between her and Blenheim Palace. There are days on which the Palace is the victor and triumphs over her; solemn and dignified she takes her walks slowly through the galleries. At other times, light as an elf, she frisks across the flower-beds, laughs, sheds sunlight on everything.' Slowly, relentlessly, the palace gained ground in its grim assault on the 13th Duchess. Gladys escaped in the autumn of 1922 to the Marlboroughs' new London house in Carlton House Terrace, but she knew it was only a temporary reprieve, and she dreaded the return to Blenheim. 'The mere thought of those huge rooms makes my aching legs ache more,' she confided to a friend. 'I wonder how long it is before I go.' Two days after a dismal Christmas, Gladys huddled despondently in the palace she had dreamed about for twenty-seven years and looked head-on at the sordid reality of her existence there. 'I am sick of life here. Convention and commonplace and selfishness alone voice themselves over us,' she wrote, 'but we will separate perhaps before long and I will then go away for good and ever.' The 9th Duke of Marlborough, Gladys concluded, was ruled by 'black, vicious, personal pride like a disease', and it was Blenheim which had infected him.

Winston came to Blenheim less often now. There were two main reasons for his neglect. Firstly, the chatelaine of Blenheim was a woman he disliked – partly, perhaps, because she 'knew him from top to bottom', as she herself said, and having lost her illusions about him, as she had about palace and owner, she saw clearly that Winston 'was entirely out for Winston'. Secondly, some of his affection and energy was being expended now on Chartwell Manor, the country house in Kent which he bought in 1922. The mid-Victorian house was built around the core of a 400-year-old dwelling and Winston characteristically chose that oldest part for his study. Chartwell was full of dry rot; Winston engaged architect Philip Tilden to cope with it, and as the years passed and the dry rot proved stubborn, relations between Churchill and his architect became almost as strained as between Sarah and Vanbrugh. Occasionally, Winston and Clemmie came down to Blenheim in response to Sunny's urging, but they found there, in the relationship of its Duke and Duchess, a different, but equally disturbing, kind of rot.

Sunny was still pathetically angling for some attention from posterity, and invited Jacob Epstein to come to Blenheim and sculpt him in bronze. When completed, the bust would be placed, the Duke decided, in the Great Hall where the white marble one of John Churchill could look down on him, gratefully and benevolently, from his place above the doorway into the Saloon. The Duke wanted Epstein to sculpt him in Roman toga; Epstein wanted him in modern dress; they couldn't agree and Epstein left in a huff. Later, they reached a compromise and Epstein modelled Sunny in all the dignity of his Garter robes, revealing him, as one critic in *New Age* put it, 'encased in aristocratic pride'. One day while Epstein was working at Blenheim, the Duke took him to see the Chapel, which he was shocked to find 'totally devoid of Christian symbolism'. 'I see nothing of Christianity,' Epstein complained. 'The Marlboroughs are worshipped here,' replied the 9th Duke tartly.

Gladys tried a new tactic in her losing war against Blenheim, and invited fellow intellectuals down for weekends, choosing them for their talent, not their blue blood. By the 1920s, the middle classes, along with their betters, had taken up the weekend habit: Monday to Thursday in town, Friday to Sunday in the country, in as imposing a house as they could manage to buy or visit. Lytton Strachey came down to Blenheim for a July weekend in 1923 and was properly impressed. He peered at everything through his thick glasses like an owl in daylight and loped about looking, as friend Cecil Beaton, another occasional Blenheim guest, noted, 'bent as a sloppy asparagus'. Strachey found Blenheim 'entrancing': 'I wish it were mine. It is enormous, but one would not feel it too big. The grounds are beautiful too, and there is a bridge over a lake which positively gives one an erection.' Arnold Bennett also came to Blenheim, but only to dine. His father had once been a pawnbroker in the Potteries town of Burslem, and Bennett had been brought up in one of its soot-laden Victorian terraced houses, but he had made enough money from his novels to buy a London house at 75 Cadogan Square. Bennett arrived at Blenheim arrayed in one of the frilled evening shirts he bought from Sulka in Bond Street, with carnation in buttonhole, and the gold watch-chain which fellow novelist H.G. Wells, a sometime Blenheim guest, called 'Arnold's gastric jewellery' strung across his front. 'Enormous house,' he enthused to his nephew, 'soup and fish off silver plate. The Duchess collects French pictures. She said I was the first person who had *any* interest in them.' In the course of the evening, the Duke pointed to a splendid Cézanne canvas and said in tones of authority, 'that's a Van Gogh.' 'The bulk of the twenty guests,' Bennett concluded, 'seemed to me to have no interest whatever except sexual.'

If sexual intrigues had remained a constant, almost everything else about Blenheim's guests had altered drastically since the week-long house parties of the 1890s and early 1900s. Edwardians did not care what they did so long as they kept it from public view; the Bright Young People of the twenties, on the other hand, didn't care what they did so long as it got talked about and reported in the *Tatler*. Appearance and manners were also radically different. The women had skirts to their knees, bare arms loaded with bangles, hair short and shingled, lips painted bright red and eyebrows plucked to a thin, interrogatory line which never seemed to get a satisfying answer. They flung their silk-stockinged legs on to sofas, twiddled with the tassels on huge magenta or jade velvet cushions, drank endless cocktails in their rooms, blew smoke-rings towards Blenheim's too-too funny painted old ceilings and said 'Sez you' in response to every remark. 'Darling, let's shimmy!' they cried, and flung their bracelets towards the nearest man in wide Oxford 'bags', while a cabinet gramophone on legs played the latest Irving Berlin hit. Sometimes they all trooped, laughing more for effect than from real merriment, down to take tea in the boat-house which million-dollar Lilian, the 8th Duke's American Duchess, had had built beside the lake, where huge razor-toothed pike lurked in the limp, brown reeds.

In addition to carefully selected guests, Gladys fought the drowning tide of ennui with a new project, begun in April 1924. She turned her back on the palace and got as far away as she could comfortably walk; near the foot of Capability Brown's Grand Cascade, she began to make a rock garden, ignoring the fact that the area was full of snakes. She engaged Bert Timms, a gardener from Hanborough, to help her, and routinely spent the day amid the dirt-piles and darting vipers, eating her lunch off a flat rock. By 1925, however, having suffered a third miscarriage in her attempt to fill Blenheim's moribund rooms with life, Gladys found the rock-garden work too strenuous and began instead to breed King Charles spaniels. She also tried to add a touch of whimsy and humour to Blenheim's grim façade. She engaged artist Colin Gill to paint six huge eyes on the ceiling of the north portico: three brown eyes (Consuelo's?) and three blue eyes (unquestionably Gladys's for she climbed the scaffold waving a blue scarf at Colin so that he could get the colour right). The disembodied eyes, however, look more sinister than saucy and stare down still as if to say: 'All hope abandon, ye who enter here.'

Maurice Ashley, a recent Oxford history graduate, came to Blenheim in 1929 to start researching the first volume of Winston's monumental biography of his ancestral hero, John Churchill, to be entitled *Marlborough, His Life and Times*. Sunny sent an estate clerk to watch Maurice while he worked in the Muniments Room, just to make sure he didn't steal any documents, for Sunny maintained that journalist and critic Hilaire Belloc had walked off with one of the 1st Duke's letters. Winston had assured Maurice airily that lunch would be provided by the Duke, but no lunch was ever forthcoming. One day the Duke talked to Maurice about the working class, whom he clearly regarded as some lower form of life, ending his little chat with the hope that unemployment figures would soon reach two million. To Maurice's fresh, young eyes, Blenheim seemed 'a disappearing world, an aristocratic oasis, an eighteenth-century relic'.

Ashley correctly perceived that the way of life revolving around Britain's great country houses had received its death-blow in the Great War. The moderates among the city-dwelling proletariat espoused the ideals of democratic self-government, and the radicals among them turned to Marx and Lenin. Gone certainly were notions of aristocratic privilege and *noblesse oblige*. Gone, indeed, was the old-style aristocracy itself, so small and élite, replaced by a proliferating peerage who bought their titles with their acquired, rather than inherited, wealth. Between 1917 and 1921, four marquisates, eight earldoms, twenty-two viscountcies and sixty-four baronies were created. (The latter, according to the Duke of Northumberland, cost £40,000.) Only dukes now were born, not made. Many of the long-term landowners had been killed in the war, leaving the problems of paying off death duties and running the estate to widows or young heirs. The *Spectator* published a series of articles in 1921 on 'How to Save the Country Houses of England', suggesting that they be opened to the public and turned into commercial operations paying their own way. Rather than adopt this radical notion, a great many estates were sold, and *The Times* in 1922 carried an article entitled 'England Changing Hands', reporting on the fact that eight million acres in Britain had changed hands in the post-war period, far more than at any other time in history. Only the largest landowners, such as the 9th Duke of Marlborough, could afford to hang on to their inherited acres and run houses as unwieldy and expensive as Blenheim.

The Duke, to be sure, had more fundamental problems on his well-manicured hands than financial ones. Worshipping and serving Blenheim had proved, over the years, to be an unsatisfactory religion for the melancholy Duke, giving little comfort or spiritual sustenance. He turned instead to the ritual and high colour of Roman Catholicism. In February, 1927, Sunny was received into the Church of Rome. Stepping inside Roman orthodoxy was Sunny's first step away from his exclusive preoccupation with Blenheim, and he would defect even further in the years to come.

Blenheim was, more and more, an unpleasant place to be, for tensions and violence between Sunny and Gladys were escalating steadily. One day the over-polite 9th Duke struck Gladys a blow that blackened her eye; after that, she placed a loaded revolver each evening beside her plate at dinner – a weird, jarring note among the orchids and the silver-gilt. When a startled guest asked her why it was there, Gladys replied: 'Oh! I don't know. I might just shoot Marlborough!'

Gladys's relationship to Blenheim had also entered a new phase. After the initial one of golden-gauze idealizing had come the sobering period of seeing the stark realities beneath; now came the third and final stage, as Gladys felt the need to strike out at the palace, to demean and deface it in retaliation for her own painful disillusionment. Her King Charles spaniels (which dog-breeders commonly called Blenheim spaniels) had always been kept in gardeners' bothies near the kitchen garden. Now she turned them loose in the staterooms and had dog-flaps cut in the fine mahogany doors. These were the dog days of Blenheim; fifty spaniels lifted their legs against gilt chairs, defecated on priceless carpets, left tufts of hair and burrs on damask settees. The entire palace reeked. Blenheim's housekeeper, Miss James, recalls that the Duke spent hours examining curtains and rugs for stains, and in the midst of this canine chaos, castigated Miss James angrily if the front and back legs of little tables deviated by so much as a quarter of an inch from their designated indentations in the carpets.

Anita Leslie, whose grandmother was Jennie Churchill's sister Leonie, has left a graphic description of a 1931 weekend visit to Blenheim. 'We all arrived in pouring rain,' she writes, referring to herself, Winston's twenty-year-old son Randolph, and an Australian, Patricia Richards.

> The Duke met us and tea was carried into one of the drawing-rooms. The Duchess did not appear for a long time. Finally, we heard, not footsteps, but the claw-clatter of many little dogs. 'Watch Sunny – he hates her guts – great sport!' whispered Randolph. In came the Duchess, surrounded by a moving carpet of King Charles spaniels. Gladys Marlborough was extraordinary to

look at. Absolutely hideous and yet exotic, with golden hair swept back in a bun, and strange blue eyes staring out of the ruin of that stretched face. She advanced in her dirty old clothes, shook hands and waved us graciously to chairs.

When the girls went to their bedrooms to dress for dinner, Patricia rang for the housemaid. 'Where is the bathroom?' she asked. 'Oh, miss, I wouldn't know that,' replied the nonplussed maid. After much exploring up and down cheerless corridors, Anita and Patricia found an ancient tub set deep in a mahogany box whose tap grudgingly yielded a little tepid water. During the dinner of lukewarm food, served by two footmen in dirty cotton gloves, the Duke 'sat looking like a rat caught in a trap' while 'the Duchess delivered her poisoned shafts'. 'I didn't marry,' she told the young people, smiling lop-sidedly into her wine, 'until I'd been to bed with every prime minister in Europe – and most of the kings.'

'Where's that pretty Miss Richards?' the Duke asked at tea-time next day while spaniels yapped and tussled everywhere. 'Couldn't you see?' snapped Gladys. 'Randolph is hoping to seduce her among the cabbages.' 'How does one get away from this dreadful place?' wailed Patricia to Anita, when they were alone, 'I shall never come again.'

Even its Duke and master had now had enough of Blenheim. Later that same year, Sunny turned his back on his once-beloved home and made an ignominious retreat. It was probably the only action of his life which paralleled that of his great hero, the 1st Duke, who had precipitously deserted the palace two hundred and eleven years before. Sunny lived henceforth in his London house, and when estate duties called him down to Blenheim, he stayed at a Woodstock hotel. He now began negotiations with his friend the Duke of Alba about the possibility of retiring permanently, as a layman, to a Benedictine monastery in Spain. Sunny also sent his cousin Shane Leslie, Anita's father, as emissary to America, that never-failing fountain of dollars, to see if he could find a buyer for the entire collection of Blenheim papers, thousands of yellowing parchments and two hundred years of prime British history packed into boxes. Sunny argued that the Blenheim archives were his personal property, not heirlooms attached irrevocably to Blenheim, and were therefore his to dispose of for hard cash, as his father had disposed of Blenheim's paintings. Shane returned to England with a proposal from Yale University to purchase the papers through a private donor for £50,000.

All these plans for ridding himself of Blenheim and its history were shelved when Sunny learned that he had developed inoperable cancer originating in his liver. Some time after this, his solicitor sent a peremptory letter to Gladys who was still living at Blenheim. She had gone a little mad;

having divided the Great Hall and some of the other rooms into dog coops, she wandered about, sometimes under the influence of drugs, dressed in Sarah's musty old court dresses held together with safety-pins. The solicitor informed its 13th Duchess that Blenheim was about to be closed down and all servants dismissed. On 29 May 1933, Gladys hired a van, loaded up her Monets and Cézannes and dogs, and as the golden balls on Blenheim's turrets twinkled at her for the last time, drove rapidly away. If, in the beginning, the palace had led her down a faerie path to dreamland, Gladys had taken her revenge. She left Blenheim dirty, stinking and befouled. It was some small consolation.

Blenheim's progenitor, John Churchill, had set the pattern, and Consuelo, Sunny and Gladys, in that order, had cemented Blenheim's strangest tradition. All of them had fled as far as possible from the bludgeoning weight, the overwhelming burden of Blenheim, Blenheim, which, like a giant incubus, sucked them dry of all devotion and all vitality, evil Blenheim which took and took – their youth, their dreams, their love, their money – and gave them nothing in return.

The wasted 9th Duke of Marlborough died on 30 June 1934, aged sixty-two. His funeral service took the form of a High Mass Requiem in the Farm Street Jesuit church near Sunny's London home. Then the crimson-draped coffin was taken down to Woodstock by train for burial that same day in Blenheim's Chapel. Shane Leslie describes how he and other mourners followed the hearse carrying the Duke's body into Blenheim park and down 'the long avenues he had planted which will probably last as long as modern England' (but which shrivelled and died forty years later). 'I found myself,' continues Shane, 'walking beside Winston who became expansive in the shadow of Blenheim' and who began debating the possibility of immortality. 'We were both in tears when we entered the family chapel,' declares Leslie. 'Below we glimpsed the Great Duke and Sarah lying in sepulchred state.' The 9th Duke's coffin was lowered slowly to join them, while a few wreaths of incense – an unfamiliar scent for the Chapel – floated above, and Father Martindale, the Duke's confessor, intoned some Latin prayers. The ceremony over, Winston walked ponderously out of the Chapel and straight up to Lord Blandford. '*Le Duc est mort. Vive le Duc*,' was his sonorous greeting to the 10th Duke of Marlborough.

The 9th Duke's obituaries droned an elegiac note. 'He was a pathetic figure, like a lonely peacock straggling through deserted gardens,' one friend concluded, a sad man 'sowing seed after seed where none can ever grow' and 'the last Duke who firmly believed that strawberry leaves could effectively cover a multitude of sins'. It was left to Winston, last remaining caretaker and polisher of Blenheim's glorious myths, to write a glowing obituary first printed in *The Times* and subsequently in its own slim volume. Winston rolled out his formal, rodomontade prose:

> Always there weighed upon him [the Duke] the size and cost of the great house which was the monument of his ancestor's victories. This he conceived to be almost his first duty in life to preserve and embellish. As the successive crashes of taxation descended upon the Old World it was only by ceaseless care and management and also frugality, that he was able to discharge his task. He sacrificed much to this – too much, but he succeeded; and at his death Blenheim passes from his care in a finer state than ever.

Winston surveyed the immediate past, and took stock:

> During the forty-two years he was Duke of Marlborough the organism of English society underwent a complete revolution. The three or four hundred families which had for three or four hundred years guided the fortunes of the nation from a small, struggling community to the headship of a vast and still unconquered Empire lost their authority and control. They became merged peacefully, insensibly, without bloodshed or strife, in a much more powerful but less coherent form of national consciousness; and the class to which the late Duke belonged were not only almost entirely relieved of their political responsibilities, but they were to a very large extent stripped of their property and in many cases driven from their homes. This process may well be adjudged inevitable and by some people salutary. But it cast a depressing shadow upon the Duke of Marlborough's life ... it saddened and chilled him, and added continually to the difficulties of his particular task of keeping the palace and its treasures together, which he had accepted as the main effort of his life.

So the faithless 9th Duke of Marlborough, unaware of cousin Winston's noble gloss, slept on in the house he had deserted, and the dirty, dishevelled house slept on in the exhaustion of old age and hard times. And if Consuelo and Sunny and Gladys had all defected, Blenheim's one true son, bone of its stone, flesh of its flint, born for gore and glory, born to bring the soiled old palace fresh fame and fortune, was still loyal and still loving.

On that July day in 1934, he stood, feet firmly planted on reverberating stone, in Blenheim Palace's north portico, tears for Sunny drying on his cheeks, cigar projecting like a small torpedo between clenched teeth. He looked beyond the 1st Duke's two cannons standing guard in the huge re-paved forecourt, beyond the high, locked black-iron gates, to threatening ranks of clouds forming up on the horizon.

Winston Churchill stood, rooted and ready, and watched the gathering storm.

5
SENILITY

What if the glory of escutcheoned doors,
And buildings that a haughtier age designed,
The pacing to and fro on polished floors
Amid great chambers and long galleries, lined
With famous portraits of our ancestors;
What if those things the greatest of mankind
Consider most to magnify, or to bless,
But take our greatness with our bitterness?

W.B. Yeats, 'Ancestral Houses'

ON THE AFTERNOON OF 30 JANUARY 1965, THE WIND WAS COLD and numbing, as if it blew straight from some sunless catacomb. Heavy shrouds of grey cloud pressed down on Blenheim from above, draining it of all colour. The palace was utterly still, with no sign of life or movement anywhere. From the middle of the south front, Louis XIV, purloined so long ago from France by John Churchill, gazed stonily at the square tower of Bladon church, a mile away across the deserted park. Tucked in behind Louis's massive ringlets was a wagtail's nest. Once it had been bursting with greedy young fledglings, jostling for dominance, thrusting open beaks towards blue sky. But the nest had been empty for many months, and, like Louis's proud features, it was falling into ruin, and rimmed with hoar frost. Behind the mouldering Sun King, on Blenheim's roof, jutted the disfiguring scaffolding which, since 1950, had been a daily reminder that at the age of two hundred and sixty, the infirm old house had need of trusses.

Blenheim's comatose condition seemed to have stretched its numb fingers all the way to the village of Bladon, for there, too, everything was silent. Its twisting streets were empty of dogs and people – except for members of the St John Ambulance Brigade, standing at the ready – and its frosty roads were empty of cars. To the east, the A4095, Bladon's main artery, was blocked off by policemen guarding the barriers. To the west, similarly sealed off, the winding road which touched the south tip of Blenheim Park was without its usual flow of traffic all the way to the village of Hanborough. Edging the road, however, on both sides, were solemn-faced people standing perfectly still and silent. The drab platform of Hanborough's railway station was draped in purple and hung with laurel wreaths. Pale-grey sky stretched like a sheet behind it and made the scarlet tunics of the two Guardsmen standing on the platform look as shocking as splashes of blood.

At 3.23 p.m. the black dot of a train appeared in the distance, its thin sound growing louder and louder, as the Battle of Britain class locomotive, the 'Winston Churchill', led its five pullman coaches into the station to disgorge their black-clad passengers. The train's heaviest burden, a flag-draped coffin, was carefully lifted out of the luggage-van by members of the Queen's Royal Irish Hussars, formerly called the 4th Hussars. Wearing navy-blue greatcoats and white gloves, they carried the coffin to a waiting hearse; the black-clad passengers, all but six of whom were Churchill relatives, climbed into nine Rolls-Royces, some of them very old, and then the whole cortège drove slowly between the rows of silent people towards Bladon village. In the back of the first Rolls sat Clementine Churchill, heavily veiled, and her plump son, Randolph, whose cadaverous eyes and white skin, according to one onlooker, made him look 'like death itself'. Looking almost as unwell, sitting beside his son in one of the older Rolls, was 'Bert', the 10th Duke of Marlborough, who had taken 'a pep pill' to get him through this gruelling day. He was still feeling chilled from 'the bitter wind', for that morning he had sat in an open brougham for the long, slow procession through London streets. His alabaster hands, those hands which had never known rough labour, were almost blue-white as they folded round the handle of his malacca cane.

The nine cars drove up the hill to St Martin's Anglican church which looked down from its slight eminence at the village of Bladon, a haphazard huddle of limestone cottages holding five hundred inhabitants. St Martin's had been rebuilt in 1802 but there had been a church on the site for eight hundred years. As Clementine climbed slowly from the Rolls, took Randolph's arm, and looked about, she was relieved and pleased to see how scrupulously her wishes had been respected. She had asked that the burial at Bladon be strictly private, with no press or television coverage, and consequently there were no crowds here as in London, no faces, even, at the windows of houses overlooking the cemetery. Coffin and mourners were met at the lych-gate of St Martin's by the rector, the Revd John Emlyn James, who led the way to the grave, its dark orifice waiting, open to grey sky. The simple ceremony of committal was so short that the nine cars barely had time to turn and manoeuvre in the narrow cul-de-sac near the lych-gate. From a mile away, Blenheim's silent towers stood watch while her favourite son, her one true son, was laid to rest close to his parents in that corner of the cemetery directly in line with the palace's south front.

Sir Winston Churchill had made his final pilgrimage to Blenheim and come home to stay.

When Vanbrugh had taken up his pencil two hundred and sixty years before, and drawn Blenheim's south-to-north axial line, he had done it better than he knew. Starting with the tower of St Martin's, near which Winston lies, the line passes through Blenheim's Saloon into the Great Hall, which adjoins Winston's birth room, and out through the north

Sir Winston Churchill's coffin being carried into Bladon church, 1965

portico to the Column of Victory where the Great Hero, from his high perch, can survey, and welcome, the grave of a descendant who also served his country with courage and high honour. 'It is this union of past and present, of tradition and progress, this golden chain, never yet broken,' Winston had written, 'that has constituted the peculiar merit and sovereign quality of English national life.'

Winston had decided six years before, in 1959, to be buried at Blenheim rather than at Chartwell, even though he loved that country house too. He had always kept his eye on history, and history had trumpeted in his ear that for Sir Winston Churchill no other burial place would do; it had to be Blenheim. His daughter Mary explains why:

> Throughout his life Winston was a frequent visitor to Blenheim. It was in a special sense his home; there he was born; there he became engaged; there he spent the first few days of his honeymoon. Later, when Winston wrote his splendid life of the great Duke of Marlborough, Blenheim epitomized for him the triumphs and magnificence of England and of his hero. And so it seemed most right and fitting that in the end he should have wished to return there.

The chapel vault within Blenheim was for dukes only; Bladon churchyard was as close as Winston could get to the palace of his dreams. Mary stood now beside her husband, Christopher Soames, as her father's coffin was lowered into the grave; next to her stood her sister Sarah, named for Blenheim's first Duchess. Not far away lay Winston's other daughter, Diana, who had been buried there two years before. Mary, wife of 'Bert', 10th Duke of Marlborough, also lay near by, as did Consuelo, wife of the 9th Duke. She had died the year before in America at the age of eighty-seven and her son Bert had flown out at once to fetch her unprotesting body back to Blenheim. At the head of Winston's grave stood the Duke of Norfolk, who had so magnificently master-minded the state funeral in London. Standing a little apart from the Churchill family were Winston's physician, Lord Moran, Grace Hamblin, who had been Clementine's secretary since 1932, and three of Winston's private secretaries: Anthony Montague Brown, John Colville and Leslie Rowan. After the committal, everyone filed past the grave to take their last farewell, led by Clementine who placed on it a wreath of red roses, carnations and tulips, bearing a card which said: 'To my darling Winston, Clemmie.' The Duke of Norfolk placed beside it a wreath of white flowers bearing, in the Queen's hand-writing, the words: 'From the Nation and Commonwealth, in grateful remembrance, Elizabeth R.'

Dusk was falling as the little party got back into the waiting cars and sped away, while Blenheim's south front across the park grew dark and doleful. No golden lights twinkled in its windows; they were blank and unseeing. The house no longer regarded the external world with a sardonic gleam; it had turned in on itself and existed now solely on a thin gruel of memories. An icy wind slid across its crippled roof and down its crumbling flues. Then night closed round it, bringing welcome, if temporary, oblivion.

INSIDE THE HOUSE, THE 10TH DUKE WAS THAWING HIS LONG LEGS before the fire in his study, an unprepossessing northern room, once Sarah's, furnished with worn, red-leather armchairs and a Victorian desk whose brass drop-handles all said 'M'. Blenheim finally had a master to match its scale, for its present Duke was six foot four inches tall. Except for his size, Bert was a mediocre man of sixty-four, living for his shooting and gardening, following the vagaries of the weather with obsessive inter-est, limping about on his cane – he often had gout – and sporting a gold watch-chain heavy with antique seals across his large front. He was as

OPPOSITE: 'Bert', 10th Duke of Marlborough, seated in the Temple of Health built by the 4th Duke

much of an anachronism in 1965 as the palace itself. When he spoke, he barely moved his lips so that almost no one could understand him; he capped every sentence with 'what?' and was never, ever heard to laugh. Oblivious to the fact that Britain had shelved its blue-bloods in a dusty, out-of-the-way corner and moved on to more mundane, modern concerns, Bert lived as Blenheim's Dukes had always lived. He once complained that his tooth-brush didn't foam as it should, not realizing that his absent valet always applied the toothpaste. He shocked an American house-guest, Lee Bouvier Radziwill, by breaking off his mumbling long enough to urinate into the nearest Blenheim fireplace, and then finished his sentence: 'what?'

Since his wife Mary's death four years before, the Duke found Blenheim far too big and quiet. It had not always been so. When his father Sunny, the 9th Duke, had died in 1934 and Bert had succeeded, the whole thing took him by surprise. He was living then at Lowesby Hall in Leicestershire where he hunted regularly with the Quorn and the Cottesmore. 'I was thoroughly enjoying life when I found myself owner of Blenheim. It was rather a shock,' he admitted. For the next six years, Blenheim had been lively enough, with four young children romping through its halls and the cries and coos of a new baby added in 1940. In the 9th Duke's time, bicycling in the park and walking on the grass had been forbidden; gardeners had to throw down their tools and disappear into the shrubbery whenever their master came into view. The 10th Duke's offspring raced round everywhere on bicycles, even in the cellars, and the Duke liked to mumble advice to his gardeners as he passed by. As one guest noted, Blenheim's corridors rang with 'childish laughter and screams' and 'huge dogs' sprawled about. Mary was a tall woman with a jaw square as a Blenheim stone. After she became Chief Commandant of the ATS (Auxiliary Territorial Service) in 1939, Bert called her 'General' and she rapped out orders to her staff and raised her children, according to the same guest, 'in a rather snappy, almost Spartan, simple way'.

Winston and Clemmie joined the Marlboroughs, as usual, for Christmas during the thirties, and for plenty of weekends as well. They were at Blenheim for an important house-party in June 1936, when the guests included Ernest and Wallis Simpson and the reigning king, Edward VIII. Christmas 1938 found Clemmie holidaying in the Leeward Islands, but Winston proved faithful to Blenheim and turned up with son Randolph and daughter Mary. He had just published, at long last, the fourth and final volume of *Marlborough, His Life and Times*, a work so gargantuan that had its pages been spread out in Blenheim's Great Court, they would have covered most of its stones. 'Writing a book is not unlike building a house,' Winston had written, 'the foundations have to be laid, the data assembled, and the premises must bear the weight of their conclusions.' When Winston wrote about his forebears, the foundation was always the same: solid praise for all previous Churchills and their august dwelling. The keystone, too, was always the same: solid praise for the author himself. 'We miss our giants. We are sorry that their age is past. There is a sense of vacancy and of fatuity, of incompleteness,' sighed Winston elsewhere, longing for modern heroes of the stature of Hannibal, Napoleon and Marlborough. In resurrecting the latter, what Winston conjured from the past was not history, but romance. 'When all that he [John Churchill] had done was belittled or written off as fully paid,' Winston writes lyrically in *Marlborough*, 'he could still reflect that he had made his fortune, that he had founded his family, and that the stones of Blenheim Palace would weather the storms of a thousand years. Such were the stubborn consolations of this virtuous and valiant builder who built noble monuments beneath the stars.' Winston completely ignores not only the clear evidence in the Wentworth Papers that Marlborough kept a mistress, but also every reference to John's stinginess and double-dealing. Malcolm Muggeridge rightly noted this lack of 'cold, aloof judgments' on Winston's part, and the fact that 'long before the end of the story' he has 'equated himself with his ancestor'.

Winston was at beloved Blenheim the following year when, in July 1939, the palace had its final careless rapture before darkness closed in and stayed. It took the form of a coming-out ball for the 10th Duke's daughter Sarah. 'The most elaborate party I ever planned,' Mary told *Woman's Journal*. 'The organization required for coping with a thousand guests was tremendous.' The whole palace was gloriously floodlit, and seemed to hang suspended, ethereal, in the dark night. Everything was bathed in gold: the lake gleaming like a large topaz in its ring of trees, the cut-velvet cedars patterning the lawns, the water terraces bespangled with strings of coloured lights and brimming, as Sunny, 9th Duke had decreed, only with water from Fair Rosamond's Well. For one magical night, Blenheim was a comely courtesan again, as in George, the 4th Duke's time. The palace looked as Winston had always seen it in his mind's eye. He smiled on it benignly, not knowing that his own golden triumph and finest hour would follow hard on the heels of Blenheim's. While a select party of adults, including Winston, dined before the dancing in the Saloon, festooned in white lilies, Sarah and her young friends dined on the terrace facing the lake, with lights shining through pomegranate-coloured awnings. Then an orchestra played Viennese waltzes till dawn in the Long Library. Guests included the Duke of Kent, the daughter of the American ambassador to London, Eunice Kennedy, sister of the future American President, and

Blenheim's 9th Duchess, Consuelo Balsan. Now that the last was living so happily with an adored husband in France, even she could smile indulgently on faerie, festive Blenheim. She sat at supper with Anthony Eden and her old friend, Winston, that irrepressible fountain of self-engrossed anecdote. Sir Sacheverell Sitwell, poet and aesthete, was at the party and penned a nostalgic description of it all: 'There was a galaxy of light upon this theatrical, but heroic building, upon this private monument that is a Roman triumph and a public pantomime; and amid those lights it was possible to admire Vanbrugh's architecture as it may never be seen again.' 'Is such a function not out of date?' asked another guest. 'Yet it was all of the England that is supposed to be dead and is not. There were literally rivers of champagne.' The thousand revellers didn't realize that the ball paralleled the Duchess of Richmond's on the eve of Waterloo. *Après nous, le déluge.* Soon, very soon, English life would be changed for ever and Blenheim would sink into permanent decline. But what a glittering string of parties had adorned the palace! The *jeune-fille* 1719 theatricals in the Bow-window Room ... the sophisticated 1787 production in the orangery ... splendid banquets in 1859 and '96 for Prince Edward ... and now, to crown it all, this brilliant jewel.

Less than two months later, on 3 September, the Second World War began and Blenheim's thousand windows went dark. Its interior, which had been refurbished and repainted for Sarah's party, would suffer worse indignities than even Gladys's spaniels had inflicted. Hundreds of marauding, obstreperous schoolboys made Blenheim quake as fifty little dogs never had. As soon as war was declared, the patriotic 10th Duke asked Malvern College if they would like to evacuate to Blenheim, since their own premises had been commandeered, and they eagerly said yes. Five weeks of drastic transformations followed while Blenheim was uniformed to suit. The three western staterooms and Long Library became dormitories, with iron cots arranged alternately head to foot. The Great Hall was turned into a dining-hall; huge black-out curtains were made for its windows and those of the Long Library (the staterooms had eighteenth-century shutters). The old laundry found itself fitted up as a laboratory and the stables as a gymnasium. Fourteen hundred square feet of linoleum and a thousand square feet of matting were laid; precious damask curtains were covered with canvas and the great mahogany doors were padded with felt. In one courtyard, shower stalls were built; in another, changing rooms took shape, with seats, shelves and clothes racks. The Duke and his family

OPPOSITE: The Long Library converted to a dormitory for Malvern College boys, 1940

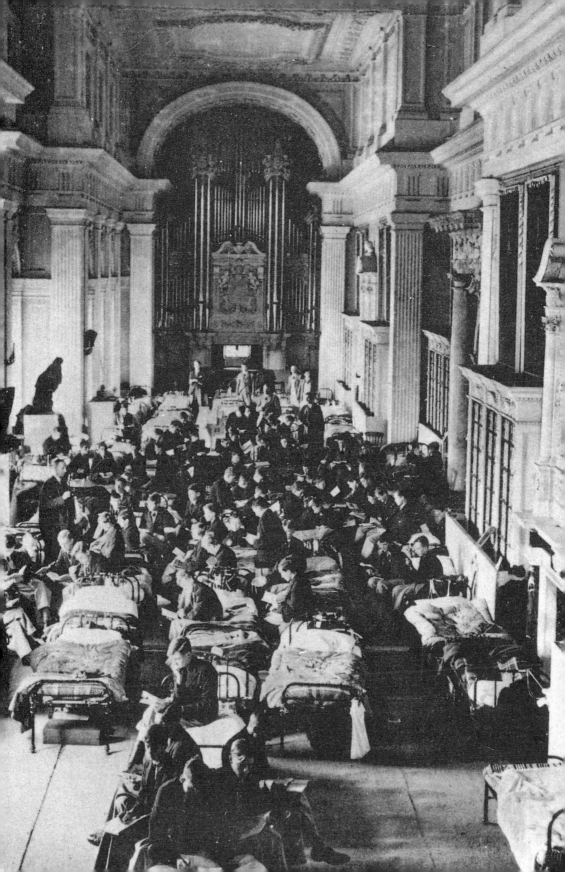

squeezed themselves – nannies, dogs, everything – into the eastern wing for the duration of the war. On 14 September the first vans rattled into the Great Court and dumped a strange cargo of desks, blackboards, crockery and cricket bats on the paving stones while textbooks and bedding piled up in the Great Hall. Finally, on 9 October the invasion took place: four hundred boys and a hundred members of staff surged through the khaki-coloured, utilitarian rooms and Vanbrugh's ghost, hovering just above his bridge, chuckled with delight; he had, had he not, always maintained that Blenheim wasn't an inch too big? 'If the war will not be won on the fields of Blenheim,' *Country Life* declared approvingly, 'they are certainly playing their part in the great business of training the nation, under the shadow of the palace that commemorates the greatest military genius our country has produced.' One year later, Malvern College rumbled away from Blenheim in straggling formation to Harrow-on-the-Hill, but before the palace could attempt to tidy itself, MI5 arrived from Wormwood Scrubs, bringing a thousand workers and turning the staterooms, which would never again be used for day-to-day living, into a hopeless maze of match-board partitions, trestles and filing-cabinets. The present was drab and depressing; the future was uncertain; it was at this point in 1940 that Blenheim began, as indeed did all of Britain, with Winston as prime mover, to feed off the past.

On 10 May 1940, Winston became Prime Minister at the age of sixty-five, and found full flowering, just as Blenheim had in the 1760s, when its character had been in perfect harmony with the times, as Winston's was now. The very qualities of overbearing single-mindedness and pig-headed stubbornness which had been liabilities for the maverick, maligned peace-time politician became assets for the courageous, revered wartime leader.

Winston came to Blenheim in September 1940 to draw strength and inspiration from its stones for the awesome struggle ahead. He spent the afternoon crawling about the Long Library floor, marshalling his fifteen hundred toy soldiers into the winning formations of the battle of Blenheim, while his cigar smoke curled upwards, and armour-clad John Churchill looked on approvingly from his marble plinth.

Winston was now fired by an extraordinary sense of mission. 'This cannot be accident,' he told Sir Charles Wilson, later Lord Moran, his physician. 'I was kept for this job.' All his energies now, his ferocious will, his autocratic bludgeoning, were focused on Victory, and the symbol of victory was, as it had always been for Winston, Blenheim Palace. Once, walking through war-torn London with his private secretary, Winston leapt over a steel girder and landed in a pool of liquid cement. 'You have now,' quipped the secretary pertly, 'met your Waterloo.' 'Certainly not,' born-to-win Winston replied at once. 'My Blenheim!' For the Battle of Britain, he had his façade ready. 'I can look very fierce when I like,' he told his physician, and proceeded to do so for the next five years. His face assumed a hard pugnacity, with scowling brow and firm mouth like the straight gash of a chisel through stone – an expression quite as belligerent as that of Blenheim's north front. Winston added the torpedo cigar and the 'V' for victory of his upraised hand, and became a living legend, Britain's best progaganda-piece. He lumbered about the bomb sites of London with his head jutting forward from hunched shoulders 'like the muzzle of a gun about to fire', as one friend put it. He took to wearing one-piece, step-in overalls like the ones he'd worn at Chartwell to build brick walls, a favourite pastime. In his bricklayer's overalls, made up in velvet or striped worsted, he reminded Lady Diana Cooper of 'the good little pig building his house with bricks'. But what Winston was building was far more formidable: a mighty fortress to keep his people safe and Hitler at bay, and the bricks he used were words. When anyone asked Clement Attlee, who succeeded him as Prime Minister, what exactly Winston Churchill *did* to win the war, Attlee always replied: 'Talk about it.' Winston set the foundation stone carefully in place: his belief, nurtured at Blenheim, that the past informs and inspirits the present. Winston convinced his countrymen that they were huge figures on the hill top of history able to make their mark there. He called forth from their hearts the panache and chivalry and patriotism of an earlier age when heroes like John Churchill charged across the fields. Winston dipped his trowel into British history and used it as mortar for all his radio talks and parliamentary speeches. And the British people heeded his words precisely because he was the product of a great house and a great tradition, a true aristocrat who wore only pink silk underwear, changed his shirt three times a day, never entered a shop and, like the 10th Duke of Marlborough, found his toothpaste ready-squeezed on the brush. Like the stately home of his birth, this Churchill, so adventurous, pugnacious and patriarchal, perfectly symbolized Britain's glorious past still vibrant in the present.

Winston's speeches were carefully, painstakingly constructed ahead of time – he couldn't speak well extemporaneously. He was as baroque and dramatic with words as Vanbrugh had been with stones: long, sweeping sentences, massed conjunctive clauses, formal symmetry of phrases, high-flying rhetoric. The grandiose language was Winston's natural idiom just as Blenheim was his natural backdrop, and as the war clouds grew darker and denser, the nation gathered round its wireless sets with their cloth fronts and took spiritual sustenance from every smooth, golden word. And Winston well knew that while monuments in real mortar and stone – the

Pyramids, the Parthenon, Blenheim Palace itself – 'crumble under the hand of Time', as he put it, words 'last for ever': 'words spoken two or three thousand years ago remain with us now, not as mere relics of the past, but with all their pristine vital force'.

Night after night, the architect of victory sat in his velvet overalls, themselves as antithetical as his character, at 10 Downing Street or at Ditchley Park, the country house of friends near Blenheim where Winston repaired when a full moon meant heavy bombing from the German Luftwaffe, and took up his pen. One clean stone piled on another: 'short words are best and the old words are best of all', he declared. 'You ask,' thundered Winston to the House of Commons on 13 May 1940, just after he became Prime Minister, 'what is our policy? I will say: ... to wage war against a monstrous tyranny, never surpassed in the dark lamentable catalogue of human crime ... You ask: What is our aim? I can answer in one word: Victory! Victory at all costs, victory in spite of all terror, victory however long and hard the road may be; for without victory there is no survival.' On 4 June, after the evacuation of the British army from Dunkirk, Winston's word-rhythms rang like great brass rings flung down on marble: 'We shall fight on the beaches, we shall fight on the landing grounds, we shall fight in the fields and in the streets, we shall fight in the hills; we shall never surrender.' When France fell, on 22 June, Winston's strong voice with its upper-class vowels and endearing lisp rallied his people: 'Let us therefore brace ourselves to our duties, and so bear ourselves that, if the British Empire and its Commonwealth last for a thousand years, men will still say, "This was their finest hour".'

Whenever he could manage it, Winston paid a short visit to Blenheim, where he and the Duchess played bézique in her sitting-room late at night. 'I won't say he's a bad loser,' Mary told a friend, 'but he much prefers to win.'

At 3 p.m. on Tuesday, 8 May 1945, Winston capped his last verbal tower with a golden ball by announcing to the nation that the war was over! Victory was theirs, and his own enduring, magnificent monument was complete. (He would leave it to others, including son Randolph, to collect his war speeches into book form.) When the seventy-year-old hero emerged from Downing Street, smiling now, not scowling, fifty thousand people were there to cheer him.

'I'm worried about this damned election. I have no message for them now,' Winston confided to Lord Moran on 22 June. 'I feel very lonely

---

OPPOSITE: Sir Winston Churchill with Duchess Mary at Blenheim

without a war.' He had reason to worry, for the aristocratic Prime Minister was swept from office to make way for Clement Attlee and the Labour Party. The common man was supreme now, and the democratization of Britain began, a new age of stronger unions, higher wages, better education and a national health service. Overnight, it seemed, Winston became an anachronism; baroque excesses and heroic vistas were unsuited to drab, plebeian post-war Britain. Like Blenheim, Winston had survived too long; history swept on by and left them both stranded, beached leviathans on an inhospitable shore.

'I think I'll go to the Riviera,' sighed Winston to Lord Moran at the end of 1945. 'I don't mind if I never see England again. Ah, Charles, blessings become curses. You kept me alive and now –'

Blenheim's prospects, too, had never looked so bleak in that new age of 'clatter and buzz', which is what Winston called it. MI5 had departed in 1944, but the brown clutter, cardboard cubby-holes and ugly huts remained. The palace's expansive grandeur made it prey to further plagues of resident bureaucrats: the British Council first, then the Ministry of Works.

In August 1949 Winston suffered his first slight stroke, caused by arterio-sclerosis. 'He will not give in without a great struggle, but there can be only one end to it,' his physician recorded dolefully in his diary. At Blenheim, the wallpaper in Dean Jones's bedroom where Winston had been born hung in tatters and the skirting-board had a large rat hole in it. In February 1950, Winston had another slight stroke just as Blenheim's roof problems became so serious that rain poured into the attics. The south-east tower was leaning so badly that it needed rebuilding from the ground up. The 10th Duke went about cursing 'the bloody roof' and worrying about where the money was to come from for repairs. Should he turn Blenheim over to the National Trust, or sell it to the highest bidder? 'Blessings become curses' ...

The Duke decided that the best solution would be to open Blenheim to the public, not, as in the eighteenth and nineteenth centuries, as a *noblesse oblige* gesture, but as a strictly money-making enterprise. The Ministry of Works did what they could to cover Blenheim's wartime scars with fresh paint and gilt-powder. On 1 April 1950, the first 230 visitors, at half a crown each, tramped through the geriatric palace. The sale of garden produce, guidebooks and souvenirs brought in more cash to pay for Blenheim's medication. 'All this is very necessary,' the 10th Duke told the *Daily Mirror*. 'Without these half-crown entrance fees we couldn't possibly keep the place going. Taxation, y'know. Crippling.' In that first year, well over 100,000 tourists came to Blenheim, which had now entered its final phase. In the 1st Duke's time, Blenheim's martial mood was full of trumpets; in the 4th Duke's day, its pastoral beauty had a flute-like pathos; in the 7th Duke's reign, its piety gave rise to hymn tunes; in the 9th Duke's queasy wane Blenheim sounded a minor note of jazz and blues. In the 10th Duke's time, Big Business and the Hard Sell came to stay; the clink of cash registers drowned all other strains. Repairs to the roof began at once, starting on the east end; they would continue for the next forty years. In 1951 *Country Life* published David Green's *Blenheim Palace*, a handsome, well-researched book which increased Blenheim's fame and its queues of sightseers.

Other stately homes shared Blenheim's commercial fate: Chatsworth and Longleat and Woburn Abbey, where Duchess Caroline had been raised. The last opened its doors in 1953 and outstripped Blenheim's first year with 181,000 visitors. 'Being a showman is much more fun than sitting about in dignity or potting pheasants,' Woburn's owner, the Duke of Bedford, declared as he mingled and joked with the crowds. The stately homes which became cold museums with resident peers were the lucky ones, for as they ceased to be viable homes, they were revered more and more as venerable institutions. 'The Stately Homes of England /Although a trifle bleak, / Historically speaking, / Are more or less unique,' sang Noël Coward, who came to Blenheim for a weekend in mid-November, 1952, and slept 'in the coldest room I have ever encountered ... glacial bathroom with a skylight that would not shut. Loo like an ice-box.' (He fled to Notley, Laurence Olivier's more modern country home.)

The mansions which weren't as famous and as fortunate as Blenheim were boarded up and left to rot, or partly shut, while the indigent owners huddled in one small wing. Other country houses became hotels, sanatoria, schools, country clubs. Some of them were turned, appropriately enough, into apartment complexes for the aged and others, also appropriately, into lunatic asylums. (Our stately homes, Virginia Woolf had declared, have always been nothing but 'comfortably padded lunatic asylums'.)

A year and a half after Blenheim gathered its tired artefacts around it and faced the public, on the last day of October 1951, Winston shuffled back into No. 10 Downing Street for his last stint as Prime Minister, with a majority of seventeen. He had had a minor stroke in February 1950, and had little heart for the task of ruling. In July 1952, he suffered another slight stroke. On good days, he still showed his fighting spirit, and did his best to prevent the Empire from slipping, like his own vitality, inevitably away. He had strenuously opposed India's independence, achieved in 1947, and now other British possessions in Asia, Africa and the western hemisphere were following India's lead. On bad days, Winston appeared 'white, comatose, flabby and almost moribund', as his doctor noted sadly in his diary.

Queen Elizabeth II was crowned on 2 June 1953. Winston liked to think of their relationship as paralleling John Churchill's initial warm rapport with Queen Anne. The new Queen made Winston a Knight of the Garter, and the new Sir Winston held court at Blenheim's grand garden party, held after the Coronation. Later that month, Winston had another, and more serious, stroke. On 5 April 1955 he tendered his resignation to the Queen.

After that, he still came occasionally to Blenheim, to sit huddled in the depths of a big chair in the Grand Cabinet, staring out at Bladon church, or into the fire, which he poked with his stick whenever an unearthly chill gripped him. They were both relics of the past now, he and beloved Blenheim, both of them superannuated, obsolete, more legend than living. Winston sat as still as the 4th Duke had in his final days, as white as the marble urns sculpted on the dark mantelpiece, while the eighteenth-century clocks chimed delicately. 'What is the time now?' Winston would ask of anyone that passed his chair. Someone would tell him. 'Oh, Lor',' he would say. Time had stopped for him ... for Blenheim, too.

Blenheim's memories wrapped him gently round and warmed him: toy soldiers on the nursery floor when he was eight ... on the Long Library floor when he was facing the worst war ever ... Christmas fun, 'French and English' rough-house in the Hall, 'F.E.', Lord Birkenhead, flailing his long arms and roaring. F.E. had been lucky, dying at fifty-eight. 'Think of the great Duke of Marlborough,' Winston had told F.E.'s son, 'how he lingered on into surly decrepitude. How much better it would have been had he been cut off in his brilliant prime, a cannon-ball at Malplaquet.' 'That was once a man,' John Churchill had said, when he had felt himself slipping into dotage. Winston's head dropped forward ... and the house held him softly, quietly.

By the early sixties, Winston's mind was largely dormant; he could no longer read or recognize his friends or speak clearly. He came no more to Blenheim, but over his study mantelpiece at Chartwell was a large, brooding painting of the palace and he often lost himself in its expansive front and everlasting arms.

Blenheim itself was quiet. Mary had died in 1961 after fifteen months of illness and Bert limped about lonely and bereft. He stared one day at the Christmas tree in the apse of Sarah's Bow-window Room, where he always dined. 'Where are the sparkling glass icicles that it's always had, for years and years?' he asked plaintively. 'Tinsel doesn't last, y' know.'

Bert tried to persuade Laura Canfield, a friend of many years, to marry him, but after several weekends at Blenheim she told him that the palace 'was so terribly gloomy' that she couldn't possibly contemplate living in it. (She would eventually marry Bert in 1972 and live only two months at Blenheim before he died.) 'Secretly,' writes Laura in her autobiography, 'Bert was in agreement with me. His reason for continuing to inhabit Blenheim – or as he came (through me) to call it, "the Dump" – was a real fear of being the first Duke not to reside there.'

So Bert and his aching joints stayed in the fusty palace with its tottering towers and ailing roof, and Winston sat silent in a comatose heap at Chartwell or at Hyde Park Gate, the London house he'd bought with book royalties, and the Empire split apart in large chunks and Britain's power and prestige in the world waned. Everything, it seems, was in decline. One day, at the beginning of January 1965, Christopher Soames, Winston's son-in-law, came to sit beside his bed. Winston's eyes were open, but he seldom spoke, and had to be fed. 'Wouldn't you like a glass of champagne?' asked Christopher, trying to kindle some spark. 'I'm so bored with it all,' replied Winston. Those were the last coherent words he ever spoke. On 10 January he suffered a severe stroke. He lay at Hyde Park Gate for fourteen days without movement, still and cold as alabaster, and on the morning of Sunday, 24 January at eight o'clock, death claimed him. A decade before, Winston's private secretary had gone to his bedroom one morning to discuss some business matter while Winston was shaving. 'Today is the twenty-fourth of January', Winston had intoned. 'It is the day my father died. It is the day that I shall die too.' And so it came to pass.

On Tuesday, a large white embossed card headed 'State Funeral at St Paul's Cathedral' arrived on Blenheim's breakfast table in the Bow-window Room. 'The Earl Marshal has it in Command from the Queen to invite the Duke of Marlborough to be present,' it read, 'on the occasion of the State Funeral shortly to be held. A reply requested on the form attached hereto ... *at the earliest possible moment.*' So Winston had gone at last; the Duke felt a chill breath on his neck as if someone – or something – had sighed.

That evening, Winston's body was taken to lie in state at Westminster Hall, with its gaunt, brown hammer-beamed ceiling and bare stone walls, where only royal dead had lain since Gladstone's state funeral in 1898. During the next three days, 320,000 people filed through the Hall to pay homage to the man who had kindled their courage, saved their honour and won their hearts. Sometimes the queue was three miles long, stretching across Lambeth Bridge to the far side of the slow-moving Thames. Inside the Hall, the people flowing soundlessly past both sides of the catafalque where Winston's body lay were themselves a mighty river, seemingly without end. Soldiers stood guard round the bier, which was draped in silver-piped black velvet. (Just after his 1953 stroke, Winston had told

Lord Moran that he didn't believe in an after-life, only in 'black velvet', eternal sleep.) The coffin was covered by the Union Jack, centred with a black silk cushion on which lay Sir Winston's Collar, Garter and Star.

'The occasion is history,' one journalist noted. 'The whole place and ceremonial breathe history.' For twenty-three hours each day, Wednesday, Thursday and Friday, the crowds flowed on and history was served, history was made.

As Big Ben struck a quarter to ten on Saturday morning, the funeral procession set out. From St James's Park came the crash of a ninety-gun salute, one for each year of Winston's life. Up the Strand, up Fleet Street, a gun-carriage bore the coffin with massed ranks of men-at-arms marching slowly behind it. Winston had told Clemmie almost twenty years before, in 1947, that he wanted to be buried as a soldier. 'Very well, dear,' she had soothed, 'you shall be.' But Winston knew that his Clemmie's utilitarian mind had no leanings to baroque. 'When it comes to my funeral, dear boy,' he told his son Randolph, 'your mother may have modest ideas, but I want troops, I want *troops*!' Lining both sides of the parade route as the soldiers marched by was a vast sea of faces – not just white ones, but black and brown and yellow, for as the Empire had drifted away, it had deposited some of its humanity on England's shores.

As St Paul's Cathedral finally came into view, Winston's daughter Sarah remembered standing with her father on the roof of the Savoy Hotel during the Battle of Britain while St Paul's was 'silhouetted in flames'. Under Sir Christopher Wren's great dome, three thousand dignitaries, including Queen Elizabeth and many kings and rulers, gathered to sing 'Fight the Good Fight' and Bunyan's 'He Who Would Valiant Be' and the great Battle Hymn of the Republic whose words Winston had known by heart. Now he lay under the opalescent dome, hard by the tombs of Nelson and Wellington, as the organ swelled, and tears fell and an additional 350 million viewers watched the ceremony on their television sets. The television lights gave the church a golden radiance which Wren could never have foreseen.

After the short service, the coffin was taken to Tower Pier and piped aboard a launch while a seventeen-gun salute sounded and Fighter Command planes roared overhead. Then Winston took his last voyage through the very core of British history: under the Tower's shadow, beneath London Bridge, past the high-vaulted Houses of Parliament where his voice still echoed, to Festival Pier, to meet his Waterloo, and begin the two-hour journey to Hanborough Station.

As the train sped forward, the Duke of Marlborough looked out at what for him was the most touching scene of the whole day. Along the tracks, and on every station platform, were knots and lines of people: families with large dogs and children on shaggy ponies waited in the cheerless winter fields; a lock-keeper saluted; a farmer doffed his worn cloth cap; they all stood silently in the bitter cold to watch Sir Winston Churchill going home to Blenheim.

O**N SATURDAY, 6 FEBRUARY, THE SUN ROSE ABOVE BLENHEIM'S** eastern wing, where the 10th Duke was gingerly rising from his bed, and the palace's mottled old stones assumed a faint pink glow. Across the frosty park, crowds of people began to file once more past Winston's grave. Since his burial one week before, 150,000 had already paid homage – more than had come to Blenheim in its first public-viewing year. The cemetery area on the north side of St Martin's tower was now one vast carpet of flowers; they covered Jennie's grave, directly behind Winston's, and Randolph's, to the left, with its large stone cross, and Consuelo's unassuming one to the right. Most of the people filing past had driven for many miles; the villagers of Bladon had come earlier in the week, their babies wrapped in blankets against the cold. Winston had been a familiar figure in their churchyard; he had often come across the park from Blenheim to visit his parents' graves, and afterwards the villagers had picked up his cigar stubs from the grass and treasured them as if they were religious relics.

The myth of Sir Winston, Grand Hero, was already building and its verbal wreaths were fashioned with descriptive words that could apply equally well to the palace that had shaped him. If 'historians are likely to argue about the achievements,' Sir Charles Petrie writes, 'there is one aspect of these achievements upon which they are likely to agree, and it is that everything he [Winston] did was in the grand manner.' He was, Isaiah Berlin decides, 'a man larger than life, composed of bigger and simpler elements than ordinary men, a gigantic historical figure during his own lifetime, superhumanly bold, strong, and imaginative, one of the two greatest men of action his nation has produced.' 'He was always expansive,' declares Maurice Ashley, 'at any rate among those he liked and trusted.' 'If the scale of Churchill's achievement was gargantuan,' Piers Brendon notes, 'his character also seemed far larger than life ... [for Winston] paraded his qualities and defects in exaggerated form, like a great actor playing to the gallery of posterity.' Jack Fishman speaks of Winston's 'legendary magnificence'; Arthur Bryant calls him a 'colossus of a man', and Violet Bonham Carter remembers his 'innate pugnacity'. 'He was not like other men,' Lord Moran declared; 'he could do nothing in moderation.' Winston became, according to Brendon, 'an ancient monument during his own lifetime'.

Sir Winston Churchill's last resting place and birthplace:
Bladon Church and Blenheim Palace

The crowds filed slowly and respectfully past the grave of their great hero on that Saturday morning one week after his funeral. The pink glow faded from Blenheim's stones and they assumed their usual jaundiced hue. Bert, the 10th Duke, having finished his solitary breakfast in his great house, stood pensive in the Saloon looking towards Bladon. Winston was certainly drawing the crowds and when 'the Dump' re-opened to the public in another month there would be more tourists than ever wanting to see his birth room. More tourists, more money. The roof repairs alone were costing £30,000 a year. Winston had been luckier than Blenheim's current master. 'Beyond question, Blenheim made for Winston the ideal background,' Bert would write. 'At times, for example, when he was researching for his life of Marlborough, it must have given him inspiration. Although before I was born he was heir to the dukedom, I doubt if he hankered much for the palace itself. Much as he cared for Blenheim, it would not have appealed to him to go down in history as its owner.' Winston had had all the beauty and fun of Blenheim with none of the burden and financial worry. He didn't have three acres of decaying roofs on his shoulders; he'd always been able to come and go at Blenheim, admiring its battle tapestries, thumbing through its archives, and then returning to 'cosy Pig', his Chartwell study. Blenheim, for Winston, was mistress, not wife. No wonder he'd been able to keep his illusions intact, to see the palace through rose-coloured glasses, what? And now it would be Winston, not its slaving Dukes, who would keep the coffers full so that the old dowager could go on existing. Bert turned his back on Winston's burial place, and on the Saloon's escutcheoned doors and polished floors. The 10th Duke of Marlborough made his way slowly and heavily towards his study where Bill Murdock, his estate agent, was waiting with a fresh pile of bills, and as he walked, no pride, only bitterness, went with him.

T EN DUKES HAD LEFT THEIR IMPRINT ON THE OLD DOWAGER, TEN active, autocratic masters. Blenheim's 1st Duke, John Churchill, had fought and won abroad, then fought and won again at home, with Sarah and Vanbrugh, to make his vision of a rich man's castle stand. The 4th Duke had decked his house-and-mistress in velvet lawns and golden lyres for his own sensual delight. The 7th Duke had stalked his halls and Chapel in full piety and pride; the 9th Duke had spread that swollen pride about the grounds, on elm-lined avenues and reflective water terraces and tortured insignia in boxwood. The 10th Duke had shrugged, and turned his dogs and children loose. Masters of Blenheim all; for every Duke the house existed to serve their needs and bring their dreams to life. Or so they thought.

The sun rose higher in the sky as the 10th Duke sat captive in his study, frowning at his pile of bills. On Blenheim's north portico, Minerva smiled her triumphant grin and behind her the two male captives writhed in their stone chains. For two hundred and sixty years, Blenheim had felt the rhythms of its masters' births and deaths, loves and loathings, devotions and defections. For two hundred and sixty years, Blenheim had nursed its secret and not a single Duke had ever found it out.

'We shape our dwellings, and afterwards our dwellings shape us,' Winston had said. Minerva's smile seemed to broaden. Winston alone had seen the truth: the ten Dukes of Marlborough were not masters in their own house, but servants. The palace wasn't there to serve their ends, whatever they might be: propaganda, pulchritude, piety or pride. The Dukes were there to serve the palace; it shaped them to its own desires. The golden balls on Blenheim's towers caught the sun, gleaming and gloating, as Blenheim's memories of its conquests unswirled and stiffened in the morning breeze: the 1st Duke building so grandly, then retreating so ignominiously from taunting halls; the 4th Duke loving and lavishing and being swallowed up by damask walls; the 7th Duke puffing up with pride in his machine-of-a-palace, which hummed and turned its wonders to perform, not knowing that he could never make it stop; the 9th Duke laying his life on Blenheim's altar, only to turn infidel and flee; the 10th Duke . . . the palace hadn't finished with the 10th Duke yet.

Dukes were servants – cosseting, cowering, sometimes cursing; Winston was different; Winston was a son. He alone had stayed loyal and loving to the end. The palace had done its work well with Winston. It had formed him to serve a greater cause than Blenheim's, given him his baroque rhetoric, his fighting spirit, his rock-like stubbornness, his omnipresent sense of history, his will to win, that above all. And he had worn the palace as central medallion on his 'golden chain', knowing that Blenheim linked past to present to future; tradition to progress; man to his most hallowed institutions. For Winston, Blenheim had been home and haven and hub of the moving cycle of his days: lived in, left, remembered, returned to, round and round; 'in my beginning is my end'. Blenheim's stones – those volatile stones which answered time and light and weather with a hundred different tones – took on a deeper, truer gold. The palace had given its whole heart and soul to Winston, who had not only loved – many, in their own crabbed way, had loved – but who had also understood.

'Victory!' he had urged. 'Victory however long and hard the road may be, for without victory there is no survival.' Blenheim's ferocious stone lions bit the sinews of their captive French cocks; Minerva grasped her shield and javelin; John Churchill, on his Column of Victory, raised high his arm and saluted the great Churchill at the far end of history's forward march. Blenheim Palace stood, a little shaky and querulous, but still triumphant, its will to win carved into every trophy, impregnating every stone. Blenheim victorious, hoary and glorious, Blenheim would survive; its vassal-Dukes would keep it alive to weather the storms of a thousand years. 'Monuments crumble under the hand of Time,' Winston had written – so be it – but words keep 'their pristine vital force'. After a thousand years, when the palace had returned to the rich humus of Woodstock Park, great armies of words – Sarah's, Vanbrugh's, Winston's, so many others' – would still trumpet Blenheim's life-story to the world.

BIBLIOGRAPHY

NOTE

Works are listed only under the heading of the earliest chapter for which they were consulted.

1. GROWING PAINS

I. *Manuscript Sources (British Library, London)*

Blenheim Papers, Additional Mss. Nos. 61353, 61354, 61355, 61359, 61466, 61472, 61479.
Private Correspondence of Archdeacon Coxe, Additional Mss. Nos. 9078 and 9079.
Coxe Papers, Additional Ms. No. 9125.

II. *Periodical Articles*

ANON., 'Blenheim Palace', *Country Life* (29 May and 5 June 1909), pp. 786–98, 834–44.
GREEN, David, 'Visitors to Blenheim', *Country Life* (10 March 1950), pp. 648–51.
GREEN, David, and HUSSEY, Christopher, 'Blenheim Palace Revisited. Grinling Gibbons at Blenheim', *Country Life* (20 May 1949), pp. 1182–6.
—— 'Blenheim Palace Revisited. The East Wing', *Country Life* (27 May 1949), pp. 1246–50.
GREEN, David, and JOURDAIN, Margaret, 'Furniture at Blenheim', *Country Life* (20 April 1951), pp. 1184–6.
HOADLY, Bishop, 'A Hasty Prologue to *All for Love* Acted at Blenheim-House', *Gentleman's Magazine* (February 1774), vol. 44, pp. 87–8.
WALPOLE, Horace, 'Journals of Visits to Country Seats', *Walpole Society* (1927–8), vol. 16, p. 26.

III. *Books*

BALLARD, Adolphus, *Chronicles of the Royal Borough of Woodstock*, Oxford, Alden, 1896.
BLANCHARD, Rae, *The Correspondence of Richard Steele*, London, Oxford University Press, 1941.
BURTON, Elizabeth, *The Georgians at Home, 1714–1830*, London, Longmans, 1967.
CAMPBELL, Colen, *Vitruvius Britannicus*, vol. I, London, n.p., 1717.
CHANCELLOR, Frank, *Sarah Churchill*, n.p., Philip Allan, 1932.
CHURCHILL, Winston S., *Marlborough, His Life and Times*, 4 vols., London, Harrap, 1938.
COLLINS, John Churton, *Bolingbroke, a Historical Study; and Voltaire in England*, London, John Murray, 1886.
COOK, Olive, *The Country House. An Art and a Way of Life*, London, Thames & Hudson, 1974.
COXE, William, *Memoirs of John Duke of Marlborough*, 6 vols., London, Longman, Hurst, Rees, Orme & Brown, 1820.

[DEFOE, Daniel], *Tour Through the Whole Island of Great Britain,* 3 vols., London, G. Strahan, 1724–7.

DELANY, Mrs, *The Autobiography and Correspondence of Mary Granville, Mrs Delany,* Second Series, 3 vols., London, Richard Bentley, 1862.

DOBRÉE, Bonamy, *Three Eighteenth-century Figures,* London, Oxford University Press, 1962.

DOWNES, Kerry, *Hawksmoor,* London, A. Zwemmer, 1959.

—— *Sir John Vanbrugh,* London, Sidgwick & Jackson, 1987.

DUTTON, Ralph, *The English Interior, 1500 to 1900,* London, Batsford, 1948.

EVANS, Herbert A., *Highways and Byways in Oxford and the Cotswolds,* London, Macmillan, 1908.

GIROUARD, Mark, *Life in the English Country House. A Social and Architectural History,* New Haven, Yale University Press, 1978; Harmondsworth, Penguin Books, 1980.

GOTCH, J. Alfred, *The Growth of the English House,* London, Batsford, 1909.

GREEN, David, *Battle of Blenheim,* London, Collins, 1974.

—— *Blenheim Palace,* London, Country Life, 1951.

—— *The Churchills of Blenheim,* London, Constable, 1984.

—— *Sarah Duchess of Marlborough,* London, Collins, 1967.

GUTTSMAN, W. L., ed., *The English Ruling Class,* London, Weidenfeld & Nicolson, 1969.

HARTCUP, Adeline, *Below Stairs in the Great Country Houses,* London, Sidgwick & Jackson, 1980.

HEARNE, Thomas, *Remarks and Collections of Thomas Hearne,* vol. VI (1 Jan. 1717–18 May 1719), printed for Oxford Historical Society at Clarendon Press, 1902.

HENDERSON, M. Sturge, *Three Centuries in North Oxfordshire,* Oxford, Blackwell, 1902.

MARLBOROUGH, Sarah, Duchess of, *Letters of Sarah Duchess of Marlborough,* from the original manuscripts at Madresfield Court, London, John Murray, 1875.

—— *Private Correspondence of Sarah Duchess of Marlborough,* 2 vols., London, Henry Colburn, 1838.

MARSHALL, Edward, *The Early History of Woodstock Manor,* Oxford and London, James Parker, 1873.

—— *A Supplement to the History of Woodstock Manor and Its Environs,* Oxford and London, James Parker, 1874.

MAVOR, Reid William Fordyce, *New Description of Blenheim,* London, T. Cadell, 1789.

MONTGOMERY-MASSINGBERD, Hugh, *Blenheim Revisited: the Spencer-Churchills and their Palace,* New York, Beaufort Books, 1985.

[NEWINGTON, Thomas], *A Butler's Recipe Book 1719,* ed. Philip James, Cambridge, Cambridge University Press, 1935.

NICHOLS, John, *The Epistolary Correspondence of Sir Richard Steele,* 2 vols., London, Longman, Hurst, Rees & Orme, 1809.

PEEL, J. H. B., *An Englishman's Home,* London, Cassell, 1972.

PINE, L. G., *Tales of the British Aristocracy,* London, Burke, 1956.

PLUMB, J. H., *The First Four Georges,* London, Batsford, 1957.

POPE, Alexander, *Poetry and Prose of Alexander Pope,* ed. Aubrey Williams, Boston, Houghton Mifflin, 1969.

—— *The Correspondence of Alexander Pope,* ed. George Sherburn, vol. I: 1704–18, Oxford, Clarendon Press, 1956.

REID, Stuart J., *John and Sarah, Duke and Duchess of Marlborough,* London, John Murray, 1914.

ROSENFELD, Sybil, *Temples of Thespis. Some Private Theatres and Theatricals in England and Wales 1700–1820,* London, Society for Theatre Research, 1978.

ROWSE, A. L., *The Early Churchills. An English Family*, London, Macmillan, 1956.

RYBCZYNSKI, Witold, *Home. A Short History of an Idea*, New York, Viking, 1986.

SACKVILLE-WEST, Vita, *English Country Houses*, London, Collins, 1941.

SCHARF, George, *Catalogue Raisonné, or A List of the Pictures in Blenheim Palace*, London, Dorrell & Son, 1862.

SNYDER, Henry L., ed., *The Marlborough-Godolphin Correspondence*, 3 vols., Oxford, Clarendon Press, 1975.

STUART, Dorothy Margaret, *The English Abigail*, London, Macmillan, 1946.

SWIFT, Jonathan, 'The Four Last Years of Queen Anne', in *The Works of Jonathan Swift*, with notes and a life of the author by Sir Walter Scott, vol. 5, *Tracts Historical and Political*, London, Bickers & Son, 1883.

THOMSON, Mrs A. T., *Memoirs of Sarah Duchess of Marlborough and of the Court of Queen Anne*, 2 vols., London, Henry Colburn, 1839.

THOMSON, Gladys Scott, ed., *Letters of a Grandmother 1732–1735*, London, Jonathan Cape, 1943.

—— *Life in a Noble Household, 1641–1700*, London, Jonathan Cape, 1937.

TURNER, E. S., *What the Butler Saw*, London, Michael Joseph, 1962.

VANBRUGH, Sir John, *The Complete Works of Sir John Vanbrugh*, vol. IV, *The Letters*, ed. Geoffrey Webb, London, Nonesuch Press, 1928.

WACE, Alan, *The Marlborough Tapestries at Blenheim Palace*, London and New York, Phaidon, 1968.

WALPOLE, Horace, *The Letters of Horace Walpole*, ed. Peter Cunningham, 9 vols., Edinburgh, John Grant, 1906.

—— *Reminiscences*, Oxford, Clarendon Press, 1924.

WHISTLER, Laurence, *The Imagination of Vanbrugh and His Fellow Artists*, London, Batsford, 1954.

—— *Sir John Vanbrugh, Architect and Dramatist*, London, Cobden-Sanderson, 1938.

YOUNG, Arthur, *A Six Weeks' Tour through the Southern Counties of England and Wales*, London, W. Nicoll, [1768].

2. GOLDEN YOUTH

I. *Manuscript Sources (British Library, London)*

Blenheim Papers, Additional Mss. Nos. 61670, 61671, 61672, 61674, 61678, 61679, 61680.
Sir William Chambers Papers, Additional Mss. Nos. 41133, 41134, 41135.

II. *Periodical Articles*

ANON., 'Blenheim Palace, Oxfordshire', *Country Life* (3 and 10 June 1899), pp. 688–92, 720–24.

ANON., *Gentleman's Magazine* (November and December 1811), vol. 81, pp. 493 and 667 (obituary of Caroline, 4th Duchess of Marlborough).

ANON., *Gentleman's Magazine* (February 1817), vol. 87, pp. 179–81 (obituary of George, 4th Duke of Marlborough).

ANON., 'Blenheim House Theatre', *Town and Country Magazine or Universal Repository* (October 1787), vol. 18, pp. 437–8.

KITSON, Sydney D., 'William Chambers. From Canton to Kew', *The Times*, 19 May 1933, pp. 15–16.

—— 'William Chambers. Somerset House', *The Times*, 20 May 1933, pp. 13–14.

III. *Books*

ANGUS, William, *The Seats of the Nobility and Gentry in Great Britain and Wales*, engraved by William Angus, London, 1787.

Annual Register for 1787, The, London, J. Dodsley, 1788.

AUCKLAND, William, Lord, *Journal and Correspondence of William Lord Auckland*, ed. the Bishop of Bath and Wells, vols. I and II, London, Richard Bentley, 1861 and 1862.

BROADLEY, A.M., and MELVILLE, Lewis, eds., *The Beautiful Lady Craven*, 2 vols., London, Bodley Head, 1914.

[BRYANT, Jacob, and COLE, W.], *Gemmarum Antiquarum Delectus*, 2 vols., [London, privately printed, 1780 and 1791].

BYNG, John, *The Torrington Diaries*, ed. C. Bruyn Andrews, 4 vols., London, Eyre & Spottiswoode, 1934.

CLARK, Kenneth, *Civilisation. A Personal View*, London, John Murray, 1971; Harmondsworth, Penguin Books, 1987.

COKE, Lady Mary, *The Letters and Journals of Lady Mary Coke*, 2 vols., Bath, Kingsmead Reprints, 1970.

COZENS-HARDY, Basil, ed., *The Diary of Sylas Neville*, London, Oxford University Press, 1950.

D'ARBLAY, Madame, *Diary and Letters of Madame D'Arblay* [Fanny Burney], edited by her niece Charlotte Barrett, vol. II, London, Macmillan, 1904.

ERSKINE, Mrs Steuart, *Lady Diana Beauclerk. Her Life and Work*, London, T. Fisher Unwin, 1903.

FARINGTON, Joseph, *The Farington Diary*, ed. James Greig, vols. I and II, London, Hutchinson, 1922 and 1923.

FITZGERALD, Brian, ed., *Correspondence of Emily, Duchess of Leinster*, 2 vols., Dublin, Stationery Office, 1949.

GILL, Richard, *Happy Rural Seat. The English Country House and the Literary Imagination*, New Haven, Yale University Press, 1972.

GRONOW, Captain, *The Reminiscences and Recollections of Captain Gronow*, 2 vols., London, John C. Nimmo, 1892.

HAMILTON, Lady Anne, *Secret History of the Court of England*, London, Reynolds Newspaper Office, 1878.

HARCOURT, Mrs, 'Mrs Harcourt's Diary of the Court of King George III', in *Miscellanies of the Philobiblon Society*, vol. 13, London, Whittingham and Wilkins, 1871–2, pp. 3–57.

HARRIS, John, *Sir William Chambers*, London, A. Zwemmer, 1970.

HARTCUP, Adeline, *Love and Marriage in the Great Country Houses*, London, Sidgwick & Jackson, 1984.

HERBERT, Lord, *Henry, Elizabeth and George. Letters and Diaries of Henry, Tenth Earl of Pembroke and His Circle*, London, Jonathan Cape, 1939.

—— *The Pembroke Papers 1780–1794*, London, Jonathan Cape, 1950.

HILLES, Frederick Whiley, ed., *Letters of Sir Joshua Reynolds*, Cambridge, Cambridge University Press, 1929.

HINDE, Thomas, *Capability Brown: the Story of a Master Gardener*, London, Hutchinson, 1986.

HYAMS, Edward, *Capability Brown and Humphry Repton*, London, J.M. Dent, 1971.

JEFFERSON, Thomas, *The Papers of Thomas Jefferson*, vol. 9, ed. Julian P. Boyd, Princeton, Princeton University Press, 1954.

JESSE, J. Heneage, *Memoirs of the Life and Reign of George III*, vol. 3, London, Tinsley Brothers, 1867.

JEWITT, Llewellyn, *The Wedgwoods: Being a Life of Josiah Wedgwood*, London, Virtue Brothers, 1865.

KELLY, Hugh, *False Delicacy*, London, R. Baldwin, 1768.

KENNY, Virginia C., *The Country-House Ethos in English Literature 1688–1750*, Sussex, Harvester Press, 1984.

LA ROCHEFOUCAULD, François de, *A Frenchman in England, 1784*, ed. Jean Marchand, trans. S. C. Roberts, Cambridge, Cambridge University Press, 1933.

LENNOX, Lady Sarah, *The Life and Letters of Lady Sarah Lennox 1745–1826*, ed. the Countess of Ilchester and Lord Stavordale, London, John Murray, 1904.

LESLIE, Charles Robert, and TAYLOR, Tom, *Life and Times of Sir Joshua Reynolds*, 2 vols., London, John Murray, 1865.

MACDONALD, John, *Memoirs of an Eighteenth-Century Footman*, ed. J. Beresford, London, Routledge, 1927.

MASKELYNE, M. H. Nevil, *The Marlborough Gems*, printed for private distribution, 1870.

MAVOR, Revd William Fordyce, *New Description of Blenheim, Containing a Picturesque Tour of Gardens and Park*, Oxford, Slatter & Munday, 1806.

MOWAT, R. B., *Americans in England*, London, Harrap, 1935.

NEVILL, Ralph, ed., *Leaves from the Note-Books of Lady Dorothy Nevill*, London, Macmillan, 1907.

POWYS, Mrs Philip Lybbe, *Passages from the Diaries of Mrs. Philip Lybbe Powys*, ed. Emily J. Climenson, London, Longmans, 1899.

PRIOR, Sir James, *Life of Edmond Malone*, London, Smith, Elder, 1860.

REYNOLDS, Frederick, *Life and Times of Frederick Reynolds*, 2 vols., London, Henry Colburn, 1826.

ROWSE, A. L., *The Later Churchills*, London, Macmillan, 1958.

RUSSELL, Lord John, *Correspondence of John, First Duke of Bedford*, 3 vols., London, Longman, Brown, Green and Longmans, 1846.

STROUD, Dorothy, *Capability Brown*, London, Faber, 1975.

THACKERY, W. M., *The Four Georges and the English Humourists of the Eighteenth Century*, London, Cassell, 1909.

TRENT, Christopher, *The Russells*, London, Frederick Muller, 1966.

WALPOLE, Horace, *Memoirs of the Reign of King George the Third*, 4 vols., London, Lawrence & Bullen, 1894.

WEDGWOOD, Josiah, *The Selected Letters of Josiah Wedgwood*, ed. Ann Finer and George Savage, London, Cory, Adams & Mackay, 1965.

WHITE, Cecil, *A Versatile Professor: Reminiscences of the Reverend Edward Nares, D.D.*, London, R. Brimley Johnson, 1903.

WILSON, Philip Whitwell, ed., *The Greville Diary*, vol. 1, London, Heinemann, 1927.

3. SMUG MATURITY

I. *Manuscript Sources (British Library, London)*

Blenheim Papers, Additional Ms. No. 61677.

II. *Periodical Articles*

ANON., *The Times*, 2 Dec. 1859, p. 12 (Blenheim Palace Banquet).
ANON., *The Times*, 12 Feb. 1861, p. 8 (fire at Blenheim Palace).

ANON., *The Times*, 6 July 1883, p. 10 (obituary of 7th Duke of Marlborough). See also items of 7, 9, 11 and 13 July 1883.

ANON., 'New Lord Lieutenant of Ireland', *Illustrated London News*, 28 Oct. 1876, p. 404.

III. *Books*

ARBUTHNOT, Harriet, *The Journal of Mrs. Arbuthnot 1820–1832*, ed. Francis Bamford and the Duke of Wellington, 2 vols., London, Macmillan, 1950.

BADEAU, Adam, *Aristocracy in England*, London, Harper, 1886.

BLAKE, Robert, *Disraeli*, London, Eyre & Spottiswoode, 1966.

BUCKLE, George Earle, *The Life of Benjamin Disraeli*, 6 vols., London, John Murray, 1916.

CHURCHILL, Peregrine, and MITCHELL, Julian, *Jennie, Lady Randolph Churchill. A Portrait with Letters*, London, Collins, 1974.

CHURCHILL, Randolph S., *Winston S. Churchill*, vol. 1, Companion, part 1: *1874–1896*, London, Heinemann, 1967.

CHURCHILL, Winston S., *Lord Randolph Churchill*, London, Odham Press, 1952.

—— *My Early Life. A Roving Commission*, London, Reprint Society, 1944.

CORNWALLIS-WEST, Mrs George [Lady Randolph Churchill], *The Reminiscences of Lady Randolph Churchill*, London, Edward Arnold, 1908.

DANA, Richard Henry, *Hospitable England in the Seventies. The Diary of a Young American 1875–76*, London, John Murray, 1921.

DISRAELI, Benjamin, *Letters from Benjamin Disraeli to Frances Anne, Marchioness of Londonderry, 1837–1861*, ed. the Marchioness of Londonderry, London, Macmillan, 1938.

—— *The Letters of Disraeli to Lady Bradford and Lady Chesterfield*, ed. the Marquis of Zetland, 2 vols., London, Ernest Benn, 1929.

DRUMMOND, J. C., and WILBRAHAM, Anne, *The Englishman's Food. A History of Five Centuries of English Diet*, London, Jonathan Cape, 1957.

GIROUARD, Mark, *The Victorian Country House*, Oxford, Clarendon Press, 1971.

HAWTHORNE, Nathaniel, *Our Old Home. A Series of English Sketches*, Boston, Ticknor & Fields, 1863.

—— *Passages from the English Notebooks of Nathaniel Hawthorne*, 2 vols., London, Strahan, 1870.

HAZLITT, William, *Criticisms on Art and Sketches of the Picture Galleries of England*, London, John Templeman, 1843.

HONE, William, *The Every Day Book or a Guide to the Year*, 2 vols., London, William Tegg, 1878.

HUGGETT, Frank E., *Life Below Stairs. Domestic Servants in England from Victorian Times*, London, John Murray, 1977.

HUSSEY, Christopher, *English Country Houses Open to the Public*, London, Country Life, 1953.

[JEUNE, Margaret Dyne], *Pages from the Diary of an Oxford Lady 1843–1862*, ed. Margaret Jeune Gifford, Oxford, Shakespeare Head Press, 1932.

KRAUS, René, *Young Lady Randolph. The Life and Times of Jennie Jerome*, London, Jarrolds Publishers, 1944.

LESLIE, Anita, *The Fabulous Leonard Jerome*, London, Hutchinson, 1954.

—— *Mr Frewen of England. A Victorian Adventurer*, London, Hutchinson, 1966.

—— *Jennie. The Life of Lady Randolph Churchill*, London, Hutchinson, 1969.

MARTIN, Ralph G., *Lady Randolph Churchill*, 2 vols., London, Cassell, 1909.

MONTAGUE, C. E., *The Right Place: A Book of Pleasures*, London, Chatto & Windus, 1926.

MÜLLER, Friedrich, *The Life and Letters of the Right Honourable Friedrich Müller*, edited by his wife, 2 vols., London, Longmans, Green, 1902.

ORWELL, George, *Selected Essays*, Harmondsworth, Penguin Books, 1957.

PAGET, Lady Walpurga, *Embassies of Other Days*, London, Hutchinson, 1923.

PEEL, Mrs C. S., *A Hundred Wonderful Years: Social and Domestic Life of a Century 1820–1920*, London, John Lane, the Bodley Head, 1926.

—— *The Stream of Time: Social and Domestic Life in England 1805–1861*, London, John Lane, the Bodley Head, 1931.

[PÜCKLER-MUSKAU, Prince H.L.N.F.], *Tour in Germany, Holland and England*, vol. III, London, Effingham Wilson, 1832.

READER, W. J., *Life in Victorian England*, ed. Peter Quennell, London, Batsford, 1964.

ROSEBERY, Lord [Archibald Philip Primrose, 5th Earl of], *Miscellanies Literary and Historical*, 2 vols., London, Hodder & Stoughton, 1921.

TAINE, H., *Notes on England*, trans. W. F. Rae, London, Strahan, 1872.

THACKERAY, William M., *The Book of Snobs. Sketches of Life and Character*, London, Smith, Elder, 1894.

THOMPSON, Revd Henry L., *Henry George Liddell, D. D., Dean of Christ Church, Oxford. A Memoir*, London, John Murray, 1899.

THOMSON, David, *England in the Nineteenth Century*, Harmondsworth, Penguin Books, 1978.

WARWICK, Earl of, *Memories of Sixty Years*, London, Cassell, 1917.

WARWICK, Frances, Countess of, *Life's Ebb and Flow*, London, Hutchinson, 1929.

WEST, Algernon, *Private Diaries of the Rt. Hon. Sir Algernon West, G.C.B.*, ed. Horace G. Hutchinson, London, John Murray, 1922.

WILLIS, N. P., *Pencillings by the Way*, London, Henry G. Bohn, 1850.

WOHL, Anthony S., ed., *The Victorian Family. Structure and Stresses*, London, Croom Helm, 1978.

WOLFF, Sir Henry Drummond, *Rambling Recollections*, 2 vols., London, Macmillan, 1908.

4. DISSIPATION

I. *Periodical Articles*

ANON., 'Lady Helen Stewart', *Country Life* (10 April 1897), pp. 367, 372.

ANON., 'Lady Randolph Churchill', *Country Life* (29 May 1897), p. 568.

ANON., 'The Royal Visit to Blenheim Palace', *Illustrated London News* (28 November 1896), pp. 722–3.

ANON., 'The Royal Visit to Blenheim', *Illustrated London News* (5 December 1896), p. 745.

HORNE, Gerald (as told to David Green), 'Blenheim Fifty Years Ago', *Country Life* (23 February 1945), pp. 326–8.

WOLTERS, Richard A., 'A Rough Shoot', *Connoisseur* (November 1987), pp. 144–51.

II. *Books*

ANDREWS, Allen, *The Follies of King Edward VII*, London, Lexington, 1975.

ASHLEY, Maurice, *Churchill as Historian*, London, Secker & Warburg, 1968.

ASQUITH, Lady Cynthia, *Diaries 1915–1918*, London, Hutchinson, 1968.

BALFOUR, Arthur James, *Chapters of Autobiography*, ed. Mrs Edgar Dugdale, London, Cassell, 1930.

BALSAN, Consuelo Vanderbilt, *The Glitter and the Gold*, London, Heinemann, 1953.

BEATON, Cecil, *The Wandering Years. Diaries: 1922–1939*, London, Weidenfeld & Nicolson, 1961.

BENNETT, Arnold, *Letters of Arnold Bennett*, edited by James Hepburn, vol. IV, *Family Letters*, Oxford, Oxford University Press, 1986.

—— *Arnold Bennett's Letters to His Nephew*, London, Heinemann, 1936.

BENSON, E. F., *As We Were. A Victorian Peep-Show*, London, Longmans, Green, 1930.

BIRKENHEAD, 2nd Earl of, *Lady Eleanor Smith. A Memoir*, London, Hutchinson, 1953.

—— *The Life of F. E. Smith, First Earl of Birkenhead*, London, Eyre & Spottiswoode, 1960.

BLUNDEN, Margaret, *The Countess of Warwick*, London, Cassell, 1967.

CAMPBELL, John, *F. E. Smith. First Earl of Birkenhead*, London, Jonathan Cape, 1983.

CARAMAN, Philip, *C. C. Martindale*, London, Longmans, 1967.

CARNARVON, Henry, 6th Earl of, *No Regrets*, London, Weidenfeld & Nicolson, 1976.

CHURCHILL, Randolph S., *Winston S. Churchill*, vol. I, *Youth. 1874–1900* (and two companion vols.); vol. II, *Young Statesman 1901–1914* (and three companion vols.), London, Heinemann, 1966, 1967 and 1969.

CHURCHILL, Winston S., *Painting as a Pastime*, London, Benn/Odhams, 1948; New York, Cornerstone Library, 1965.

CORNWALLIS-WEST, G., *Edwardian Hey-Days*, London, Putnam, 1930.

COURTNEY, Nicholas, *'In Society'. The Brideshead Years*, London, Michael Joseph, 1986.

COWLES, Virginia, *Edward VII and His Circle*, London, Hamish Hamilton, 1956.

D'ABERNON, Viscount, *Portraits and Appreciations*, London, Hodder & Stoughton, 1931.

DUGDALE, Blanche E. C., *Arthur James Balfour*, vol. I, London, Hutchinson, 1936.

EPSTEIN, Jacob, *An Autobiography*, London, Hulton Press, 1955.

FIELDING, Daphne, *The Duchess of Jermyn Street*, London, Eyre & Spottiswoode, 1964.

GALSWORTHY, John, *The Country House*, London, Heinemann, 1907.

GILBERT, Martin, *Winston S. Churchill*, vol. III, *1914–1916*, and vol. IV, *1916–1922*, London, William Heinemann, 1971 and 1975.

DE GRAMONT, E. (ex-Duchesse de Clermont-Tonnerre), *Pomp and Circumstance*, trans. Brian W. Downs, London, Jonathan Cape, 1929.

HEARNSHAW, F. J. C., ed., *Edwardian England. A. D. 1901–1910*, London, Ernest Benn, 1933.

HOLROYD, Michael, *Lytton Strachey. A Critical Biography*, vol. II, *The Years of Achievement (1910–1932)*, London, Heinemann, 1968.

HOYT, Edwin P., *The Vanderbilts and their Fortunes*, London, Frederick Muller, 1963.

HYNES, Samuel, *Edwardian Occasions*, London, Routledge & Kegan Paul, 1972.

JAMES, Robert Rhodes, ed., *Chips: the Diaries of Sir Henry Channon*, London, Weidenfeld & Nicolson, 1967.

JULLIAN, Philippe, *Edward and the Edwardians*, trans. Peter Dawnay, London, Sidgwick & Jackson, 1967.

LEES-MILNE, James, *Ancestral Voices*, London, Chatto & Windus, 1975.

LESLIE, Anita, *Edwardians in Love*, London, Hutchinson, 1972.

—— *The Gilt and the Gingerbread*, London, Hutchinson, 1981.

LESLIE, Shane, *Long Shadows*, London, John Murray, 1966.

McCARTHY, Lillah [Lady Keeble], *Myself and My Friends*, London, Thornton Butterworth, 1933.

MAGNUS, Philip, *King Edward the Seventh*, London, John Murray, 1964.

MALAN, A. H., ed., *Famous Homes of Great Britain and Their Stories*, New York, G. P. Putnam, 1900.

MALCOLM, Sir Ian, *Lord Balfour. A Memory*, London, Macmillan, 1930.

MARGETSON, Stella, *The Long Party. High Society in the Twenties and Thirties*, Farnborough, Saxon House, 1974.

MASTERMAN, C. F. G., *The Condition of England*, London, Methuen, 1909.

MASTERS, Anthony, *Rosa Lewis. An Exceptional Edwardian*, London, Weidenfeld & Nicolson, 1977.

MONTGOMERY, John, 1900. *The End of an Era*, London, Allen & Unwin, 1968.

NICOLSON, Nigel, *Great Houses of Britain*, London, Weidenfeld & Nicolson, 1965.

OLSON, Stanley, *John Singer Sargent. His Portrait*, London, Macmillan, 1986.

PEARSON, John, *Edward the Rake*, London, Weidenfeld & Nicolson, 1975.

PLESS, Daisy, Princess of, *Daisy, Princess of Pless by Herself*, ed. Major Desmond Chapman-Huston, London, John Murray, 1928.

—— *From My Private Diary*, ed. Major Desmond Chapman-Huston, London, John Murray, 1931.

QUELCH, Eileen, *Perfect Darling. The Life and Times of George Cornwallis-West*, London, Cecil and Amelia Woolf, 1972.

SACKVILLE-WEST, V., *The Edwardians*, London, Hogarth Press, 1930.

SITWELL, Sacheverell, *British Architects and Craftsmen. A Survey of Taste, Design and Style during Three Centuries, 1600 to 1830*, 2nd ed., London, Batsford, 1946.

SMITH, Eleanor, *Life's a Circus*, London, Longmans, Green, 1939.

SOAMES, Mary, *Clementine Churchill*, London, Cassell, 1979.

SPENCER-CHURCHILL, Winston, and MARTINDALE, C. C., S. J., *Charles IXth Duke of Marlborough, K. G. Tributes . . .*, London, Burns Oates & Washbourne, 1934.

VICKERS, Hugo, *Cecil Beaton. The Authorized Biography*, London, Weidenfeld & Nicolson, 1985.

—— *Gladys Duchess of Marlborough*, London, Weidenfeld & Nicolson, 1979.

WATSON, Alfred E. T., *King Edward VII as a Sportsman*, London, Longmans, Green, 1911.

WESTMINSTER, Loelia, Duchess of, *Grace and Favour*, London, Weidenfeld & Nicolson, 1961.

WORTHAM, H. E., *Edward VII*, London, Duckworth (Great Lives Series), 1933.

YOUNG, Kenneth, *Arthur James Balfour*, London, G. Bell, 1963.

5. SENILITY

I. *Periodical Articles*

ANON., 'Malvern at Blenheim', *Country Life* (3 February 1940), pp. 118–22.

ANON., 'The Valiant Fighter', *Illustrated London News* (23 January 1965), pp. 3–7.

ANON., 'Sir Winston Churchill Lies in State', and other articles, *Illustrated London News* (6 February 1965), pp. 3–42.

BRYANT, Arthur, Sir Charles Petrie, *et al.*, 'Sir Winston Churchill', *Illustrated London News* (30 January 1965), pp. 4–29.

The Times (30 January 1965), p. 12; (1 February 1965), p. 8.

Witney Gazette (29 January 1965), p. 1; (5 February 1965), p. 3.

II. *Books*

BEDFORD, John, 13th Duke of, *A Silver-Plated Spoon*, London, Cassell, 1959.

BERLIN, Isaiah, *Mr. Churchill in 1940*, London, John Murray, 1964.

BIBESCO, Princess, *Sir Winston Churchill: Master of Courage*, trans. Vladimir Kean, London, Robert Hale, 1957.

BIRKENHEAD, the Earl of [F.E.S.], *Contemporary Personalities*, London, Cassell, 1924.

BONHAM CARTER, Violet [Lady Helen], *Winston Churchill as I Knew Him*, London, Eyre & Spottiswoode and Collins, 1965.

BRENDON, Piers, *Winston Churchill. A Brief Life*, London, Secker & Warburg, 1984.

BROAD, Lewis, *Winston Churchill. The Years of Preparation*, London, Sidgwick & Jackson, 1963.

CHURCHILL, Randolph S., *Fifteen Famous English Houses*, London, Derek Verschoyle, 1954.

—— *Twenty-One Years*, London, Weidenfeld & Nicolson, 1965.

CHURCHILL, Randolph S., and GILBERT, Martin, *Winston S. Churchill*, 7 vols. and companion vols. II to V, London, Heinemann, 1966–86.

CHURCHILL, Sarah, *A Thread in the Tapestry*, London, André Deutsch, 1967.

CHURCHILL, Sir Winston S., *If I Lived My Life Again*, ed. Jack Fishman, London, W. H. Allen, 1974.

—— *Into Battle* (speeches by Winston Churchill compiled by Randolph S. Churchill, MP), London, Cassell, 1941.

—— *Onwards to Victory* (war speeches of Winston S. Churchill compiled by Charles Eade), London, Cassell, 1944.

—— *Thoughts and Adventures*, London, Thornton Butterworth, 1932.

COLVILLE, John, *The Churchillians*, London, Weidenfeld & Nicolson, 1981.

COOTE, Colin R., *Sir Winston Churchill: A Self-Portrait Constructed from His Own Sayings and Writings*, London, Eyre & Spottiswoode, 1954.

COWARD, Noël, *Diaries*, ed. Graham Payn and Sheridan Morley, Boston, Little Brown, 1982.

MARLBOROUGH, Laura, Duchess of, *Laughter from a Cloud*, London, Weidenfeld & Nicolson, 1980.

MASTERMAN, Charles F. G., *England after War. A Study*, London, Hodder & Stoughton, 1922.

MORAN, Lord [Charles M. Wilson, 1st Baron], *Winston Churchill: the Struggle for Survival, 1940–1965*, London, Constable, 1966.

SOAMES, Mary, *A Churchill Family Album*, London, Allen Lane, 1982.

WOOLF, Virginia, *Collected Essays*, vol. 4, London, Hogarth Press, 1967.

INDEX